DECODING
THE REVELATION OF SAINT JOHN THE DIVINE
UNDERSTAND THE ROLE YOU INHERIT

O.M. KELLY

COPYRIGHT

Copyright © 2025 Margret Ann Kelly/O.M. Kelly
Decoding The Revelation Of Saint John The Divine: Understand The Role You Inherit (Revised and Republished),
First published in 2015,
Margret Ann Kelly/O.M. Kelly, Copyright © 2015.
ISBN: 978-0-6459905-1-5

All rights reserved. This book may not be reproduced, wholly or in part, or transmitted in any form whatsoever without written permission from the author, O.M. Kelly, www.elanea.com.

The author of this book does not dispense medical advice or prescribe the use of any technique as a form of treatment for physical, emotional, or medical problems without the advice of a physician, either directly or indirectly. The intent of the author is only to offer information of a general nature to help you in your quest for emotional and spiritual well-being. In the event you use any of the information in this book for yourself, which is your constitutional right, the author assumes no responsibility for your actions.

AUTHOR

Author O. M. Kelly, known as Omni to her clients and students is an accomplished author and international lecturer, on Metaphysics, Philosophy and understanding the Collective Consciousness. Omni consults for Member States of the European Commission as a Conciliation Advisor and Rhetoric Counsellor for other International Companies throughout Europe. Omni now resides on Australia's beautiful Gold Coast, writing books, and works as a Life Mentor and Business Coach.

Omni has dedicated her life to decoding the mysteries of the universe. With a deep knowledge of the biblical agenda, mythologies including ancient Egyptology, Asian principles, and metaphysical insights, Omni has discovered the secret that all stories share a coded hidden metaphysical language. Her seminal work, *Decoding The Mind Of God*, is a compilation of nine volumes of metaphysical information based on the research into the coded information of the Laws of the Universe, also known as the Collective Consciousness, and represents a groundbreaking contribution to our understanding of the metaphysical universe. Now, all nine volumes have been as separate, revised books, each offering a unique perspective on the universe's workings. Omni's work has been widely acclaimed for its depth of insight, and her contributions to the field of metaphysics have been groundbreaking.

THIS BOOK

Decoding The Revelation Of Saint John The Divine: Understand The Role You Inherit by International Author and Lecturer O.M. Kelly.

What if the Book of Revelation was never about the end of the world, but the beginning of a higher consciousness?

After more than 48 years of meticulous research and metaphysical inquiry, O.M. Kelly (also known as Omni) presents a groundbreaking, revised edition of her renowned work that will change everything you thought you knew about the final book of the Bible. Drawing from ancient mythology and ancient traditions from Egypt, Mesopotamia, Assyria, and early Israel, O.M. Kelly reveals a metaphysical symbolic system that serves as a universal blueprint of human identity and evolving consciousness.

Inside this revelatory book, you will explore:

- The genetic role humanity inherits through the coded symbols of Revelation.
- Uncover the secrets of the Ark of the Covenant.
- Unlock the mystery behind the 144,000 and the sacred codes of their salvation.
- How you open up to the information stored in your Seven Seals.
- The true implications of the mark of the Beast.
- The ancient wisdom of the Egyptian pyramids and their connection to your consciousness.
- The truth behind Armageddon, not as destruction, but as revelation.
- Learn how to access the Recorded History of Your DNA and the Library of the Universal Mind.
- Understand the symbolic Fall of Babylon and its impact on our collective psyche.

- The process of clearing the channels of human consciousness to awaken the Divine Self.
- Explore the connection between Greek mythology, Egyptian pyramids, and early Israelite traditions.
- Understanding the genetics behind the role you inherit in Revelation.
- Stepping through The Doorway of the Divine Self.

This is more than a book. It is a sacred map. O.M. Kelly deciphers the ancient texts and opens a doorway to understanding the mystery of life through metaphysical interpretation. Decode your destiny. Remember who you are. Awaken the divine within. Let the Book of Revelation become your guide to the evolution of consciousness.

CONTENT

Introduction

SERIES ONE: MY INTRODUCTION

Chapter One
When We Take The Metaphysical Journey — Page 1

Chapter Two
Reflections — Page 22

Chapter Three
The Hidden Language — Page 30

Chapter Four
The Library Of The Universal Mind — Page 45

Chapter Five
The Mystery Of Life — Page 51

SERIES TWO: THE ARK OF THE COVENANT

Chapter One
Our Creed Is The Covenant We Ark — Page 62

Chapter Two
Your Divine AN — Page 73

Chapter Three
The Language Of The Metaphysical Interpretation — Page 79

Chapter Four
The Hidden Collection Seal Of Conscious Recognition — Page 85

Chapter Five
Stringing Ourselves Together — Page 87

SERIES THREE: REVELATIONS

Chapter One
Revealing The Inner Knowledge — Page 105

Chapter Two
Explaining The Angelic Vibration Of The First Four Seals
Page 134

Chapter Three
Continuing The Seven Seals   Page 137

Chapter Four
The Entrance Into The Throne of God   Page 140

Chapter Five
The Book Sealed With Seven Seals   Page 145

Chapter Six
Opening Six Of The Seals   Page 152

Chapter Seven
The Original Story   Page 160

Chapter Eight
The Opening Of The Seventh Seal That Created The
Great Plagues   Page 172

Chapter Nine
Entering Up Into The Royal Chambers   Page 182

Chapter Ten
The Recorded History Of Your DNA   Page 185

Chapter Eleven
Understanding The Differences In The Biblical Teachings
Page 190

Chapter Twelve
The Doorway Of The Divine Self   Page 199

Chapter Thirteen
The Beast   Page 208

Chapter Fourteen
The Fall Of Babylon   Page 218

Chapter Fifteen
The Wrath Of God   Page 223

Chapter Sixteen
Clearing The Channels Of Our Collective Consciousness
Page 227

Chapter Seventeen
We Are Finally Waking Up   Page 234

Chapter Eighteen
Final Rendition Of The Fall Of Babylon   Page 242

Chapter Nineteen
The Search Of The Cosmos   Page 252

Chapter Twenty
The Inner Journey Of You Discovering Your Soul   Page 256

Chapter Twenty One
Viewing Through The Mind's Eye   Page 261

Chapter Twenty Two
Your Inner Library Becomes More Than Your Inner Light
Page 268

Chapter Twenty Three
In Closing   Page 274

Chapter Twenty Four
Final Synopsis   Page 283

Books By O.M. Kelly (Omni)   Page 320

INTRODUCTION

It is with great pleasure that I present this revised edition of *Decoding the Revelation of Saint John the Divine: Understand the role you inherit*—a profound exploration of the metaphysical significance hidden within the text often referred to as the Book of Revelation in the Bible.

Building upon the foundation of my original work, this updated edition offers fresh insights, expanded interpretations, and a perspective on the metaphysical messages embedded in the Book of Revelation. This book is the result of over 48 eight years of dedicated research and personal exploration. It reflects my lifelong commitment to uncovering the hidden codes of ancient times, particularly through the construct of language, mythology, and metaphysical understanding—insights that remain largely unknown to many, even across the diverse stages of human development.

Through years of training and disciplined inquiry, a new pattern of understanding began to emerge—one that revealed deeper layers of meaning related to self-realisation and consciousness. The text of Revelation, I discovered, was encoded using a metaphysical symbolic system grounded in Greek mythology and interwoven with Egyptian, Mesopotamian, Assyrian, and early Israelite traditions. These ancient influences offer a compelling key to decoding the hidden wisdom within the biblical narrative. The Elders of this sacred text drew upon mythological archetypes and symbolic ancient codes to formulate a universal blueprint—a metaphysical map of human identity and the evolving consciousness of our species.

Today, more than ever, this knowledge is vital. It offers a perspective through which we can begin to understand the story encoded within us during our own gestation. This book is not merely a transcription or interpretation of biblical passages; it is a guide to transformational insight. It reveals how the Book of Revelation can become a personal mirror—in essence, it shows you how to reveal your inner 'nations': your thoughts, emotions, personality, and inner world. Such understanding can nurture self-awareness, emotional intelligence, and spiritual growth.

For some, the ideas within these pages may offer a radically new perspective. I invite you to approach this work with openness, curiosity, and courage. Step boldly into the ancient wisdom it presents.

Each of us is here to live out our own myth—to unfold our personal mythology. Interpreted as 'my theology,' this unique way of life has been seeded into our very cells and genes. We each play a vital role in the grand design—a cosmic game authored by what I was taught to call the **G**reatest **O**rder of the **D**ivine (God), or the unity of the self. The letter 'D' in 'Divine' may be seen as symbolising our innate Divinity, echoing the sacred language we have inherited over 64 generations of ancestral lineage. This knowledge, our DNA, is a living thread connecting us back to the original Source.

These are the Universal Laws, etched into the human experience. Consider yourself a piece on the grand chessboard of life. It is your move. Are you ready to embrace the role you were born to play? The next step waiting just ahead? Please enjoy the read. May you inherit the wind, known to me as the breath of God, for us to know that we can all inherit the earth.
O. M. Kelly.

SERIES ONE: MY INTRODUCTION

CHAPTER ONE

When We Take The Metaphysical Journey

The biblical stories were collected and condensed through the understanding of their time—particularly influenced by the Greek myths and the evolving field of Egyptology. Both Greece and Egypt contributed to how these ancient codes were interpreted. The King James Bible, first published in 1611, was England's authorized version, translated from the original Hebrew and Greek texts into English at the request of King James I.

This book is presented to you in three sections.

Series One builds upon the journey of my previous works, *Decoding the Mind of God*, which I have recently revised into nine individual books. These updates reflect my evolving understanding, leading to the next step in uncovering the hidden agenda embedded in the nucleus of every cell in your body. This is where you begin to understand the dictionary of how the ancient ones wrote in their hidden language—language that was foretold to us from the beginning. Once again, I reveal more secrets encoded through the Mystery Schools across time.

It makes a tremendous difference how our inner dictionary (our DNA—also referred to as our inner Bible, for the stories within the Bible reflect this code) creates its mathematics autonomically (self-governed). As we place more responsibility on the right hemisphere of the brain, it must balance the emotional weight of each sentence. More of our cells release their own antennae to dichotomize the emotional factor of the thoughts released, as each thought is measured and tested to be either positive or negative to the conversation. When we think a word, our cellular antennae search for a compatible, computable companion within our inner sentience—how we feel and perceive each thought before we speak.

We must remember that our right brain interfaces with the universal mind once the ego, or left hemisphere, retracts its critical stance and learns to bow to itself. This is the essence of the Bible stories. Each story serves as a codex, guiding us through the metaphysical journey of our inner mathematics, where every thought we think is carefully measured. This is the second stage of our life that we are presented with, to live and evolve through, as it is the next world beyond our third dimensional intelligence, where we release the commitment to begin again to learn and then earn how to advance our inner truth to ourselves, as our inner truth was implanted during the first three months of your gestation before you were born. We begin by climbing the ladder of the last 64 generations of our own DNA, which through our intelligence awakening become our blood lines, as we learn to ascend up into living within this superior language to create our own ever-lasting life. My aim is for you to learn to understand what role you inherit in the divine plan of revealing to yourself the inner nations of your world, that are shepherded by the glandular system throughout the language of Revelation.

This amazing system is also referred to as the 'Gods Lands', later explained as the Prophets in the Old Testament, which then advances to the Disciples in the New Testament. These are the caretakers of the twelve strands of our DNA, which are responsible for governing our thoughts and generate an accumulation of ideas to support the thought of our present moment. Our Inner University which is situated two fingers above our navel, has a vocabulary many thousands of years older than us, which when unfurled (opened up) through us earning our inner intelligence, they speak through us, to give us a direction to aspire to.

Series Two explains the responsibility you can accept for self as you earn the interpretation of the 'Ark of the Covenant'. The term was originally pronounced in Old Latin as 'earc' or 'arcere', meaning a coffer or chest used to enclose. Our body represents the ark, with each cell embedded with the creed we autonomically made with God before birth. I hope you enjoy my explanations of the metaphysical language within the stories written about the Ark.

Series Three reveals the inner knowledge behind the language that St. John was initially trained to write the Book of Revelation. This book, with all its gore and depravity as well as its inner beauty, helps you understand the depths to which your ego abides. The ego believes it commands everything you say and do, always placing itself at the forefront while refusing to understand and accept the consequences of its actions. Instead of judging itself, it chooses to judge others, continually building and creating its own karma due to a lack of responsibility.

I refer to the ego as the rebellious child, as it can only countenance up to thirteen words in a sentence—just as a hen in a henhouse cannot fly beyond thirteen feet. The hen serves us by providing eggs rich in protein and minerals that are difficult to obtain from other species. The ego must be coaxed into self-discovery. One of its favourite sayings is: *"Do I have to? I would much prefer to shift the responsibility onto someone else!"* So, let us begin this momentous journey of decoding the hidden codes written in the final book of the Bible and uncover its original meaning.

Allow me to write to you in the first person. Yes, I understand it places responsibility onto you, the reader, but that is how I introduce you to the divine unity of metaphysical language. I refer to it as the 'matter' downloaded into us—our inner physics. This allows you to explore the wonder of a mathematical, hidden language passed down to us during gestation, biblically referred to as 'in the first time'. I aim to explain the unified language of heart and brain, and how ancient authors threaded their intelligence throughout their minds. This is the universal language of the mind: everything that has evolved from the beginning of time. All is one. Every thought is layered, and it is only through intellectually evolving through these layers—formed by past thoughts and insecurities—that you can reveal this sacred mathematical language inscribed in our genetics by the Greatest Oracle, which I have renamed as the 'Order of the Divinity' within every human.

After 26 years of studying the map of Egypt with my Masters of Time, I came to understand that the cities, temples, obelisks and pyramids are all explaining the inner evolution of our central nervous system. It represents a perfect blueprint of our inner road map that we can unfurl through releasing our past fears of the unknowable energy that was still trapped within ourselves, where we walked on by through our innocence, which at that time was also our intelligence, through us not knowing or understanding this inner language every human had inherited during our gestation. These amazing caretakers have explained to us through their languages of the past 200,000 years to the present day, what they have created for every human to view within, the more we get to know ourself!

Over time, I came to understand this also included the names of people and places across the planet. To unlock their meaning, I had to learn the Sacred Alphabet and decode every word passed down through generations. These words carry the wisdom of earlier intellects, whose insights we now build upon. Once a priest earned his rites of passage, he could then share this language with others. We spend one-third of our lives observing, another unfolding our inner intellect, and the final third expanding our perspectives—enabling all of humanity to grasp the whole picture.

I am introducing to you the three Gods—EL, AN, and EA—who came from the East (within), and who continually ascend into their enlightenment. It is within our temple mind that we are gifted the past, present, and future—often before we even complete our sentence.

It begins with your feelings, which must always vibrate through your heart, that we are showered with the truth. The truth has always been present, working on your behalf. It awakens only when you allow yourself time to discover who you are. That is what destiny means: the cause of your inner action. This intuitive aspect is delivered to us through universal laws, which continually shift and rearrange the mind, moment by moment, until you learn and earn the understanding to accept what is your God-given right to achieve.

Just as the totality of the universe expands moment by moment, so do we. There is no easy way out. These are the mathematics permanently at work through this hidden language of numbers that are measuring every form of energy we think, through the creation of these natural laws of the universe. We cannot divert them as they have always been here measuring each moment of each universe's existence. They keep us stabilized. When we do not adhere to them, they keep on broadening the excuses we create and bring down their furore or wrath for us to overcome. The planetary wholeness becomes more destitute which buckles your knees and you begin to falter. As we all think, we create for ourselves to inherit! In the beginning we add and subtract and as we notice that we are adding more to our own equation, we begin to multiply our energy which broadens our horizons for us to realize there is so much more to add to our own portfolio which binds us to our inner responsibility of self.

From a young age, I shared many conversations with my father about Einstein's theories of relativity. He explained them to me in childlike terms. I listened to his gentleness and there were many times I had difficulties hearing his words, as I tried desperately to keep up with him. We also shared a love for Egyptology. For my ninth birthday, I received black-and-white photos of King Tutankhamun's tomb. Along with them, he gave me a challenge: when I found time, I should discover why "God does not play dice with the universe."

As I grew into adulthood, life took precedence—finishing school, starting work, falling in love, getting married, raising a family, paying off a mortgage, and funding higher education. Life brought illness, accidents, and the inevitable discoveries of self. We entered self-employment, believing ourselves wiser, yet always spending or saving for the unknown.

When the last child was adult enough to stake his own claim in the world, my father's words returned to me. I could not find any more excuses to deter me, so I began to challenge myself to do his bidding. He believed that there were no mistakes in the original plan which was delivered to us through these unseen and unknown laws, we just had to find out what they were representing to us and how they were all connected throughout us. We had all been given a lifetime to explore this hidden agenda. There was an answer to everything the human mind could create, if only we could take the time to enquire. It wasn't just the ability I had to believe in to bring through this hidden information over the years of my training, it was the added responsibility I had to bring forth to make sure that to announce to myself my truth, that the next thought correctly followed on from the previous one!

We have written the greatest treasury of information—still unfolding through the 'Great Memoriam', as it was called when Christianity was first introduced to us. We have come a long way since then. Now it is time for the next equation to be filtered through. To present the future to ourselves, we must first repair the fractures of the past. This gives us the expediency to then become available to help and explain to those less fortunate than ourselves.

Over the next twenty years, as I immersed myself in this hidden language, I discovered the answer: no, God does not play dice with the universe. Everything is mathematically correct and above board, just as it should be. There is a mathematical answer to every thought we release—each one an expression of our personal accountability.

The consequences of every thought we release from our mind, whether positive or negative, are automatically created through our thinking. This thinking, generated through the porous section surrounding our ears, forms our words, which automatically weaves an etheric web around our body. We must always equate and be answerable to this web. It is through the telepathic convergence of our harmonics, rearranging and balancing themselves, that we are able to continue on. This syntax creates a séance of music that is vibrated and felt throughout every gene in our body, to create each individual's opera of intellectual balance.

If we collapse in our thinking, these universal laws must release the mathematical equation back to us so that we may earn the opportunity to understand exactly how and where to place our responsibility in every thought we release from our mind. These universal laws are presenting to us a continuous clue that is hidden underneath our veils of innocence; and yet we are unconsciously perusing each thought at the same time. It is right in front of our eyes, if only we could learn to see through this amazing world, not just look at it.

*

The universe is governed entirely by energy. Energy is what we release as we think. Therefore, as we think our thoughts, we are also governing the universe in how it must add our thoughts to retaliate (the universe must incorporate and respond to our thoughts accordingly, adjusting itself based on the energy we contribute). By now, we are aware that one human thought holds ultimate power and strength to accomplish anything that hu-man (the **h**eavenly or higher **u**nderstanding of each gene—through the language of the Ancient Sanskrit, the word '**man**' is each gene; and the word 'men' (plural) are representing our genes), can produce. It is the mathematical strength within each thought that sets the scene, becoming the act in motion. Every thought you are thinking right now is the most important moment in the history of mankind.

Now this paragraph requires more of our attention. Just imagine if every thought we produced came through an open heart, free of fear, to be digested (absorbed) throughout the body of the universe. What a difference we could make for future generations. Many dismiss this emotional thinking, claiming the world would become too blasé. Yet, they have never experienced the freedom of becoming it. If I could imagine a world without starving or thirsty children—future generations of this planet—I could see how this energy could eradicate the word 'forfeit' from our dictionary.

These hidden universal laws will only be revealed when you have undertaken the initiation process of understanding and accepting the importance of the self. These are the teachings found in the principles of Egypt, Greek philosophies, and thousands of others who walked the Earth before us, many of whom we continue to unearth today. They all explaining the same story, including how the Bible collected into the stories we read, which explain the inner education gained through understanding these so-called secrets. We remain unaware of this intelligence, layered within our innocence, until we become fully aware of accepting our own responsibilities.

We have named these the hidden teachings, the unknown—a word that collects into a language that many of us have become afraid of. What we can't see, we assume is not really there! What if we changed the word 'unknown' with 'inner known'? Would that change your perspective? Consider the other four senses we have inherited: hearing, touch, taste, smell. They are just as important! We automatically place barriers around that we do not understand! Releasing this information allows us to transform fear into wisdom, shaping the experiences we gain throughout life's journey. My hope is that you release this so-called fear and view it as the journey of your previous existence, opening up the doorways to the next journey, which will introduce you to your next educated life.

More importantly, it is how you discover the principles that lay behind Egyptology, Mayan and Asian writings, the Biblical agenda and even our medical sciences written in Latin, that are all explaining the same identical story. These natural laws remain hidden from us until we realize the importance of learning to understand who, what, and why we are in relation to the self. This realisation brings us to see that this language is something that we mathematically earn. Meanwhile, our ego tries heretically to walk away from allowing us to unravel our genetic inheritance. There is nothing magical about this. It is simply the next evolutionary step of human intelligence!

When one begins to read their own story, they open themselves up to the subject at hand. The more they relax into who they wish to become, the more their inner storehouse of information opens to explain their biblical agenda, which is the blueprint of their own DNA. Recorded in this blueprint is every experience that their previous generations have already lived. This information is freely available, in concordance with the subject at hand. The unconscious mind automatically clicks in to assist us, as it has every recorded moment of their existence.

Over the years, I have found that we all share the same experiences throughout our lives, it is just that some express them more eloquently than others. Hopefully, you will exemplify the following conversations to serve you well. I would like you to gain many new experiences from reading these words. Otherwise, you are only listening; in other words, you have not heard a word that I have written.

There have been many times I have thought I have written too much. The totality of this information is vast. It can be draining on your ego, which, while reading these words, still believes it is in control. Your ego may become affronted with each word you read and attempt to turn you away. You may start yawning five minutes in. Then come the itches, the headache, the toothache, on and on, until you notice you are being had by yourself. I know, as many thousands have told me the same. Tell your ego to remain quiet and allow itself to learn something new. These words do not interfere with your emotions. So how can I explain only half of this amazing story? Until you hear it in its entirety, you are susceptible to argue and disbelieve everything I have written for you to inherit.

*

We have been informed that the Holy Bible contains all our answers, if only we could exalt our thinking into the hierarchical mind, by accepting that every word we think must first echo throughout our cells, our selves, before being spoken to others. It sounds prolific, doesn't it? The parables in the Bible explain the language of your genetic inheritance. Each book has been correlated through you understanding just how through each forthcoming generation, your DNA has collected as to how it has reinvested in itself; which is all through the creation of your unconscious mind. They are one and the same.

We seem to struggle with discovering ourselves, yet we have no qualms about delving into the lives of others. Is your ego in command again? Think of it as attending the 'University of Your Life', the most exalted university on Earth. While we focus on someone else, we hold the planet in abeyance—where periodically we keep releasing and reliving the same thoughts and experiences over and over again.

That is why I chose to write most of my works in the first person. I could not explain my teachings properly using the third. I saw a million excuses arise as each reader avoided their challenges, through thinking this information was just too much, and placed in the 'too hard' basket behind the door. But when you close that door, there it is in all of its glory, right in front of your eyes. It still requires your attention! The truth disguises itself when we shift the onus to someone else. This way, you are learning, not just earning the rights to your own passage.

I would like you to gain many new experiences from reading these words. Otherwise, you are only listening to what is being explained. In other words, you have accepted, but not truly heard. Listening through the left ear informs the ego and aligns with the brain's left hemisphere. Through listening, we learn. Hearing, however, is where we become attracted to the words and is through the right ear, which is in alignment with our emotional responsibilities, our right hemisphere of the brain. Through hearing, we earn. Note the difference. Only by hearing your thoughts can your future unfold.

Yes, I know this differs from the medical establishment's view of the brain. I am explaining the energetic information delivered by the unconscious mind. This is where the divine equation reverberates every message, concisely appeasing us when the mind is silent and still.

*

To accept the teachings of the Bible correctly, we must realize that every story within its pages speaks to us the evolution of the self. That is why these narratives were passed down to us!

When we open the first chapter of the remarkable book that our predecessors have named 'Revelation,' we begin to read the words of St. John the Divine, the final book of the New Testament. Once we understand this ancient language, we discover it is used in every moment of our existence. It is the highest form of intellectual awareness, where we can become fully absorbed into this hidden language, though many find it difficult to understand. And yet, on page one of Genesis, the codes begin to introduce us to these secrets. The stories are all there, recorded and explained to us in each page, written many thousands of years ago. Every hieroglyph scribed on the walls explains the same story! That is worth thinking about!

Once understood, these philosophical principles can create electromagnetic waves that stabilize the self and ripple outward to the rest of the planet as a whole. The written word is decoded and reveals that everything ever evolved is embedded within our cells, including the rocks and crystals of the Earth and all that grows from it, animals, fish, birds, and more. All have reached their own antenna. In ancient language, this was pronounced 'wyrd' meaning destiny. Allow me to now add this word to 'read' and 'write' and reverse the sentence: It is our destiny to see from within what we have already accomplished, and then to act upon it!

*

The Universal mind is the life force of the planet and each individual has their own unconscious energy that is identical to this information and surrounds them, which automatically tunes them into the planetary result, where we are all symbolically representing one, or 'same mind'. Every person that you meet in this lifetime; you will find that the previous generations of your family have already met before! This is the eternal wisdom reconnecting you back to the source; represented to us symbolically, as the twelve tribes of Israel. As a seasoned global traveller over the last 50 years, I can relate to countless stories on this matter, where you will find that one of your previous generations that you have been seeded with, over the last 64 generations of your family tribe—once found themselves in a distant land and formed a friendship. Generations later, a descendent of that very friend has now appeared before you!

All are equating to the twelve strands of the universal DNA. Over many years of research, my students—primarily from Europe and China, along with others from the globe, explored their genetic inheritance alongside mine. Through this journey, we traced our ancestral connections and came to terms with the points in time when our families encountered one another in past generations. Needless to say, the life force of this planet has a very important job to do and is busily reflecting to us our inner truth, through every thought we think.

When we raise our voice in judgment regarding others, we must also remember that this person is reflecting back to us an image, of what we are refusing to bring into realization regarding our self! In other words, we are both doing exactly the same thing. One on an inner level and one mirroring back to us through an experience of the moment.

*

I would like to bring to your attention, the final synopsis of my book as I reveal to you, how I was trained to exuberantly bring forth my understanding to earning the language of the hidden word of God. The hidden one was originally known as Amon Re, throughout the Egyptian Philosophies; who supposedly represented the sun. That draws our attention to the third person. Once we begin to understand this hidden revenue that we are all endowed with, it brings the onus back into the first person. In other words, he is representing the hidden God within. This is the intellectual light which is exuded from the pineal gland situated in our brain. Once we have earned the layer of intelligence we are currently working on, we are measured for our truth through the inner mathematics that harmonize and balance within us. As this process unfolds, the pineal gland takes over. It is situated just below the gene which is referred to as the 'head of God' also known as the 'Godhead' throughout various languages. This earning opens up our third eye, allowing us to see from within. Simultaneously, our peripheral vision expands, guiding us towards the next stage of our inner journey. Much like an eagle, which broadens its vision as it glides through the air, we become far more attuned to our surroundings. We begin to see through things, not just look at them.

When we understand these sacred metaphysical philosophies in the way they were first described to us; we will realize that their philosophy was initiating us into understanding how we are connected throughout, as to who we become, so that we could learn to accept this higher temperament of our inner language to tune us into the unconscious recognition of our self!

The story of Genesis began with the evolution of the Earth. Or was it just accepted as that, at that time of our intelligence? Now that I have completed the path of Ascension, into the afterlife as it is referred to; knowing now that it is the next evolutionary step of our intelligence, we release through our DNA by being right here. I believe that their wisdom, explaining their stories, initiates us into the evolution of the human body. Where their hieroglyphs are introducing and revealing to us the permanence of the collective consciousness.

How was the Bible collected, and for what reason? We have a tendency to think that these stories narrate the historical evolution of humanity at that time. However, through years of research into the origins of this metaphysical language, I realized that each story is a collection of every mythical story that has been passed down through each generation and, more importantly, across every spoken language on this planet. The word 'mythology' was originally referred to as 'my theology', meaning 'my religion'—an interpretation of my way of life! As it is out there, so too does it unfold within the cyclic evolution of every human being. Each author, once trained in the language of metaphysics, was asked to write a story explaining their version of the evolution of the human mind—how we first began to evolve through the collection of our thoughts. This became our future intelligence, revealing the possibilities of releasing our inner wisdom. The word 'Genesis' is interpreted through the sacred codex of language as follows: Our **Genes** are manifesting through the internal relationship of our self, revealing to each one of us, how one can begin to listen to oneself. Through this process, we begin to listen within, allowing us to understand the truthful teachings of the '**I**ntelligence of our **S**oul'.

Or are the stories a precursor explaining the Genes of Isis, which, of course, serves as a symbolic reference to the emotional, heavenly mind? It is also known as Maria or the Meer (ocean) of EA, representing the consciousness of the right hemisphere of the brain.

Over the last 48 years, I have had to earn each step of my intellect firstly through my earthly teachers, and then my Masters of Time who came from other realms, stepped into my life to introduce me into the internal-ness of our cellular inheritance, which is identical to the intellect of eternalness of the universe; I have had to release the intellectual light of my own collective consciousness. A priority part of my education into the journey entailed me reading the New Testament of the Holy Bible backwards, which took me around seven years to complete, to understand the codex of the hidden language, that is sealed until you begin to open up your inner self through your self-realization that you have initiated yourself into accepting that you are more important than you ever thought you could be.

As I earned each section; I then had to live the equivalent of how we as a whole can evolve up into our higher realms of intelligence; to explain how others can benefit for themselves. We have named this realm 'Religion'. Through the Latin language this word religio, decoded, is referred to as linking us back into the sacred laws of self.

Through taking on this responsibility, I learned and earned a different story. My new mentors over the next two years introduced me into understanding the many different levels or layers of the great memoriam, as to how I was to view these stories through the mind's eye, not the eyes of the mind. Remember the eyes of the mind look at what we think is there in front of us, whereas the mind's eye has the ability to look through the truth of all, for us to be shown how the story reveals the truth of what we see. Both create a different level for us to view. The mathematics that originally created the great memoriam had to be revealed in their correct mathematical order for each ark to connect and harmonize with one another. All of which explains how mathematics, geometry, and numerology, were created for us in the beginning. Now you can understand the words written in the bible, "*The days of thy (your inner) kingdom are numbered*".

These mathematical layers we autonomically weave must lift one layer at a time; for us to create the fabric of the garment we finally wear (metaphysically). The same as science does when explaining the fabric of space which must be flexible for it to ark or bend with each glyph of energetic light that is created throughout the universe. This garment surrounds us to become our future intelligence. The mind's eye is our connection into the fourth dimension, known to us as the Eye of God. The eyes of the mind are in reference to our third dimensional reality, before we have undertaken the responsibility to accept the teachings of this metaphysical explanation of our inner language. Through the Egyptian Principles, the 'Eye of Horus' is known as a symbolic representation of the one who sees from above. This concept is conveyed throughout all religions, releasing the Metaphysical language embedded within each of our genes—protected and embedded within every one of our cells.

This language that is delivered to us through the original source autonomically creates the laws of nature, which every species of land, sea and air, that has evolved on this planet of ours, must coincide with. These quantum laws are always explaining to us how they multiply themselves through their antennas reaching their own limits to become the ever changing, universal mind. Once the antenna has reached its peak of performance, we find that it has the opportunity to rebirth and a new life or thought autonomically (self-governed) begins to advance our inner dictionary!

We find an answer to my words in the Book of Luke, chapter 2, verse 46, when Joseph and Mary were searching for their son after the feast of the Passover. After three days, they found him in the Temple, sitting among the doctors and physicians, both listening to them and asking them questions. Now we can begin to understand this word, metaphysician, which of course is the mathematical measurement of the inner physician. We earn every vision we think we see, until we connect to the hidden mathematics and then we realize that we're on our way, we are on standby for the rest of our lives! We find that we are always in the right place at the right time to assist ourselves and others who are innocently drawn towards our intellectual light.

Scientifically we can bring this explanation back into saying that the word 'Metaphysics' is explaining to us, the 'Matter or

Measurement of the inner Physics'.

Symbolically this story is informing us that Zeus as well as Jesus took the time to listen to their inner voice that they heard from within, which has many references in today's language to become our guardian angel, also named as our inner teacher, as well as our intuition or exalted mind.

Humanity as a whole is finally waking up to understand that the Bible was written and explained to us metaphorically by the educated minds of that era, their version of the original understanding of the myths in this ancient language of the unconscious recognition of self. The unconscious recognition of self is the language that our central nervous system abides by. We are permanently sending our messages to our brain to satisfy our own personal needs, even we need updating every now and then to keep our ego stimulated and satisfied. After years of research—reading, reversing and re-reading each parable—I have come to believe this to be so. The cities, as well as the names of people and places mentioned, are all codes within the collective alphabetical language, autonomically embedded in our genes to align with the sacred numerology, which has been genetically passed down to us for thousands of years.

The in-depth studies that I have conducted through researching the mythical agenda has proven to me that the same stories are repeated time and time again. Finally, after many years of corroboration I came to the conclusion that there is only one story of evolution, and all branches are still connected to the same original source that we began with; our biblical history refers to it as Babylon—or is it referred to today as to how we babble on.

Also, symbolically this is known to us as our tree of knowledge. And it totally depended on the orator or author as to which personality of themselves or branch of intellect that they were connected to, explaining how these stories were written and passed down through the genetic DNA of the planet. We are still running around out there looking and searching for proof of the written word. The proof is now being revealed to us that these places or words came to our notice hundreds of years later, through our own assumption, searching for its own release and contentment. We are finally beginning to wake up, it is all scribed within your genes which you will unfurl and understand when you have taken the time to turn within and relook at you!

Why did I have to wait until I had learned to open my heart to myself in order to release my inheritance—the ultimate collective of my own consciousness—before being given this test from what we now refer and understand as Extra-Terrestrial Intelligence? It is no longer alien to me; I have discovered that it is an energetic language, reflected back to us from above. And there, inscribed on the temple wall, stands the god Thoth, holding the scales of justice in his hands, measuring our hearts against the feather of flight—where both must weigh the same. Anubis is also present in his station as gatekeeper to the underworld, which, through the Sacred Language, represents the loyalty we must endure of our past.

I came to realize over 30 years ago, that these subtle vibrations which lead us into cosmic consciousness pick up and multiply once our heart has been refined through our present understanding where it becomes a substance formed of fibres, in other words we gain a strength of character through every thought we now think! Once this fibrous character has blended throughout our heart it is opened permanently through it being constantly stimulated into earning its own intelligence, where it harmonizes its own behaviour through to our brain, to reflect back to our self. All of which creates a progressive arching from one ventricle to the other. The vibrations that are autonomically created through this action create feelings which are stimulated from our pituitary gland where they are rendered throughout the body.

The action from this behaviour produces an eclectic life force throughout the DNA which opens up the intelligence barriers that we still have furled tightly or could they be still trapped through our fear of the unknown or maybe they held on to for support through our own innocence. The centurions are briefly relieved of their duty, where we have the possibility to rearrange our guardians; thought I would add that in to attract your attention! These centurions or centaurs are explained to us through the myths as half horse, half man and they are metaphorically explaining the responsibility that our inner strength has to stimulate to activate our glands into action. And remember horse represents the emotion of 'Spiritual or inner Action'.

This energy travels throughout our glandular systems up to the pineal gland which automatically retracts a chemical substance or essence which realigns our alchemy to reimburse our nervous system. All of which creates a void or space through time where the cellular structure has the possibility to re-construe the mathematics of bipolarization. And our heart continues to pulse in alignment to our thoughts.

I cannot go back on my own 'Graduation' which was taught to me from the highest education or altered minds of this planet, and beyond. Many of my teachers were brought from their land to appear at my front door, there were no invitations sent out by me on a conscious level, I just heard the knock on my door and there they were; and yet they overheard the questions I was asking of myself! Finally, my destiny was being brought to my attention.

This is the miracle of the universal mind, which is continually working on our behalf every second of our life, twenty-four hours per day. There is no time for smoko or tea-breaks; by looking through each thought we think, the answer is given to us immediately. My colleagues, to whom I reach out and mentally touch holographically every day, collect their words in their language from the same dictionary of the sacred narratives as I do. I had a huge thirst for knowledge and wanted to know how and why it appeared before me; for what reason and more importantly how did it concern me! As I understood my education, I then had to reverse everything back to the given point of conception to release the mathematical realization, through the gestation of its original truth.

As we create each positive thought step by step; we begin to release our truth which is embedded in each cell to become our new found belief which highlights and restores our faith in ourselves. Our purpose becomes a much stronger energetic force as it filters throughout our body; all of which creates a higher vibration of intellect that releases outside of our own personal boundaries. Each one of my teachers taught me the examples of their teachings and over time, through isolating myself for nine years in total, my task was to bring these many thousands of stories together. Now you realize how difficult it is for me to bring these stories back into your level of understanding. The more you know, the more you respect your past and your present; and through your respect to self, it all adds up to become your future; there is no doubt left in my mind!

Each question I asked was shown to me from within, similarly scribed in an Italic formula, which is the written language of the upper chambers; as it has been automatically registered with the universal mind, where I had to hear each word and as my father explained and taught me to break each word up into syllables to accept the consequences of how each thought had created and released itself. Living this sequence automatically released my inner truth to bring me back into a balance of perpendicular motion within myself. Are you becoming more aware of the two teachings of the inner sacredness of the alphabet and language coming together as to how they begin to coincide and arrange your inner dictionary, through your geometric superiority to alter and add to your thinking?

Once I had equalized the mathematics of each letter of the alphabet, I realized how we had created each spoken language and the next step was there for me to move up into. It depended on the emotional value each member of your tribe had for themselves and the rest of their nation, as to how they constantly communicated with one another, in same mind. And as one member had the courage to step out from the crowd, this person through silencing their mind to endless chatter, heard a different consonant that autonomically rearranged their inner dictionary, and a new word was formed. We had created a new branch to the original tree of good and evil. I could see how these natural laws were created mathematically on our behalf!

Through this equation I was then introduced to the next exalted language of numbers; which is where I could watch the mathematics delivering unto me a clearer and more concise picture that could be used for my benefit eternally. Yes, it does sound spectacular, but that was, is, and will be, the rest of my time that I spend on the earth.

For me to understand and accept the infusion of these natural Laws of God, this **G**reatest **O**rder of our inner **D**ivinity has been a magnificent teacher to me. They are an identical connection with these universal laws, where I know that we have both become the illusion of one another. One is delivered to us on an inner level and the other one refines my wisdom, as to how I can communicate on the outer perimeters, with others. Through my understanding of Einstein's insights on mass and energy which are both sides of the same coin, so too, I could understand how these universal theories worked continuously throughout our body.

They both must correlate to every thought to give us what our heart and mind desire. There are no maybe's, everything we could possibly think, must equate and balance. Our intelligence expedites itself. We are automatically registered up into the hierarchical mind and the program of what and where we are to be placed for future reference; this equation redesigns our future! If our mind is still, it mathematically sets its self out to become. Therefore, we are automatically staking our claim on tomorrow.

Derivatively we are purposely shown on an inner level, what is available and the opportunities we can use to ignite our next step. This is transferred to us through our visions, which are those inner pictures that some of us still like to refer to as our imagination; when these pictures are understood metaphysically; they become the image inside our nation. These pictures are being delivered back to us from our mind's eye, through the chelation of our cellular inheritance releasing from our memory bank of our own accountability. The image that we receive is in relationship to answer us through the respect that each one of us has for ourselves.

If you ask yourself a silly question, then you will receive a silly answer. You ask a positive question you will receive a positive answer. There is never a wasted moment regarding God or these natural laws, as we are now aware that both are measuring each moment. Time waits for no man. Why? We have busily collected it as a reprieve for our ego through our thinking, every moment of our life. There is never a mistake; the mathematics do not lie; the responsibility of what we want to accomplish, we must take care of all by ourselves.

Throughout all of my books there are many Biblical references explaining the hidden wisdom of different parables that have been collected and scribed of certain names and places of the collective DNA. I am not going to interpret the whole book; I will leave that to the future intelligence of this planet, to unravel as they evoke their intellect to themselves. My aim is to drop in a slice of information every now and then, to explain this hidden code of intelligence; that is in its natural sequence to what I am endeavouring to explain. There are only a certain number of words you can explain as you write your book! And this information will only release in you when you unfold the inner creation of your next level of the collective.

CHAPTER TWO

Reflections

At one stage of my life, I lived for many years and completely renovated a château in Germany into a Teaching Academy. The main Ballroom could hold 250 seated students, with sleeping accommodation on the third and fourth floors, for those students who had travelled from many other lands to attend. I remember looking out through the window of my château, watching my royal stag tread softly on the fallen leaves as autumn concluded, preparing for winter. A sculptured parkland of approximately ten acres surrounded the château, with outer buildings nestled among the towering, century-old trees. At this time of year, the only trees still holding onto their leaves were the magnificent oak trees; they seemed to consider themselves the Elders of the deciduous tribe, they have earned the position of being at the end of the line.

Why? After the snow has melted and winter has finished its service to us, the oak trees still retain the last few leaves of the previous season. Only when the first new leaf has birthed on the twig does the last one release itself to the past. This tree reminds me of the words of the Lord Buddha, who said, "Never throw out your bucket of used water until you have another bucket of clean water to replace it". The oak tree lives this parable repeatedly. These sentinels stand on the earth in their complete divine intelligence, always in service to themselves first. Only after they have measured themselves can they send their message through their root system to support those trees that are devout of their own nature.

I have watched as the first tree shed its leaves, which was the maple, and this instigated the next tree to do likewise. There was the linden tree, which I adore, the birch and the beech trees, and so it went on down the line. The autumn colours these trees created are embedded in my memories; as coming from the tropical north of Australia, the colours they produced were stupendous—never to be forgotten through my mind's eye or the eyes of my mind. It all depends on the sap, i.e., how strong and powerful its DNA has evolved through the strength of how its chemical elements created themselves. They inherited their coats of many colours and wear them proudly at the end of each season, just like Joseph did. And please remember—the name Joseph, when interpreted through the sacred ancient languages, is interpreted as 'yourself'. This same transformation happens to you, the reader, when your mind is occupied with thoughts. Your colours manifest throughout your auric fields. The more collective your thinking becomes, the more this explains the biblical story of Joseph and his coat of many colours his mother made for him.

It is exactly the same life force as embedded in our brain. Energy connects from one branch to the next; therefore, it works with the same vibration as to how our central nervous system collects and connects to our thoughts swimming around in our own consciousness.

The magnificent pine tree does not have leaves; it is one of the oldest trees and also one of the first to have evolved into its educational completeness of enlightenment. The leaves of these magnificent species have earned their needles or spines that hold them firm through the evolution of their own belief. Their leaves have curled themselves back into their original source. Perfect! Now that is explaining who they are! This is where its gravity can supersede itself. Therefore, its intensity or life force (*wisdom*) increases itself! That is exactly what the black hole does in the universe, doesn't it!

What holds the pages of the book together? It is the spine of course—which has no need to shed itself. Metaphorically, the pages represent the leaves on a tree. The pine tree has birthed itself up to its pineal (pine-al or oil) gland. This gland is the symbolised by ancient Egyptians as Amon Re! He is presented to us as the Hidden God, or the Head of God throughout the English language, which is where the eye, situated on top of the pineal gland, looks permanently up to this gene, referred to as the God Head throughout many of the ancient languages. It knows, and has accepted who it is! Now we know why the symbol of the pine cone is situated in the front of the Vatican, representing the Fibonacci through the sacred mathematics of the third eye, as this last gland has inherited the doorway to our inner wisdom—to explain to us the power and strength of how we are absorbing our own manifestation, for us to absorb our inner light as to how we continue to absorb the continuation of our own enlightenment!

This is why pine sap is so thick, and why its mathematical vibrational is so valuable in medicine today—to heal rampant diseases which of course, is the bacterial response given to us through our God self. These diseases are automatically collected to release back to us, through our un-abbreviated thinking (disharmony in our thinking) not being measured correctly.

We are now using this ancient energy of the pine tree's new growth to find a replacement to heal the latest evolution of diseases that humanity has created for itself, through our animals with foot and mouth disease and bird flu. The bird flu virus, returning roughly every hundred years or so, has been known for over five centuries. Why does it keep on returning?

It brings us a message we still fail to understand. Please don't blame it on the weather. These incidents are alerting us to the facts of how the mathematics continually rephrase themselves as to how or where our thinking has never harmonically balanced itself! (Incidents highlight how mathematics, as consciousness, continually rephrases itself).

Once we slip down beneath our own agenda as the wholeness (if our thinking slips out of harmony), back comes a virus to remind us of our failures. Where it returns on the planet is also an important message about what level of intellectuality we need to stimulate (needs awakening). When we fear our self, we look for a retainer to pass on our responsibilities (we look for someone else to carry our responsibility). This clears our moment. We are not realizing that the retainer must also be balanced harmonically.

The old women knew of these healing methods long ago. Passed along from mother to daughter, and is still being carried out to this day. It was when they walked through the forest after the snow began to melt and collected the tips of the new growth of the pine tree, which were just beginning to sprout.

These trees emit a mauve aura as the new tips emerge—after winter's end. It is the collection of its past season which will create its new life force and reinvest in itself to support the tree for the following season. The mauve represents higher wisdom. Again, we are being shown how we arc our information into a positive outcome each time we come to the end of an experience. The information of the pine tree (the pine tree's wisdom) is already embedded in us to know that this plant heals the collective mind. It is such a magical lesson that the species of the trees have earned for us to be able to inherit. These pine tips were collected, brought back to the house and gently brought to the boil, so that the oil or essence could release and then, as this was rendered down, the oil was skimmed, mixed with honey or molasses, and taken by the spoonful. I still do this today—only now I also like it spread on a slice of crunchy bread. Of course, my mind and body benefit either way. When something repeats or mirrors back to us, it is supposedly a learning that we have not yet fully heard and accepted (understood the lesson). It reflects our abbreviated thinking—toward ourselves or others of the same mind.

Now, returning to my forest. Once the snow melts and spring begins to bloom, thousands of snowdrops pop up their heads, followed by crocuses, daffodils, tulips, and wild strawberries. Their purple-blues and golds carpet the lawns—a sight to behold!

There will be thousands of seeds regenerating throughout the parkland and they will be carried to their resting place by the wind, or the squirrel who has just one acorn too many shoved into his mouth as it scampers back to its nest. I am amazed at how many young trees sprout from the Oak tree. Does it relate to the many leaves they retain from the prior season? Is this why the seed factor is so much more prolific than the other trees? What is its divine equation? Perhaps it stems from inner strength. I do know that this is delivered unto us through the breath of God, and so it is the same within ourselves!

In time we will find the same vibration in the Sperm Whale that the pine tree has already accomplished; the whale commits its energy back to itself, regarding the spermaceti gland on the top of its head. This wax-type substance is also the collected nectar of its gods, reaching up to release their 'royal' achievement—just like the bees create the wax that protects their honey. It is the result of each species' ultimate earnings, protecting the intellect it has already acclaimed. The whale vibration throughout the Shamanic language is recorded throughout the Universal Mind as representing the words 'conversation and communication'. When brought back into today's language, I realised that the whale used their inner conversation through their vibration to sound.

And the bee is decoded as producing the nectar of the gods. The more we collect our inner communication, the more intellectually we converse through ourselves to others—through spreading the nectar around and sweetening those who still innocently do not know how to sweeten themselves. Slowly we are becoming more aware of how to allow the silence we have created to tune into our inner mind.

If our mind is still, there is nothing that can attach itself to us. Did you hear that last sentence? Will I write it again? If our mind is still, there is nothing on or in our world of thought that can attach itself to us. We now see how the whale's conversation is carried right throughout the waters through their sonic sound of the planet, as to how its sound is heard by every other whale in the ocean, which is all through this wonderful species reaching the peak of their telepathic inheritance through their antenna; just the same earnings has evolved as the elephant can also pass along an important message to every other elephant on the land, as to how they can work together through their telepathic enhancement to reach the same climax as the whale. Could they have both earned their telepathic agreement with God through the expediency of their pineal gland? My belief is yes, as I have taken particular attention to my own telepathic expediency and growth, where I can communicate and talk to all species. And I come back to one of my first encounters when it was explained to me that once we reached a perpendicular motion, or synchronisation of same mind, we are all united with the same transcription or language as one!

Now, are you becoming more aware of how we communicate on a telepathic level once we unfurl the layers of our intellect? Why do we have to delete the whales for the sake of our own insecurities? Why can't we learn to bring our thoughts up to their levels of consciousness and set a challenge for ourselves?

Remember that throughout the ancient languages, and also through the mythical stories, these lesser gods are our own personalities that have climbed their own internal ladder and achieved their own wisdom and success. They are then free to march on into discovering their next educational step. They then become a leader for those less fortunate than themselves.

As it is written, and also explained throughout the gift that Egyptology left for us, these gods are pertaining to the twelve strands of our DNA, where they originated symbolically from the ancient ones into the twelve tribes of Israel in the Old Testament and then became the twelve Disciples, or Apostles, in the New Testament. These stories are also explaining to us the twelve tribes of Israel, multiplying themselves as to how our glandular systems have inherited an identikit of the earthly body. Over time they grow up and create the substance of teaching us into becoming at one with the oneness or **G**reatest **O**rder of our inner **D**ivinity. Now can you understand by learning to look through instead of looking at, how these 144,000 personalities that you have within will be saved! This information makes us accountable to revealing the hidden revelations through the security of understanding the alphabet of the sacred language.

Is this why the Bible is still our recorded futuristic history, all through what we have not yet understood and accepted of the past? To the innocent mind, these religious stories that are foretold in the Bible have been delivered to us from our parents or Sunday school, or maybe it was from the religious instruction at school; these stories are still stored in our memory banks while we grew up to become the adult. Through these stories reflecting themselves back to us, we have the opportunity to keep realigning ourselves as we sometimes feel the need to reimburse back to our self. The progress of our future depends on how we have understood our past. We therefore have the opportunity to open up these stories to their next exalted level, which will automatically tune us in to the intellectual awareness that awaits us!

Again, you can understand why my words are written to you in the first person and not the third! I am bringing this information into your own personal diary, which becomes your awareness—not where you can think about it and put it in the too-hard basket to peruse at a later date, or leave it to others! The information threaded throughout these laws that have been furled within you most of your life can now become your responsibility alone.

This is why the Bible has been delivered to us in two sections: the Old Testament, and then the information has been revised and updated to explain the New Testament. The Old Testament is explaining through symbolism how we first began. It is explaining the ecology of the human body as to how it collected to create us in the beginning. It is an identical picture of how the universe began through what some term as the Big Bang! Remember through the original source: what is out there is also within you! The New Testament is explaining to us how we learn to handle our ego self, which bounces along through our sympathetic nervous system to create our own experiences through how we understand ourselves. This is the same identical story scribed on the walls of Egypt for us to open up to become the benefit to mature within ourselves!

To those of you who are on your path of earning the metaphysical understanding (the measurement of the inner physician, whose stories are best explained in the Gospel according to Luke), we read how we can create the next evolution of man's capabilities and intelligence. Now do you understand the parables in the Bible where Jesus went into the temple to hear the physicians speak?

He went up into his hierarchical mind and asked himself his own questions. The Lord Buddha, so the story is told, also did the same thing by sitting under his own tree of knowledge five hundred and forty years before to release his own information. Muhammad did the same in the seven hundreds (700s) by sitting on his mountain and revealing to himself his own understanding of his quest. They are all explaining exactly the same story. Why? There is only one! It all depends on how you understand your inner dictionary through the language you were born into.

Through my many years of Shamanic education, I have also been trained to view these biblical stories as to how the evolution and understanding of my central nervous system came into being a source of its own. It has become the creation of the hierarchical mind of self, where the branches of this wonderful tree of knowledge filtered throughout my body; where the information collected in my glands; and metaphorically, we understand that these glands are representing the lesser gods as explained throughout Egyptology and the myths. And remember from my earlier writings: until I had understood each story in its fullness, I was stopped and could not move on. Back to the beginning I went and started over again— until I got it right! The challenges kept on being presented to me, and I could and would not allow myself to falter. Once my inner mirror was clear, I then had to allow each memory to seat itself in its correct alignment. There was only time to honour myself and then, the next lesson began.

CHAPTER THREE

The Hidden Language

Allow me to explain to you a little more of the derivative behind the hidden language that is explained to us in the first book of the Holy Bible, Genesis, and reiterate to you why it is still hidden:

1st Dimensional Mind:
"And the earth was without form, and void; and darkness was upon the face of the deep. And the Spirit of God moved upon the face of the waters. And God said, Let there be light: and there was light. And God saw the light, that it was good: and God divided the light from the darkness. And called the light Day, and the darkness he called Night. And the evening and the morning were the first day".

Are you now better prepared through reading the previous pages to step up here with me and understand the metaphysical interpretation? God is introducing us to the foetus which is created in the darkness of the womb. Let there be light is introducing us to the first glyph of intellectual light to create the human body. When the female egg is fertilized by the male, the conception of the light begins to radiate out through the waters, which is referring to the fluidic waters of our cells. God divided the light from the darkness and called the light—day—he was referring to the gestation period creating its own responsibility to become the next generation. The darkness is at that time the past, where our ego will place itself to rest! It is the unknown, and he called it night.

2nd Dimensional Mind:
"And God said, Let there be a firmament" (Is God talking about the human brain here?) *"in the midst of the waters, and let it divide the waters from the waters".*

"And God made the firmament, and divided the waters which were under the firmament" (the Brain) *"from the waters which were above the firmament: and it was so".*

"And God called the firmament Heaven. And the evening and the morning were the second day. And God said, Let the waters under the heaven be gathered together unto one place, and let the dry land appear: and it was so. And God called the dry land Earth; and the gathering together of the waters called he Seas: and God saw that it was good".

Are we seeing how God is introducing us to the evolution of the brain as to how it was first produced in the midst of the waters; the midst is the cellular structure and is the second stage of gestation. From here it was divided again to become the two separate hemispheres of the brain, where it divides the waters from the waters?

God called this heaven! Let the waters under the heaven be gathered together unto one place. Here we see how the three minds of God collected for the rest of the body to become a sealed unit. Our body up to the neck is referred to as the dry land known as the earth. I refer to this in my teachings as the uninitiated disciple; through our own innocence we know not who we are. We muddle and puddle along through the upheaval of our inner emotions, which makes us envy others who can keep their life in order, where we must learn to keep our mind focused on self for us to become aware of our own shortcomings. And as always in our hour of need, someone will step in front of us to offer us their strength and guide us on to stepping onto our own pathway. We have named this enterprise our imagination, or through the metaphysical language we are being tuned into the image inside our nation, or what is on standby as it is already created within every human, from before we were born.

The gathering of the waters, he called the seas. In other words, we are capable of becoming the heaven and the earth both at the same time! We are being informed that we are entitled to earn our free will to become our own universe, or our complete self!

To take you back through the sacredness of the ancient language, many thousands of years ago in the Mesopotamia region of Iraq, the planet was pronounced as UR-T, which we now pronounce as earth, and is denoted as 'Understanding and Releasing the Truth'. We know that in the past, as foretold throughout the Mayan, Arabic, and Asian chronicles and also the Nordic regions, each tribal elder that took on the responsibility of the tribe was given the name of URT. More information is explained throughout my book *Decoding the Shaman Within*.

As each person evolved intellectually, they connected up into the exalted language of the etheric connection of the consciousness. Once they had connected their intelligence up into the great memoriam of consciousness and could accept the responsibility to believe in themselves, their light stood out where the clan had someone to look up to. They then had to take on the responsibility of the village. Therefore, these elders were all given the same name. So, their tribal councils between one another were collected from the earth. This same word is pronounced as 'Airte' or 'Erte' in the Aboriginal language in my land. Now can you understand how they telepathically heard the same name, right around the planet?

All of these stories are interpreting to us how, through our relationship of understanding, our inner self began as to the thoughts we could release; which became our personalities, which gave us the confidence to use and rely on the information filtering throughout our brain. Our inner light or day grew and expanded each time we changed our mind! I realize that this information is unknown to many of you; it all sounds new! Please trust me as I release this information to you, for you to release the empowered confidence that is within every human to read on.

*

3rd Dimensional Mind:
"And God said, Let the earth bring forth grass, the herb yielding seed, and the fruit tree yielding fruit after his kind, whose seed is in itself". We can view how we created our many personalities through the collection of our thoughts releasing themselves; these personalities become our ideas, as to how we blend each thought to create a sentence? We are being informed that every thought we release is already instilled in our mind, and everything is embedded in each gene from the

time of our gestation. We are our own perfect hologram. The number 3 denotes our collective mind. Biblically this is known to us as the written word of God, in other words, we are being reminded that everything we need to know is already waiting for us and is on standby, and more importantly, it is only revealed to us on an inner level when we feel that we have lost ourself in all directions. All of which creates the first Arking of the Covenant, which is this sacred order of our inner divinity that we have already made with God! More information on this subject as you read on.

*

4th Dimensional Mind:
"And God said; Let there be lights in the firmament of the heaven to divide the day from the night; and let them be for signs, and for seasons, and for days and years. And God made two great lights; the greater light to rule the day, and the lesser light to rule the night. And God set them in the firmament of the heaven to give light upon the earth. And to rule over the day and over the night, and to divide the light from the darkness: and God saw that it was good".

Is this explaining to us our inner strength that comes from our heart and is autonomically (self-governing) collected through the neural system or nerves of the brain? We view now how your light became the support of your emotional stability, which is the right hemisphere of your brain, as this area interfaces with the collective, and your darkness is your past or fear that is still embedded in the left hemisphere of the brain to create the two eyes we normally see with? The number 4 in the sacred numerology is represented as our temple mind, which, when decoded, is the explanation of both brains earning the right to meld as one, where they are being equalized to represent both our dark and light worlds. Throughout the Asian influences, the number four denotes death or a significant sign of a completed moment. Therefore, don't give up—give in to the truth of your inner self; there is more work for you to attend to!

*

5th Dimensional Mind:
"And God said, Let the waters bring forth abundantly the moving creature that hath life, and fowl that may fly above the earth in the open firmament of heaven." Stay close with this one and see the changes of intellect for our inner growth. "And God created great whales".

In the Shamanic language, the whale represents the words 'conversation and communication'. They have already earned their telepathic freedom through their language of becoming one another throughout the oceans with same mind. Hence the size of their spermaceti gland, which is their pineal gland. Compared to ours, theirs is monstrous; therefore, we have a long way to go before we have earned our telepathic agreement with one another.

This amazing gland we have all inherited creates the essence for us to move our intelligence up into the doorway of our unconscious mind for us to inherit ever-lasting life. Through the exemplified codex of self, we have left the earth and have journeyed up into the 'Heavenly Kingdoms,' where it brings a foreclosure to our third-dimensional thinking, which gives our cells the final incentive for them to receive the recognition of our completeness of both our inner as well as our outer self, to be free to combine as one. The smaller species of fish represent our next thought and follow on with the same inheritance, in a smaller version. When the whale wishes to communicate or make a sound, every whale in the ocean can hear their call. If we look at the whale, it is a huge fish at that time of the Biblical spoken language. *"And every living creature that moveth which the waters brought forth abundantly, after their kind"*. Please remember that the evolution of the human brain is the first organ to manifest in our body during our gestation, which was created through the energy of every living species that has evolved before us—*"and every winged fowl"*—(the bird kingdom represents the freedom our inner personalities can adhere to through the flight of the mind which shows us the way to open our heart to ourselves; which is symbolic of the stories of the Angels, that we see on an inner level)—*"after his kind: and God saw that it was good. And God blessed them, saying, 'Be fruitful and multiply, and fill the waters in the seas, and let fowl multiply in the earth'"*. The exemplified code is in the words 'in the earth'—not 'on the earth'. Now can you accept my findings on what was written previously, regarding how we should read the Bible? It is not about the earth or the planet as a whole. The magic appears when you understand the gift that the metaphysical language, which is the highest branch of philosophy we can attain through us dealing with the nature of existence and knowledge, is accepted throughout us. As we earn the information of our inner quest, which has been passed down to us informing us that our body is the earth up to our neck before we journey up into the heavens. The correct interpretation is to allow your thoughts to multiply through you being receptive to your angelic self. Are you now beginning to collect this metaphysical language through this new understanding; all explaining to us the multiplication of our intelligence, as to how we earn our inner freedom?

Remember that through the explanations of the hieroglyphs of the Egyptian Principles, the God Horus represents the third eye, which equates to this aspect of self. He is the Peregrine Falcon who can see much further into the distance from greater heights or an elevated mind. This species has earned their intellect of being great hunters, and through the words of my students—of whom many of them are Professors of the Latin Language—and after many lengthy discussions, we have come up with the word 'Peregrine', which is through the Ancient Aramaic language which was passed down to the Arabic language or Persian Principles and is decoded as: coming from beyond one's own land. The word 'beyond' is the key to the doorway here, as it explains to us that it interprets as: outside the range of. Now the story begins to come together. Another inference to this word is 'Pereae' or 'Perea'—through the codes this word is informing us of the '**p**ower **e**ternally **r**eleasing up into the crown of our head,' which is symbolically known to us through the collection of many thousands of myths as EA.

This area is supposedly a region of Ancient Palestine—it is east of the River Jordan and is recorded as the Dead Sea. Also, this information is recorded throughout the Dead Sea Scrolls, when read correctly. When we read this through the metaphysical language, we see how we are being informed that we have left our past behind us and ventured up into the doorway of our next step through releasing or walking towards us receiving our own intellectual contentment.

When one is still trapped in the folds of their ego, they look for a form of reality that supports their thoughts. They have not yet released the intellect to believe in the science that has laid behind the language, hence the area they thought this information revealed. Many of us still believe in the old adage that if it is not seen, then it is not there!

Do you now see how the matter of physics or this amazing metaphysical language is being brought back home to you? There are many other birds of this family tribe of similarity inheritance, some of which are called 'Rafters'. Now we understand where this word came from, as we know that the rafters are the support beams that hold up the roof of our house or home.

Can you see how the Angel entered into the language of our mind through the art of symbolism? Our intuition is designed autonomously through appropriation to search for similar sequences to explain to us logically in the moment of how like attracts like.

This is the wisdom of our divine heavenly energy. Once the inner eye is fully opened, we have the possibilities to become the matrix or hologram of each species, where we are able to view our inner freedom through the horizons of our mind.

*

6th Dimensional Mind:
"And God said; Let the earth bring forth the living creature after his kind, cattle and creeping thing, and beast of the earth after his kind: and it was so".

We have come to the evolution of the 6th day, as explained in Genesis 1, Verse 24. Again, we are unravelling another important code for us to accept. God said, Let the earth bring forth the living creature after his kind. Now what have you previously read as to how the base of the human brain was firstly correlated (be-connected to systematically) as to how we have been ignited through our own intellectual light with the living species that had evolved before us.

"And God made the beast of the earth after his kind, (we now begin to realise that this verse has been brought back to the left hemisphere of our brain, which our ego has a tight rein on, also often referred to as the child within every one of us, until it has succumbed to the greater good, as it does not wish to be told or controlled as to what its journey has to be responsible for.) *and cattle* (once decoded means our inner contentment that we are all able to achieve once we can honour and respect ourself) *after their kind, and everything that creepeth upon the earth after his kind: and God saw that it was good".*

We are becoming more aware of how we are bringing this journey of the hidden information that the Bible stories have collected over the millennium of time together.

"And God said, 'Let us make man in our own image, after our likeness: and let them have dominion over the fish of the sea, and over the fowl of the air, and over the cattle, and over all of the earth, and over every creeping thing that creepeth upon the earth.' So God created man in his own image, in the image of God created he him; male and female created he them".

Now, how are we beginning to change our understanding in all of this metaphysical interpretation? Are we the creation of every fish, animal, fowl, and creeping thing? Is this how evolution explains itself? *"Let us make man in our own image, after our likeness".* The human brain is now being understood correctly.

Wow! Sounds good to me! Remember that through the language of the Ancient Sanskrit, the word 'man' is each gene; and the word 'men' (plural) are representing our genes.

Now we are being informed that we are made up of every aspect that God has already created through the origin of the species on this planet before we evolved. All of which is explaining to us that the species of everything that was previously created before we evolved represents an emotion that we are able to add to our own personal dictionary, for us to use to the best of our ability. More is explained in my book *Decoding the Shaman Within*. We have been endowed with this bountiful knowledge to expand our feelings, which will support and explain to us how to use these potentialities to explore and add to our own resources.

I remember learning thirty-odd years ago how the human foetus began in the womb of our inner creation; as the head of the child began to shape itself and grow, it produced many different faces that all looked like fish. Fish are metaphorically representing the next thought. And as we ventured forward to create our medical inheritance, we brought forth the radar scanner. This amazing machine could create a picture into elements of lights and shadows for the reproduction of the unborn children, where we could see how each child had a different species of fish projected through its face; they were representing the emotional personalities the child would inherit one thought at a time, in the right hemisphere of the brain.

As the foetus grew stronger and became more pronounced, the faces then changed to reflect the animal races; which created the haughty and superior personalities of the left hemisphere of the brain, one thought at a time, that it could attach itself to for it to be able to defend itself and use for its own excuses. The fish of the ocean are reflecting our future; the animals of the land are reflecting our past! We are becoming more aware of how the gestation of our DNA, our recorded history, those 64 generations, were answering to the sound of the mother's thoughts when her mathematics had collected to balance and reply to those ninety days previous to the pregnancy being collected telepathically, through her not living up to her ideas she was trying to educate through to herself.

Now which fish or animal ruled supreme in this child's life? What is their inner totem now at this stage of their gestation? I will leave that up to you young medical students of the future! There's your challenge to release this metaphysical language and once it begins to unfurl itself, you're well on your way to igniting your inner light which stimulates the lymph nodes to send impulse messages through to the cells and genes where your inner body begins to radiate with an inner smile. Do you see how when we understand the makeup of the species, whether land through our ego, or sea through our emotions, we have the ability to predict the future disease that is created from the species; we can also dissolve it as well! Let's move back into the story.

"And God blessed them, and God said unto them, 'Be fruitful and multiply and replenish the earth and subdue it: and have dominion over the fish of the sea and over the fowl of the earth and over every living thing that moveth upon the earth".

It's getting better! I understand that this information means that I can nourish myself from my thoughts and bear my own fruit, which will sustain me through the sweetness I return back into myself. Yes, I am qualified to know and can accept now, that the Earth is me!

"And God said, 'Behold, I have given you every herb bearing seed, which is upon the face of all the earth, and every tree, in which the fruit has a tree yielding seed; to you it shall be for meat. And to every beast of the earth, and to every fowl of the air, and to everything that creepeth on the earth, wherein there is life, I have given every green herb for meat'; and it was so".

We now come to terms with how this is explaining to us that this is the energy of our ideas and our emotional thoughts, that we can abide by? Are we mirroring one another or are we learning to balance our mind to create the family of the God—this greatest order of our inner divinity—which has already been gifted to us from within. For us to earn our freedom in both mind and body, which allows us to balance our mind for us to 'Master' our self?

*

7th Dimensional Mind:
"Thus the heavens and the earth were finished, and all the

host of them. And on the seventh day God ended his work, which he had made, and he rested. And God blessed the seventh day and sanctified it, because in it he had rested from all his work, which God created and made".

Slowly, over the seven years of reading the Bible backwards in the early nineties, I came to understand and accept the metaphysical language that the Bible was originally written in; it is explaining the relationship to me, it is who I am, and as you read through this book, my aim is to support you into realising, you are also. It is not the birthing of the world! It was teaching me by explaining the concordance of my body and my brain working in unison with one another, which by now you have become more aware of, are the heavens and the earth, plus the added evolution of the species of the planet that are foretold to us all.

It is explained to us through the stories of the myths that the Gods travelled to earth from the skies; I now fully understand the myths through my own interest and many years of earning the hidden codes to Egyptology. I found that it was explaining to me an identikit picture of the codes of the Bible! After many trips to Egypt, I gathered more information each time and more importantly, my clarity deepened through my understanding of why this area has been gifted to us, that we have named Egyptology, thousands of years before Christianity was brought to the surface for us to view.

I then had the confidence to move on through the other myths of the Anunnaki, where once again I had to unfurl their hidden agenda, which became our language that they left for us to view through their pictograms that were carved on the walls, and many other popular myths that have held the majority of us at bay for thousands of years, through our innocence of not understanding the hidden agenda of both the Sacred Alphabet and Language much more eloquently. Now I fully realise that I was repeating the same story over and over again, that the earth is my body right up to my neck and the stars and skies, in other words, they are all situated in my brain, where we are free, while still on the earth, to evolve up into our own next educated step. Now that is the explanation of the world engraved on the walls and temples for us, known as the story of Egyptology.

As I stepped up each rung of my intellectual ladder, my DNA, I realized that all of these Gods traversed from my head down throughout my body. Jacob's dream was also about the ladder when he saw through his vision world the angelic kingdoms, which metaphysically are our next thoughts traveling up and down our system. My glands send the information to the brain, which are known as the God's Lands, where they have the responsibility to filter the information throughout our central nervous system, which takes over and places every thought we think back into its rightful position, for us to begin again. A thought that has become expedient explains to you that the thought became advantageous in that moment, rather than right or just for you to use. Therefore, it is no longer required, unless you find it difficult to surrender to it, as this is where your ego, left brain, lays in abeyance until the next time you go back into your past to refresh itself and relive the same experience, where it has once again regained its own control. For those of you still in doubt, would you like to refresh your mind by reading this paragraph again?

We learn to adjust our frequencies through our newfound belief in self, where we learn to come into a more compatible unison with one another through the unconscious recognition of humanity's awareness. We become aware of the educated shift of our thoughts that create the differences between the words that produce our sentences, the land, country, nations and cities, as we journey into understanding this new language of the Bible. Each word is explaining different facets or faces of our personalities that nourish our energy to supply us with our newfound spiritual strength, as to how these words all resonate through our DNA to prepare our mind for its next sentence.

Chapter 2, verse 4: *"These are the generations (the genes rations, called the saeculum as explained through the Latin language, meaning forever, that were passed to us through the previous thought being measured through the hierarchical mind) of the heavens and of the earth, when they were created in the day that the Lord God made the earth and the heavens".*

"And every plant of the field before it was in the earth (not on the earth) and every herb (the healers of our nation) of the earth before it grew; for the Lord God had not caused to rain upon the earth, and there was not a man (gene) to till the ground. But there went up a mist from the earth, and watered the whole face of the ground. And the Lord God formed man of the dust of the ground (or is this, the gathering of the energy from all the previous species, that have been heralded onto us, before we were born?) and breathed into his nostrils the breath of life, and man became a living soul".

The seven seals written in the book of Revelations are taking shape and are beginning to evolve; we are informed that it took seven days to create the earth; for us to live our life to be able to inherit the information stored in these seven seals. We realise that our seals were closed when we birthed into the family and we know that these seals metaphorically begin to open up as our intelligence evolves throughout our life.

Why? It becomes our responsibility to open them; as they are the doorways into us discovering the hidden intelligence that is embedded within our cells and genes. Remember, this is Biblically explaining to us the written word! Let's run by this thinking again. We are able to understand how it took seven days to create the earth; this earth is our body and then we step up the ladder which is situated around our neck area into the heavens which is our brain. Actually, it took six days and we rested on the seventh! These seven days are our divine inheritance which are sealed to us at birth and are represented as the seven seals clasped on the back of the book. This book holds the keys to the recorded information of our DNA, that we need to open on our journey to reach the heavenly realms or what some term as the afterlife. Please read this paragraph again until you understand how I am bringing this information through.

All of which becomes our genetic fulfilment in our body as these seven seals are explaining to us the relationship we have to our soul. Where did they come from? We have seven layers of skin that protect our body. These skins are our first garment that we wear. They sublimate themselves together to strengthen and support us. Our moment of earned rest comes, when we have ascended intellectually through releasing the ego of its fear. The metaphysical language is explaining to every one of us the inner dictionary we all have; it has nothing to do with what we create outside of ourselves!

When I came to the readings of the Old Testament, I realized that I was repeating the same story as I had read in the New Testament. I came to the conclusion that the Old Testament was nourishing the self; and the New Testament was through we had finally earned the nurturing of self. The word 'nourish' through the codes interprets as to how we feed and nourish ourself by bringing together through digesting our thoughts; and to 'nurture' interprets as giving of our inner self to others, which is released through what we have already gained. I kept finding the same story written throughout both Testaments. They were explaining a different evolution of our intellectual body as to how we have unfolded our DNA, to release our emotional (our energy in motion) self. The explanation I give to my students is that the Old Testament is our understanding of who we are, yearning to succeed; and the New Testament is accomplished through accepting our learnings, where we have finally earned the right to deliver our message to support and strengthen others. Let us return to Genesis, chapter 2.

*

8th Dimensional Mind:
"And the Lord God planted a garden eastward in Eden" (the east is within us, please make note that the Bible is explaining to us the 'Garden of Eden,' also the story of 'Adam and Eve,' through the growth of our inner intelligence that is already imprinted within) *"and there he put the man whom he had formed"* (remember, the word 'man' is interpreted as a gene, the word 'men' is representing the plurality of the word, which becomes the genes contemplating our intelligence) *"And out of the ground made the Lord God to grow every tree that is pleasant to the sight"* (through the seeds he implanted in our cellular memories; is where we are able to see through the written word (right brain), not just look at (left brain) from within, as to how our truth releases itself, through our newfound belief) *"and good for food;"* (explaining the nourishment we attract to self) *"the tree of life in the midst of*

the garden and the tree of knowledge of good and evil". Inside each one of our genes is the neuron; pronounced dendron in the Greek language, which interprets as the word 'tree'; each dendron transmits impulses throughout our body through its cytoplasmic processes where they create their own branches; commonly known as dendrites. All of which stimulate our motor neurons which are responsible for carrying out our responses throughout the central nervous system. Could this be one of the reasons as to how the written word first interpreted the story of the tree of knowledge?

Both of these trees mentioned are in relationship to the double helix of our DNA. One is for the left brain and the other is for the right brain. When explaining the eight dimensions of the mind, we are metaphorically honouring the infinite truth we have within; where we learn to balance and harmonize our mind.

We now understand why the unicorn (the horse is decoded as our inner spiritual strength) has the spiral horn coming out of the brow, which is representing the eye of God, showing us how we have earned our freedom to gain our own inner spiritual strength. It is metaphorical in showing us the results of our DNA being free to search the universe. My sincere thanks for your patience in reading through to the end of this chapter.

CHAPTER FOUR

The Library Of The Universal Mind

Ten generations later came 'The Noah', who was told by God to build an Ark and to gather the animals, one male and one female times seven of the clean beasts, and one of each of the unclean. Do you see the familiarities between the seven seals or the seven chakras as explained throughout the Indo-Asiatic principles, with regard to the clean beasts? Now don't forget, that thousands of years before Christianity came into being, the knowledge was heralded down to us that Noah was also known as the 'Knower of Ways' as foretold throughout the Egyptian Philosophies, as he was the head Physician to the Pharaoh's wives. His position was to make sure that when the wives came to their birthing time, the new child had both sections of the brain intact and that they were harmonized and balanced with the complete memory of all the species that had evolved before us, as we could find comfort and support through their aptitude, through how they found their way up into the royal house.

In other words, the Garden of Eden that had been planted with all of the species, one of each of the unclean to create the inner library of their DNA, then by sevens to create the seals on the back of the book, which as our intellect climbs our internal ladder, we leave the earth (our body) through the doorway which elevates our intelligence up into the heavenly kingdoms, is in connection to the seven vertebrae of our neck which has the ability to support and hold our DNA together. All had to be complete.

The Bibliography that is written in all of our scrolls and myths will never go out of date; although it could take us many years to understand and come to terms with this inner metaphysical language as to what has already been written. It is the completed compilation of the library of the sacredness of the universal mind. This library is a reflection that mirrors itself to every human on the planet; where on an inner level, not one of us is any different to the other.

It all depends on you as to how you view yourself on an inner level through the preparation of your thoughts, which will become your aims and expectations of how you would like to prepare your own future.

No matter what language we speak or what religion we wish to serve; we are all born with the same hidden agenda embedded in every cell. When someone is born with a gene that has been disturbed and distorted, it is an eclectic answer of intrinsic behaviour that is valued through the intuitive management of the Divine language. The word 'eclectic' through the codes, interprets as a religious experience. A religious experience is you linking back to yourself! These are the laments that were written in the Egyptian Book of the Dead. Always the blessings are to be returned back to the self! We are being delivered the information of our DNA as foretold through the twelve tribes of Israel, right through to the twelve Apostles (the Apostolates) who become through their earnings, the Disciples (the Disciplines) of those who walked before us, also Jesus Christ.

*

Through our understanding of the Old Testament, we are earning the right to release our twelve Disciples of the New Testament where they walk hand in hand with us throughout our life's journey. There is no other book that has been collected and written to surpass its supremacy. Why? We have still not understood the hidden codes of the unexplained. Now do you understand that the symbolic form of information presented to us, opens up and allows us to create our reality? It is all just a matter of physics or the measurement we have earned, through the mathematical right to unfurl and open up of our inner physics named Metaphysics.

The Books of the Old Testament are symbolic stories about the evolution of man understanding himself—not a record of the journey of the land or the planet. These stories were passed down to us, written in the language of the universal mind, through the collected wisdom of Egyptology and echoed in many other lands as mythology. And this wonderful word bears thinking about: 'my-thology'. Was it once 'my theology'—my religion—which, through Latin interpretation, becomes *religio*: 'my way of life' or 'linking back to the self'? Learn to bring everything you know back to the first degree. Make it your responsibility. We have automatically placed our thoughts out there, in our innocence and lack of self-understanding. More importantly, we have neglected our inner dictionary of self. The land mentioned in the myths and biblical stories represents you—discovering the mathematical formula of your own mind and inner body. This becomes your 'land-gauge-ing' (language): the way you process thoughts to shape your future.

Through your innocence yearning for its own release, you are finally beginning to learn and earn the codes of this wonderful hidden God that has always been our intellectual light; this light is the compulsive positive energy or irresistible urge that surges through our life force. Again, I am repeating myself to you until you are able to hear, not just listen to my words. In other words, you are now beginning to look through your thoughts, not just looking at them! Isn't the meaning of our life a majestic story? We are all finally waking up.

Through the training I received from my Masters of Time, I am now more aware of the metaphysical explanation to most of the stories in the 'Holy Bible', and more importantly I understand that each story repeats itself over and over right throughout the whole book and why? It is a separate message for every one of your personalities to feel important; to feel as if they belong in the family of your mind.

Metaphorically we all have 144,000 personalities that can or will be saved as we journey throughout our life, or the 12 x 12 which is relating to the twelve tribes of Israel throughout the Bible, through multiplying their own thoughts and more importantly accepting who they are, or another explanation is to bring that information back inside yourself for you to accept that it is explaining the twelve strands of your DNA multiplying themselves as you earn the right to accept your own responsibilities. All of which allows us the satisfaction of feeling complete through this sacred code of the numbers magnifying our inner light. This light encourages us to search and explore up higher into our exalted mind. I also know how it was explained for you to urge yourself forward to release the inheritance of how your soul collected itself to become your Oracle; which we now understand is your intellectual light being measured from within. Remember that these same numbers were embedded into the skulls of two of the famous Kings; both of them through the principles of the Mayan and Egyptian Philosophies, many thousands of years ago, long before the bible was written.

*

Written in the Book of St. John in the New Testament, the words are beautifully explained in chapter 1, verses 6-11: *"There was a man sent from God, whose name was John"*. (This is explained through the manuscript of our DNA and is denoted as our inner light.) *"The same came for a witness, to bear witness of the Light, that all men (genes) through him might believe. He was not that Light, but was sent to bear witness of that Light. That was the true Light, which lighteth every man that cometh into the world. He was in the world, and the world was made by him, and the world knew him not. He came unto his own, and his own received him not"*.

Are we beginning to understand the meta or the measurement of the physics here? In the first section of these verses, we are informed through our innocence, that John is a reflection of the intellectual light, and all men (genes, nourishing themselves) may believe through understanding his light. Now we notice how we are being addressed and spoken to. Allow me to remind you that, through the ancient Sanskrit language; this knowledge was embedded in the energy of the oracle, scribed in the sand of one's self. The sand is the ancient interpretation of the second God AN, who is responsible for our Divine Education.

John was not the ultra-light but an affinity of it. *"But to bear witness of that light"* explains that he carried this truth in his heart—embedded also in his collective mind—as evidence to introduce us to this light. This was his highest intellectual and brightest gene. He tells us that we are all created from the same mould. The word 'world', when interpreted through the language of metaphysics, refers to the body. It also represents the light within one's words. *"The world was made by him, but did not know him"*. Through our innocence and a deep yearning for self-improvement, we have been given the opportunity to become like him.

Now to understand this next important code *"He came unto his own"* is explaining to us that he came from above, this is where we begin to understand that this is explaining our heavenly home. Also, this information is an added value explaining our soul or seals.

My goodness, this story is turning into shades of Genesis, chapter 1: *"In the beginning God created the heaven and the earth"*. It all sounds very familiar, doesn't it? Are you keeping up with me? Can you begin to see how and where we have not yet fully understood what is termed the written word? We are not realizing that we have had to bring our language up into the next equation, for us to fully realize that the written word is our flesh. Have we therefore misconstrued the science within the written word of God?

I get so excited when releasing these codes to you that I could go on and on. Another memory from my childhood returns to me—when my father read this chapter at the table after we had finished our roast dinner one Sunday. As a child, I was busily concocting a story unfolding somewhere in my mind. To me, it was always a story that had happened in the past. I could not bring this story inside myself to realize that John was being explained as a part of me! In my innocence, I was listening, but at that time, I did not yet have the knowledge to truly hear the words. Oh, I am eternally grateful to consciousness for blessing me with my Father and Mother, who taught me how to become the woman I am today.

If we go on to verses 12–14, it begins to reveal an important level: *"But as many as received him, to them gave he power to become the sons of God, even to them that believe on his name; which were born, not of blood, nor of the will of the flesh, nor of the will of man, but of God. And the Word was made flesh, and dwelt among us (and we beheld his glory, the glory as of the only begotten of the Father), full of grace and truth"*.

Now we are bringing the narrative together where John is explaining to us that we are all the 'sons and daughters of God'. And remember that through the marriage of the mind between one another; meaning both hemispheres of our brain realigning with one another; we learn to open our heart where we become a fully-fledged united being. As we raise up our arms our wings are beginning to fly. In other words, we are becoming every species that has evolved before us! The written word is interpreted as every cell in our body, which releases our destiny!

When we birth our son into the family, he represents our ego as well as our next positive thought! He is the results of our power, our power begins with our strength, our strength begins with our intelligence, and our intelligence begins with our light. A daughter represents our emotions as well as our next emotional thought and when our ego overrides our emotions, she surrenders under the weight and our strength becomes an overbearing factor that places us out in the wilderness, where loneliness isolates us from becoming our truth.

Again, another code is released in this narrative: *"Which were born, not of blood, nor on the will of man, but of God. And the word was made flesh and dwelt amongst us"*. It is the world of the Divine equation that we are here to inherit and all of these stories are transcribed to us through the subject of matter. Hear how he describes our genes; our inheritance is imploded and written in our genes.

And please feel free to read on, and on.

CHAPTER FIVE

The Mystery Of Life

My inner desire in the beginning of my quest was to draw your attention to this wonderful mystery of life, so that we can see, hear, feel, taste and know ourselves, through the veils we are so quick to pick up and wrap around ourselves for protection and security; especially when there is something we do not understand or have difficulties in coming to terms with. When we feel comfortable in the moment; we act like sheep, we allow others to lead us, and we meekly follow. Is this our innocence or do you think it is our ignorance? I have a definitive ambition to help you release in yourself the garments, not veils; that you have earned the right to wear.

The information of this language is extremely hard for those of you still caught up in the 3rd dimensional reality, where humanity finds safety in others numbers; it can only awaken when you have out lived your desires to your ego's satisfaction. The next challenge is to learn to open your heart to yourself, which leads you up into the divine language that has already been invested within you.

This is where we evoke ourselves up into the language of this universal mind, which is housed up in the temple area of the head. It is where we have earned the gift of looking through our written words; not just looking at them! This is the law that the Priests within have been seeded with and must always abide by.

Remember our thoughts collect exactly the same as cosmic dust! Also remember that cosmic dust is porous; the same can be said regarding our bone matter that surrounds our upper cheek bones and around the back of our ears; this is the responsibility our future thoughts have, as to how they are prepared on your behalf. It is through our own cosmic dust, where our magnetic force fields integrate with each other to produce your next sentence! If not, we produce turbulence throughout our mind which is where the heart and brain combine to send a signal to step in to disrupt our energy flow as our mathematics are becoming weaker, which sets the scene to create our futuristic diseases in the body. I call it fate!

It is up in this area, how we begin to release the nectar of the Gods. We are able to see how we as humanity have evolved, when we notice the millions of people who have stepped up into what is termed as the alternative healing worlds, since the end of the last world war. We are finally beginning to heal our self; and what was, is no longer advantageous enough for us to satisfy our curiosity.

There are many years of Biblical research involved here, to finally bring these codes of historical significance to fruition and then to release them out to you. I would like to speak Goethe's words when he wrote: *"The moment one makes a commitment to oneself, is when the Universe conspires to help you"*. And I finally had to realize within myself: *"That which releases through my heart, will automatically be accepted by my heart"*.

You will become more aware of yourself when you can hear your inner truth. Every word I have spoken and written to you in these tutorials—you will recognize as your truth. It is truly wonderful when so many of you approach me at the end of a seminar, regardless of the language you speak, and say, *"I understand every word you have spoken. It resonates deeply within me, and I feel as if I am coming home to myself."*

This information had been protected and stored in our cells. These stories originated from the inner library of those who walked before us, who had earned the right to open up their inner storehouse which was already stored in one's mind before they drew their first breath. We also understand that this information created the basic foundation of all Medical Sciences which were also written in Latin, as each philosopher researched and released his detailed information. Note the symbol that was created for the Medical Association of the twin serpents spiralling up on their staff with the orb on top; with the outstretched wings of Ma'at, protecting them where they are facing one another.

Through the explanation of the Egyptian Philosophies this same symbol represents the balanced mind of a Pharaoh who had reached an attainment of discovering himself where he could release the twin serpents at the same time; both representing the double helix of our DNA coming out of the upper mind, known as our forehead. Now you note the horn of the unicorn written previously. The Greeks have named this metaphor Aesculapius, the Romans brought this word through into the Latin language where it is informing us of EA the heavenly home, also there is the word 'skull' where we attain the piousness of self. To reverse this word, I honour you with a sentence that explains: through the religion of one's own mind, we create our piousness, which is housed in the skull and known as our heavenly home.

The Biblical language evolved through the wholeness of the collective consciousness measuring itself. Our intellectual light from this inner library brought forth new words for us to inherit.

You are now aware that this information is inside you; every story is registered within your genes. We have named it 'intuition' a word that many of you still do not trust, for what you can accomplish up to this point in your life. Therefore, it will take time for you to accept my version of how I explain the written word. In many areas of consciousness, it will take some of you, generations.

In the first place, many of you will want to argue with what I have written to you. I know, I had to argue with myself for years, over and over again when I was placed in isolation, in the outback. No one could give me the answers! The messages came through the cosmic laws of the universe. I watched the birds who were always with me flying in unison to my thoughts, coming from the left of me or the right to giving me confidence for me to allow them to show me my answers. And then the animals who arrived at my door uninvited, be they snakes or kangaroos, foxes, dingoes, huge goanna's which I knew would not harm me, who were there to guide me into calmer waters. I watched which way the wind blew, as to how the trees rustled through my thoughts, informing me of the right or wrong direction I was leading myself into.

The clouds in the sky became my inner screens, as they also changed through my thinking, giving me a picture in an animated form for me to watch and learn how I could learn to laugh at my own folly; until I could trust myself enough to open my own. Please refer to my revised book *Decoding Extra-Terrestrial Intelligence,* explaining the codes of Extra-Terrestrial Intelligence.

I seemed to spend so much time reading and revealing the codes backwards, as well as forwards; even at times turning them inside out for me to realize how this energy had mathematized itself to become our truth. These are the testimonials or tutorials, that I am writing to explain these ancient codes of the consciousness to you; and are my total responsibility. For many of you, they will become your periodicals in the future, where you can open up the books of your mind to any page; to find an immediate answer.

Society has 'portended' that we write a story explaining the third person. We either have to create a story that is happening to someone else; rather than place the responsibility into our own circle of light. I will now change the word 'portend' to 'portent' and offer you a significant sign or more to the point, an omen to help you understand yourself. It is as though we must be there on the sidelines, taking notice of someone else's expectations and experiences, where we are watching their game being played; in this way we can exchange ideas and write the story as to how we came to view their situation. That is excellent for the ego! It can turn the other cheek at any time. I am pleased to report that it takes a considerable amount of time to earn our self, through someone else's demise!

In the beginning, I was asked by many thousands of you to please write my story and share my teachings with you. "We need your words written; to remind us of the importance of who we really are?" Throughout my seminars the students arrived with their blank pages to write my words; as to how they understood what was being spoken to them. To add to this information, there were many thousands of hours of researching after each seminar to equate to the notes that they had written. They wanted to see more clearly and understand the message as to how their words were being conveyed to themself so that they could use this information when needed. After each seminar, I sat on the side lines to give them confirmation when they were in doubt, so that they could fully understand, how the message was delivered to them, the first time. This sometimes took many of them years for them to comprehend!

I was also told by many people that we are not supposed to confuse people by speaking too much of the original truth. Is this another excuse we have created? Why would the truth confuse you, it is the truth! Can someone explain to me why you have to keep walking on tenterhooks; who are you protecting? It is only your ego self! And that is only one half of your brain! You have a birthday every year to celebrate the ending of your past year on this planet. We have named it a ritual. This same day is also a celebration for the accomplishments that you can achieve for the forthcoming year. In other words, you do not stay the child; there comes a time when you have to grow up to become the adult, so why should you inhibit your dreams, your desires, of what you would like to accomplish for yourself; they too, are all a part of your divine equation, known as your personal intelligence! You personally thought of those ideas!

All of this written information will take some of you years to understand in its fullness, others will connect straight away. Please do not allow your ego to step in and confront you and try to lure you away. I am sharing this information to both hemispheres of your brain; not just one! Allow your inner truth to see through your demise, to set you free!

Can you see why there are still people running around the planet searching for the answer to these stories that are supposedly hidden either underground, or embedded in a mountain? No wonder they are still searching. The figures have already proven that nothing has ever been officially unearthed as yet! Until we can evolve up into this language, all is just surmised!

The only name that can be brought forth and understood in today's language; is the word 'Israel' and it is carved at the base of a column in the Temple of Luxor, which is one of the first Temples of educated light that is still standing. The Principles of Egypt are slowly revealing to us, parts of our futuristic self. The tombs in the Valley of the Kings that have been uncovered over the last one hundred years should be proving to us that we have not caught up with our own history. We are still in the process of learning to reveal the past; how can these things be forgotten? How come we can't remember these stories? What has happened to us to make us forget them! We are hell bent on trying to discover something new to take place in our lives, before we have fully understood how we have earned the right to be here! Bring it all back into the first person; you will reveal a different story!

Also, look at the thousands who are searching for the lost cities which are supposed to be hidden in the past somewhere? We have lived on this planet for thousands of years; these are our Grandparents, who have left us a trail of their intellectual conception, and we are now coming to terms with just how intellectually aware they were. We are the culmination of their expectations of what they had lived, learned and earned; their memories are here to support us each moment of our existence. These symbolic 'lost cities' are you arching yourself into your next evolution of attaining the Divine Intellectual Language. Remember through the Greek rendition that the 'lost city of Atlantis' or is it spelt Atlantes, as it is known through the Italian word for Atlas, which in today's language is a map! I remember throughout my journey searching these age-old mysteries for answers and once understood I found that I was discovering new ones instead!

The crown of your head is your Heavenly Kingdom. This is where all of the 'Cities of Light' come home to release and become one. The word 'light' means intelligence. Let us get this original story understood correctly; as it was written in the first time. In other words, switch this inner light within yourself on!

When I was conducting a series of lectures in Egypt, it was amazing how each neighbouring land all thought that they had the responsibility of guarding the Ark of the Covenant. Each language thought that this was their responsibility alone.

I am again reminding you, that you are that Ark and every word you think has the responsibility of arching you up into your heavenly home. God (this **G**reatest **O**rder of the **D**ivine) never placed boundaries around the planet; we have made this submission through our own control over what we have thought was unruly behaviour; isn't this the way we react when rearing our children?

So maybe now you can understand the torment I went through in the beginning to release my information to you. Until I could reverse my truth and come back to the original point of conception; to see how I came to the decision, there were years of not one word spoken, to others. Do you think that it makes it easier for you to listen to my words; rather than hear them? Through listening, (left brain) we are looking at; through hearing (right brain) we are looking through, where we learn to become the eagle which expands our peripheral vision to see from a greater height a totally different and expanded picture!

I am explaining to you, that the way we are heading, we are giving ourselves the opportunity to inherit more fatal diseases for each forthcoming generation to inherit on our behalf.

A dis-ease is also created through you walking backwards over your own 'Holy Ground' where you have repeatedly taken your mind back to a previous experience that created pain. This was not a happy time in your life, otherwise your energy would not collect this experience to disturb you. Some of us do not want to let the past go.

Why do we hang on to the negative; why does our ego grasp these memories to inhibit our own freedom? Why can't we truthfully say to our self "Enough is enough! This pain was created for me to learn. And I must remember that my pain stimulates and feeds the ego." There comes a time when you realize that you have given it, its own life force; you have allowed it to control you; and through its own momentous gain; it begins to consume you! All through you keeping yesterday's thoughts alive. Where are your earnings throughout all of these past experiences? This is why the Book of Revelations was created in code, for us to read in all of its gory detail that the whole story is explaining to us the rejection our ego tries to confuse us into believing that it all comes from outside of us. When the truth is finally revealed, this seven headed ten horned bestial left brain thinks it has priority right to rule and control us, for the rest of our life. Now read about the seven candlesticks with an opened mind, also understand why the seven seals were placed to inhibit you in understanding the importance of who you are in regards to the book of your life?

There were so many sayings of others that sustained me and gave me the confidence to go on. The words that my father explained from Einstein in the beginning of my journey, was a great help that it is only 'Matter transcends light'. I had to realize that my previous conceptions of life were no longer applicable to me now. I had to search and research; to be constantly aware of my new sense of reality, to release the courage to go on. Through courage, I could reveal to myself a sense of confidence to reinvest in myself; for my education to collect as matter. I needed to search my inner self to create the right answers to my questions, which have released from the collective consciousness of the one original truth. For the first time I understood that mathematics was the original word. This symbol is on the front cover of all of my books.

Always remember the most powerful energy on this planet is just one thought and if that thought is positive, we can all in time, realize the changes that we can make for ourself as well as explain back to the future of all mankind. Our telepathic inheritance awaits us all.

We have accumulated our ethics through understanding our intelligence; over the last fifteen hundred years, it has been through listening to someone else's story and trying to understand the previous recorded history of this wonderful word called Mythology, (my theology, my way of life) that has been passed down to us, throughout the earnings of the last 64 generations of our family tribes, as they are in their new kingdom and yet are still watching over us, to now assist us into discovering ourself! It is only those who still have their ego controlling them, that do not want to accept the truth of their own reality! Reality is a momentous gain to bring an end to a sentence you have in your life, in this God given moment.

We have brought forth the age of Christianity and have all of these 'Holy Books' that were written by the masters at that time, explaining to us in a hidden code just what our future inheritance, truthfully is. Our journey is to earn the wisdom to know how to release this hidden language, it is not passed down to us; it is already threaded throughout us, during our gestation from before we were born.

What more can we do for us to be able to reveal our true self? Turn our self - inside out? Is this how God programmed our life for us to inherit our earth? So back to the beginning we go where we yearn, to learn, to earn! Now that is a different explanation, isn't it? Therefore, when we begin to unfold this metaphysical language, we find out that all of these stories that we have correlated up to this point; are exactly what all of those previous stories have been trying to explain to us all along! It is just that we were not smart enough to view each situation. In other words, we had not earned the trust in ourself to become intellectually aware enough!

Many thousands of people who have attended my seminars have been helped and I can count on one hand that only a few of them have walked away; usually they attended through someone else's invitation. They did not come of their own accord. Those who walked away were not yet ready to accept themselves; life is as simple as that! They were out there still yearning to accept the word of others, rather than releasing their inner confidence to unlock the key to the 'doorway of their own heart' for them to trust more in themselves.

We have created divisions in our thinking; we have set up fences, you stay on your side and I will stay on mine. These barriers have been created only through our lack of understanding through not believing enough in ourselves!

This planet is my home, I live here and I am self-endowed with different levels in my inner dictionary; these languages explain to me, how I have evolved through my belief in understanding my own education.

I do not have any boundaries and there is no need for me to protect myself; I am free to travel completely around the fields of this small planet and know that I am fully protected. If there is no negativity in my thoughts, how can I attract them to me? So how can I explain my words more copiously; to place the onus of your life on to you?

My dilemmas presented themselves to me in regards to how I could relay these important messages out to you? There were times when my confusion reigned supreme, when I wondered if I was placing too much information on their shoulders, until many of my students alerted me to the fact that their years of education had not been in vain. Their intellect had changed dramatically through them listening to me explain the wisdom of the ages as to how they could and earn their hidden truth. They began to take note and hear their thoughts for the first time in their life. And now they are out there amongst the flock of lambs, who have the opportunity to grow up and become the ram, the Pharaoh Rameses, explaining and teaching the written word that is already scribed in their own genetic inheritance of what is our 'God Given' right to speak; they are explaining their stories right up to the universal commitment as to how one can accept one's self; to fully understand their responsibilities and earn their acceptance to serve themselves first. They now have the freedom of mind as well as the free will, to be of service to the rest of humanity.

I then realized that to explain this inner wisdom; I was totally on my own! I have had to bear witness to myself first, through hearing myself babble on, and now you know how this word came into our language which means Babylon. When there is no chattering or babbling on, we become more aware of knowing and understanding ourselves; it is only then that we earn the silence of our mind. Throughout my journey of many years, decoding the language that the bible was written in it gave me the sustenance I craved for; it seemed to symbolically represent and become my big brother and sister, my spiritual mother and father, as I walked through my many worlds. I had the book right beside me and every morning when I opened my eyes, I opened it to any page and was drawn to the thought for the day. The words that I read, kept my faith and belief intact. I had to remember that these Universal Laws will last, as Dynasties will pass. Ever so slowly I climbed each rung of the ladder that I had inherited at birth.

I could not step down as I had already been there, I could only step up, where I realized that my support team was on standby waiting to guide me towards my next experience. Please allow me to continue with your educational training to alert you to the word of the hidden God or initiate you into the language of the sacredness of the mathematical laws that we can abide by; so, I would like you to give me your right hand and let us continue the walk down 'Memory Lane' together.

SERIES TWO: THE ARK OF THE CONVENANT

CHAPTER ONE

Our Creed Is The Covenant We Ark

For us to begin to understand the Book of Revelations we should now have some semblance of understanding these hidden codes that presented themselves to you, before you were born. Most of us are aware subconsciously, that the Ark of the Covenant is the creed we make between ourselves and God. Why? It is written.

We begin to read in the book of Hebrew chapter 11, verse 1: *"Now faith is the substance of things hoped for, the evidence of things not seen".*

I move on to verses 7, through to 10:

Verse 7: *"By faith, Noah being warned of God of things not seen as yet, moved with fear, prepared an ark to the saving of his house; (himself) by which he condemned the world, and became heir of the righteousness which is by faith".*

Verse 8: *"By faith Abraham, when he was called to go out into a place which he should after receive an inheritance, obeyed; and he went out not knowing wither he went".*

Verse 9: *"And by faith he sojourned in the land of promise as in a strange country, dwelling in the tabernacles with Isaac and Jacob, the heirs with him of the same promise".*

Verse 10: *"For he looked for a city which hath foundations, whose builder and maker is God".*

In verse 9: We are introduced to Isaac and Jacob who were also given the same promise as Abraham. It is all explained so precisely in Genesis from chapter 15 onwards, where we note that Abram by whom he was previously known, had taken Sarah's handmaiden who was named Hagar to be the mother of his first child, who was given the name of Esau.

Come with me now and allow me to explain these hidden codes to you! Remember that the human form is divided into three sections; beginning with our understanding which is our feet up to the navel. From there we begin to accept our learned intellect to bring our education up through our heart. Once we have reached the upper echelons, we have earned the confidence to act out our belief. This releases our truth! The sacred number 3, relates to how we collect our mind. It is explaining to us how we bring the journey of one thought up into its fruition.

We know that Abraham was the father of Isaac, who became the father of Jacob. When we first read this story, we become aware that it is explaining the three generations of the same family, as to how we have always understood the bible. Through the metaphorical interpretation we read a different story! Once we begin to understand the inner language of the unconscious mind, we find it is explaining to us the interpretation of the same person growing up into becoming his own kingdom! Throughout every myth that has been explained as well as the stories relating to the biblical agenda, we are informed that all of these stories are explaining the intellectual advancement of self.

Now we can see why Abram was 100 years of age and his wife Sarah was 90 years of age when they birthed their first child, who became Isaac. Sarah is representing his wife, which is his balanced mind, where both hemispheres of our brain become harmonized with one another. As to how he brings his emotional intellect up into his thinking which will automatically release his truth. His mind becomes balanced when his ego is brought under control through his emotions. Hagar who did not have the same emotional responsibility was insecure and she represents an emotional thought that is not fully matured. Abraham wasn't either! In other words, this personality that she represents is in close contact with Sarah as she is there to do Sarah's bidding. Can you see how we have been confused by the language of the unconscious explanation in all of the stories that have been previously told regarding the marriage of brother and sister? Also explained throughout the stories we have been taught regarding the Egyptian philosophies?

This gene called Abraham, previously called Abram, at this stage, is on his path of learning how to grow up to become mature. All of these stories are explaining the responsibility that both the left and right hemispheres of our brain must finally adhere too. This support naturally balances our thinking as to how the DNA releases our next positive advancement. Our advanced computer is ticking away through every thought we release. These thoughts are being placed in the correct formula where they have been brought together through the glandular system up into the pituitary gland where our thoughts are measured through this gland and weighed and measured through your inner mathematics as they keep adding and or subtracting autonomically (again explained as self-governing) on our behalf. All of which is then forwarded on to our hypothalamus gland, referred to as the gland that oversees our thoughts, it measures our inner stress, our body temp, our hunger and thirst, blood pressure, sex drive and more importantly our collective moods, which was explained to me during my training with my Masters of Time, was consumed by our ego, left brain, screaming for its own attention as it did not want to bow before itself! More explanations are in my first volume of books titled Decoding the Mind of God. Once our ego comes into its own abeyance the results are then passed on to our master system our pineal gland, which continually anoints us by opening up our inner vision worlds, where we have birthed into understanding our added value of who we are. We then become aware that we are beginning to realise the majestic beauty we have been born with, known as the doorway to our unconscious recognition of our inner self. The light we have released through this endeavour is then passed on to our pineal gland and the measuring is complete! We really are a marvel, aren't we?

Do you recall in chapter 15, when Abraham received a vision from God that he must inherit his own land? In verse 9, God instructed Abraham to take him a heifer, a she-goat, and a ram, each of three years old, and a turtle dove, and a young

Pigeon. Then he had to divide them in the midst and lay them against one another. The birds he had to leave alone. And then we read on about the darkness that fell upon him.

What does the young heifer represent? Cow means contentment. Goat represents foraging, taking a nibble here and there. It can survive in the desert! And the ram, the male sheep, represents our innocence learning to understand itself! And then lastly the turtle dove and the young Pidgeon which are all portending to the power we create in our thinking. They were all three years old which denotes that they had reached their higher mind. They knew themselves. Do you also note that they had to be divided into three? One for each section of our mind as it collected itself! The EL- AN and the EA. What about the birds? The turtledove represents the heart. The first angel, it is the gift one gives oneself! And of course, the pigeon is the messenger. So, we can see how Abraham had to inherit himself through the species he had embedded in his genes.

Abraham was originally known as Abram until he had grown up enough intellectually to sire his own child with his wife Sarah. And then his name changed to Abraham. The added letters of HA represent through the codes—in the name of—or maturing into the—heavenly ascension. The codes are explaining to us that Abraham was 100 years old when he had finally formed a relationship with his soul. The number one denotes as—I AM. The zero and there are two of them denote the relationship he had with his soul. He had to attain these advanced changes through his intellect birthing its self. Sarah was 90 years of age, the nine denotes as the inner knowing and of course the zero represents her soul. This is explaining how she relates to her inner knowing through her finally understanding her soul. Now you can understand how my name kept on changing throughout my journey as my intelligence unfolded itself!

These three names are introducing us to how the story came together to create a personality full of its own strength who later became a prophet of the mind of God. Abraham relates to the first God EL, who was childless which is our initial introduction into understanding ourselves and his experiences finish just below our navel! He relates to our ego and is in charge of our sexual administration. This area of our mind is known for its abbreviated energy where as it thinks, it expects! And of course it is totally controlled by our ego! He must learn to become his own executive where he can control these personalities of himself, who refuse to listen and hear the word of God.

Isaac relates to the second God AN, he is the child of Abraham or the next thought, he is male not female, therefore he represents the strength or power of Abraham. The God AN, or Ang as it known throughout the Asian philosophies is our educational system where our truth releases to exalt us up into the energy of our higher learning. We can begin to understand how to exalt our sexuality through ourselves and the reasoning for this precious gift we have attained. The last is Jacob who relates to the final ascension as we leave the earthly realms and evolve up into our heavenly aspects where we are tuned into the unconscious mind. This mighty realm is referred to through the thousands of stories explaining the myth as EA, known as everlasting ascension. We can all become these paragraphs written in the Book of Hebrew in chapter 11 explaining this city which hath foundations when we have exalted our own belief in self! Thank you for reading this story.

I can relate to this word 'Faith' as it took me years to bring it into my own fruition. I never knew from one moment to the next what was placed in front of me. I could not see ahead of me, and the more stressed out I became, the more I clouded up my past! I could not make heads or tails of this crazy language in the beginning, that I found myself speaking, and often wondered how my thoughts could collect and support me! I had to keep on retraining my mind to look only at each moment. It was like I was reading a book one word at a time! I felt like I was stretching my memory levels beyond their own boundaries. I was afraid of losing my knowledge as I could not keep up with my inner language releasing itself!

Everything was segmented. My father suggested to me to break each word up into syllables for me to understand how the word came together in the first place! As I matured into the way of thinking my life became easier, no longer were the words broken up into fractions. Then came the realization as to when did each sentence have enough information to explain my story? Where did I put the comma or create the full stop, to know that enough was enough? I had previously tried keeping everything at arm's length away from me. I just had to trust that all would be revealed, when I could finally bring myself together. It took a long time for me to earn my own house. And that is where the word 'faith' came to assist me and all was well as the years passed. What I am endeavouring to do is a momentous story explaining our evolution and to explain it all in these few pages really does require your undivided attention. Once you have read the book it can be closed and put away until next month or next year when you can open to any page when needed to refresh your mind. The story does not change. It can't, it is already written in your genes! The miracle is that you are the one to change!

You are more aware of how quickly I have been sidetracked again, there are so many memories supporting me, so back we come to also note that the ark is mentioned in regards to a balanced relationship in 1st Peter, chapter 3, explaining the courage that both wives and husbands will learn how to respect and face one another. Also on this journey, how both brains once united, support one another where we can receive and accomplish our own endowment. Again, I remind you to remember Peter, the Apostle, explains us how we are mathematically measured by God in relation to our feelings being released through our ego and emotions. Both metaphorically represents the marriage, or joining, of each individual's mind. This same Peter is the story inscribed on the walls of the God P'tah throughout the Egyptian philosophy.

We find that the ark is mentioned again in both verses 19-20:

"By which also he went and preached unto the spirits in prison.

Which sometime were disobedient, when once the longsuffering of God waited in the days of Noah, while the ark was a preparing, wherein few, that is, eight souls were saved by water".

The disobedience mentioned here are our thoughts that refuse to listen. They are locked up in their own prison, their own confinement, where they feel secure yet still hide among their fears. Noah had to speak to himself, before he could accept the next level of his intellect, enabling him to hear what God was expecting of him.

These eight souls, we understand are Noah, his wife, their three sons and their wives. Now we look at the sacred numerology where we note the source of the two parents, and their next positive thought, which are represented as their three sons, one for each of the Gods; denote the inner strength available to the mind of Noah. Their three wives, one for each of the three Gods, represent the emotional mind that both Noah and his wife are able to use to support them. Now let us bring both our strength and emotions together and there is the combined strength that Noah had earned. These are the eight souls that were saved by water. The number eight represents harmony and balance into the infinity, and the water of course represents the ultimate consciousness.

We again read of the Ark in Genesis in chapter 6, verse 14: *"Make thee an ark of gopher wood; rooms shalt thou make in the ark, and shalt pitch it within and without with pitch"*. I have never heard of gopher wood or a plant named after this animal, so I had to understand why the gopher has been mentioned. Wood represents nature! This little animal lives underground and feeds off the tuber and plants that survive under the soil. It is nourished by the next generation of seeds. Could this be the explanation of writing this paragraph? Remember that these words are continued in the next phase in Exodus regarding the vessel that held and protected Moses in Exodus chapter 2, verse 3: *"And when she could no longer hide him, and daubed it with slime and with pitch, and put the child therein; and she laid it in the flags by the rivers brink"*.

I understand that the word 'pitch' means a substance called bitumen, that we create when building roads to carry a heavy load, it makes the road waterproof; or a cricket pitch to play on, or to erect or pitch a tent to create a temporary home. Also, when a truck starts to pitch from side to side on an uneven road, the momentum of the weight could tip the truck over if it is not rebalanced. Another rendition of this word 'pitch' through the intelligence of the metaphysical language is through the vibrations of our mucus. Also, could this verse be portending to us a story of the child in the womb?

This paragraph is very important so pay attention! Our mucus which we have named slime in many different languages, supports us when we are in a stressful mode; it thickens when it is automatically tuned in to a reverse mode, where we keep on supporting our weaknesses through our fear of stepping up into a positive thought. When they are positive, it flows in a fluidic movement throughout the body; but when we panic, it stops and reverses its flow to try and counterbalance our negativity and gathers itself to form a convection of adulation. In other words, through a reversal of energy, we have named this a fat cell.

The skin of the human body is also collected this way. When we have reached a perpendicular motion through the intellectual peaking of our antennas; which is representing the twelve strands of our DNA; our skin begins to collect its layers which creates its own strength and becomes our protection, or our first garment that we use to support our own strength. Some of us are born with thick skins and thick hair; others are born with thin skins and thin hair. Those with thick have a substance that sustains them throughout any direction; where those with thin, have to reach up and endow themselves with their intellectual light. I call these the horizontal and vertical movements; both are needed to create and bring our thoughts back into balance.

Then the Ark begins to show itself to us again and is mentioned in Exodus in chapter 25, where we begin to see more information coming through. This begins in verse 2, where God asked Moses to speak to the children of Israel and ask them to bring an offering; of every man that bringeth willingly with his heart.

He asked for *"Gold, Silver, and Brass"*. These are the hidden elements of our own alchemy that we have within us, to create our inner strength for the journey ahead. Remember that the Bible is written through the interpretation of the metaphysical language, which comes from above; the home of the unconscious mind! Therefore, they write back to front. Now you can understand the reasoning behind the upper and the lower regions of Egypt. Also, the Asian Principles are explained the same way! The Brass represents from our thighs, and hips, up to the navel area, where we can balance our understanding and nourish ourselves. Our feet are explained further on.

The Silver is the education one releases as we go back into our past or fear, known as the darkness or underworld; it is situated in our solar plexus area, up to our breast or chest and represents the moon. It is the moon which opens up our psyche. Where we can begin to measure our thoughts!

Finally, we come to the crown of Gold we have earned, which is released out through our arms to represent the final result of our actions. This attainment is accomplished through how we accept the wisdom of our inner knowledge. Our glands have measured our thoughts where they release up into the pineal gland where everything is magnified into becoming our intellectual freedom. This is our alchemy at work.

These references are also explained in the book of Daniel, chapter 2, verses 31 and 32. I like to relate to these elements as our **Desire**, to **Defining**, the **Divine**.

Our lower legs are made of half iron and clay; we can realize that this area is the strength we have inherited in our basic foundations. The clay is the ground we walk on and the iron is the strength we have embedded in our bones. Remember our bones hold all the information known to the universe that is why they are so strong! The Egyptian philosophies explain this as the Bjah. In other words, he wanted us to inherit all of our faith. He wanted us to give him the best we had to offer!

"God asked for the colours of Blue and Purple and Scarlet". The colour Blue is resonated and collects as we prepare to ark (arc) ourselves up into producing our conversation and communication; this colour represents our forthcoming speech. The colour Purple is a reflection of the penitent feelings that are still caught up in our past. We are able to

watch how these thoughts can evolve through processing them to form a sentence where we are seeing the image of our invisible worlds collect together in their own light. We see through the forehead of our mind as we ark ourselves up to connect to our divine intellect.

And the scarlet is made up of the red and blue to create the colour cerise and remember that the first colour is red, which again represents the eternal balance, where as we create our cycle of life we are permanently brought back to the beginning. This colour is representing a celebration we ignite upon ourselves to speak our thoughts with confidence. Remember we are anointing our inner church!

Therefore, what are we accomplishing for our self by arching these colours? We are preparing to release each thought which is still caught in the past, for the success of our future! We automatically begin to arch or curve our new found perspective, which is dependent on the strength of the thought to release the colour spectrum. The more positive the thought; the higher we climb.

Remember Einstein's explanation in his 'Theory of Relativity', where we are able to produce space time through the confidence we feel; which autonomically releases the curve or ark, which creates gravity. All of which comes through the right hemisphere of the brain through our intellect reaching for the stars. We become lighter and more profound in our speech; where our inner light can magnify itself! All of our Holy Books are explaining the same story. God is within you; therefore, the more confident you grow within, the stronger your inner light, exudes out to others! You are becoming more aware of the matter of physics; as to how it is also created within you, which was previously known as Metaphysics. The colours that God is asking of you, reflects back to him; through your faith surmounting your belief in yourself.

In Beijing in China, the 'Holy City' is represented to the nation as the Purple Royal Palace, which is the ultimate story of man's evolution regaling through the symbolism of metaphysics. It is surrounded by TI-AN-AN-MEN Square. Can you decipher this word? **TI**—is my **T**ruth and **I**ntelligence,

AN—is the education, reflecting the light, **AN**—is repeated again, so therefore it becomes a relationship with self and—**MEN**— we know represent our genes. Now let us bring the sentence together. Through my truth and intelligence, I form a relationship with my education, to discover the evolution of my genes. Now we reverse this sentence. Through the light of my genes, I form a relationship with my inner education which becomes my intelligence and truth. Now that sounds interesting! This square has the four cardinal points of north, south, east, and west, which also represent our global inheritance.

CHAPTER TWO

Your Divine AN

Now we begin to understand in the Book of Exodus, why the ram's skin was died in red; our innocence has reached up for a higher level of attainment which is becoming our wisdom showing us how our intellect has matured. I have heard many different interpretations regarding this story and I still prefer my own. So please bear with me. Scarlet is the colour that is produced through your innocence maturing, through the resurrection of your past. We note here, how the colour blue has been added to the red. So, the sound we speak; has been reinforced through the growth of how we have accepted our self. Does this help you understand why the land of China heralds the colour RED as the most important one of all? Life through their language is a permanent celebration where you are continually moving forward. Therefore, you are not holding on to yesterday's thinking, which can only deter your future!

It is the culmination of the inner and outer self-maturing and coming together, which is the reflected colour of our genetic oracle. What colour is our blood? Depending on the elements we produce through our thinking, it can be many shades of red. Also, the colours red and blue are the colours that we receive in our vision world once we have ascended into the heavenly realms and these two colours represent how we are able to view the original blue print of life. All of which creates our geometrical convergence of everything we create! The mathematics are at work! Now you know why we refer to our Royalty as the blue blood. Also, throughout every myth as the royalty of self, the Blue Buddha etc; which is showing us how we are earning the crown we wear.

"God asked for fine Linen", which is produced from the flax plant and is one of the softest natural cloths that we have ever produced. The more it is washed and worn, the softer the fabric becomes. *"And he asked for goat's hair"* to represent our sturdiness. *"He asked for ram and badger skins"*, the ram's skin is for the emotional responses and the badger

who is always foraging for itself in our rubbish, represents support for the ego. And remember our ego can only sustain itself through reinvesting in its past. We can see here how our strength was collecting for us to create our first garment through these species, which were collected on our behalf.

"And shit-tim wood, oil for the light, spices for the anointing oil and sweet incense"; which explains how our odours collect and release, on behalf of our thoughts which breathe through our skin. *"He wanted onyx stones and stones to be set in the e'-phod and in the breastplate"* and in God's words, *"let them make me a sanctuary; that I may dwell among them".* Our garment is now strengthening and becoming ornately decorated; where we are reflecting out to others how we have taken the time to reimburse our self!

While we read of the commitment Moses made with God to build the tabernacle or the home of God; this story is carried right through to the end of the book. We can see how we are creating ourselves and endowing ourselves with the gifts that support us to release our lighted intelligence, so that we may fend for ourselves.

Through the energy that releases from the collection of these gems, and from the support of the other species, we can understand how we naturally produce the colours which become our support teams; all of which add to the awakening of our responses of the nervous system to become the intellectual alchemy of our brain. I will leave it up to you to read this wonderful book and bring through the clarification of your mind, to understand this Tabernacle that you have unconsciously made between you and with God.

*

We move on to the next evocation at the Jordan river, in the book of Joshua, chapter 3, verse 15 and 17: *"And as they that bare the ark were come unto Jordan and the feet of the priests that bare the ark were dipped in the brim of the water, (for Jordan overfloweth all his banks all the time of harvest).*

And the priests that bare the ark of the covenant of the Lord stood firm on dry ground in the midst of Jordan and all the Israelites passed over on dry ground until all the people were passed clean over Jordan".

Again, we read in chapter 4, verse 11: *"And it came to pass, when all the people were clean passed over, that the ark of the Lord passed over, and the priests, in the presence of the people".*

This brilliant chapter explains so much to us regarding our DNA and the twelve strands or the double helix, as it is known today. The Lord was speaking to Joshua regarding the river of Jordan. In verse 2 we read: *"Take you twelve men out of the people, out of every tribe a man".* It may be better if I explain this chapter through the metaphysical interpretation. The twelve men are representing one of the tribes of Israel, mentioned in the Old Testament; which later evolves up into becoming the twelve strands of our DNA.

These are our forthcoming Disciples or through the Arabic and Asian interpretation become our twelve Disciples. The final outcome is twelve genes; one from each tribe. The word 'people' represent a group or a multitude of genes. Each man or gene had to carry a stone (a personality of his mind) on his shoulders and place it where the priests stood firm and they were to place these stones in their footsteps. The Priests are represented as the glands which are our integral collection points of power, all the way up to our neck; these substations relay the energy up into the base of the skull; where they connect up into God's land. These nodes or glands are connected to our lymphatic system; which is known to us as the umbrella of God that filters throughout our body to support us.

*

I previously mentioned the idol made of iron and clay, which formed the foundations for creating Brass—earning its light to transition into Silver—where the elements evolved, investing in themselves to become the essence of Gold. This iron mixed with clay is the basic structure of stone, symbolising our fundamental understanding of self. Do you recall Peter's words when he said, *"Upon this rock I will build my church"*?

And until each man could believe in himself, they could not cross the river Jordan which is pronounced in the Arabic language as Yor-di-an. When we take this word through the ancient scrolls of the alphabet, this word interprets in the Arabic language as, Jor or 'Your Divine AN'. This area reaches its peak half way along the bridge of your nose and represents crossing the rivers into the unconscious area of the brain. Is this the four rivers that release in our mind?

Also in regards to the Chinese Principles, this story is represented on their dinner sets known to us all as the willow pattern, which is one of the most popular patterns to ever travel the planet. Why? It is explaining the metaphysical journey, it is mirroring in a nutshell the evolution of self, earning its freedom! It explains the willow tree, which is representing the sacrifice one makes to oneself; both the male and female crossing the bridge, are representing both hemispheres of the brain that have finally harmonized with one another; once they had crossed over the bridge to the other side they became angels, which are represented as the two swallows. These tiny little birds that we have named Swallows, have earned through their shamanic inheritance and through my Shamanic language as both represent the word 'endurance'.

When they migrate from Russia to Australia to rear their young, they travel over the ocean for thousands of kilometres, for months flying 24 hours per day, no sleep, or they would fall into the ocean and drown, snatching an insect passing by to sustain themselves in their moment, they are fixed on their horizon, their end result, back to their nest where they were born, whether their birthing was under a bridge, or in the wall of your bedroom near the doorway, so they could see out. It was an exciting time for me to see them flying in the sky as their migration was nearing its end! They had finally returned home, back to where they had evolved from. Does the story sound familiar? Then, both male and female would begin to repair last year's nest that had been vacant for around twelve months with the first layer of fresh mud from around the water tank to fortify and strengthen the original nest in place, once dry, they would gather the tips of dead grass and weave it with their spittle, which set the second layer like glue, once dry they would then remove their breast feathers and weave them in amongst the grass and then cover them with spiders webs as the third and final layer to keep their eggs at a constant temperature. Finally, their nest was ready and they could nestle in to their home for the hen to lay their eggs. This is when my diary came out to count off the days, waiting to hear the first new cheap. Now you can understand more eloquently the meaning of the word 'endurance'. Australia is a huge country and yet they remembered where they were born, even if it was out in the outback. If the parent had died the next generation took over the nest, as it remembered where it was born. Now that is a story of our inner sonar at work!

Another story, as to how we come together is told through the myth of King Arthur, and the twelve Knights of the Round Table; who were there to support him. This fable began through the Aramaic Language in Egypt through the Coptic religion many eons before-hand, which was used as a children's story for them to relate to the young man who could grow up to learn and earn his believe in himself; as to how he found his inner strength and was able to remove the sword from the stone.

The double-edged sword of course is the same explanation in every myth; it is the final result of how our ego has finally surrendered to its second dimensional mind to become an inheritor of the third dimensional reality, for it to walk hand in hand with the right brain in a balanced mind. It is the final result which when we are measured, stems from our soul's word! All of which is explaining the stories of the twelve Apostles, who served and supported Jesus Christ, also explaining to us the twelve strands of our DNA as each strand becomes a Disciple or Discipline we can abide by. Throughout the Greek Philosophies, it is the journey that Homer describes in the Odyssey or I like to refer to it as the 'ode to see'. Through the Greek interpretation it is pronounced as the ODES-TZEUS; brought back into English are explaining the identical stories written of Jesus.

And then we find the ark is placed in this wonderful house

in Solomon's Temple (in the –solo- or -soul of mans- which becomes our intellectual light) written in I Kings, chapter 8, verse 3, and again in 2nd Chronicles, chapter 5.

And finally, we read of the opening of the ark in Revelations, in chapter 11, verse 19: *"And the temple of God was opened in heaven, and there was seen in his temple the ark of his testament and there were lightening and voices and thunderings and an earthquake and great hail"*.

Have a rest before reading on and let these sentences filter through your mind. A glass of water will assist you to allow your collected thinking to flow naturally, which is also a reflection of our inner light explaining the river of Jordan.

CHAPTER THREE

The Language Of The Metaphysical Interpretation

Are you ready for another overview? Come along with me while we step through into the language of the metaphysical alignment.

We find that society sometimes has difficulties in accepting the paramount version in the Bible. Why? It is all through you not having earned the next step of your own intellectual education; which can only begin to support you, when you have mirrored yourself to yourself? Many of you are still relying on others to support your inner strength.

Through your innocence there has been no commitment by you, to accept the deeper relationship of self, all through you not yet having been deprived enough of your emotional upheavals which you constantly create. For us to reveal our inner truth, every cell of our body which has already made a commitment to itself from before we were born is sealed. The information is hidden away from our momentary thinking until we take command of our thoughts in a positive way. These cells can only begin to awaken through their own transformation to become our inner light. This light carries us up into the hierarchical levels of our unconscious mind, where it becomes our inner sight! And those who can see are realizing how much more of the world they can view; in other words, their peripheral vision expands beyond the old boundaries.

We come to the first step of the inquiry: What does it mean when it is written that the ark was covered in animal skins. The species that are mentioned in Exodus are the animal skin of the ram, which are died red and the skin of the badger. Both of these species also represent the energy of both the left and the right hemispheres of our brain. The badger which forages on the dead represents the ego or left hemisphere; it can only survive through reinvesting in the past as it cannot decipher the moment or the future. The Ram which keeps on plodding along represents the inner strength that we endow upon ourselves through our innocence, which belongs to our emotional right hemisphere.

They are representing the garments we wear of our primal past. And then we read how the ark was covered with the blue cloth. The colour blue represents how we speak to release the royal-ness of our spoken words. We begin to understand the colour spectrum more clearly as to the colours of the mask that was initially placed over Tut Ankh Amen's or Tutankhamen's head. And we are informed that not even the Levi Priests were allowed to look on the completed ark.

We are realizing the importance of the information, as to how this story is presenting itself to us. It is the evolution of the human brain; it is the language of the unconscious mind, which is the pre-recorded message of our DNA.

One of the stories that are foretold is that two of Moses nephews tried through bribery to make an offering before the ark, where they were both incinerated. Why? Neither one of them had earned the right to look upon the ark, as they had not yet earned their own intelligence. They had to be resurrected by their soul. That is what the word 'resurrect' interprets. Remember we earn every step of our intellect, it cannot be given to us by someone else, it is all up to how you begin to understand you! Again, I refer to the words in the book of Revelations chapter 11, verse 19.

Supposedly no person was allowed to touch the ark with their hands. Remember that our hands represent the results of our action; until they had earned their own ark within. The bible explains that Moses had already passed his test and had earned his intelligence. He carried the ark through the wilderness for forty years, until he had evolved up into and had earned the intellectual office of his unconscious mind. And his children followed him. Through the metaphysical these children represent every positive thought of this story. They represented every personality that he had purposely designed to follow him through his inner education of himself. They represented his forthcoming intelligence.

We then hear the stories of how the ark was carried by the Priests in the front line of the army during battle in the land of Ca'anan (do you see the similarity to the Asian word Ti-an-an-men Square. Also, through the Arabic interpretation it is pronounced as Kha-Anna-An which is also a wonderful word that needs to be explained. **Kha** is our inner knowledge, **Anna** is our education being mirrored back to us, and then the final **An**, where we become our educated mind) and it emitted a humming sound, while the Israelites were conquering the Promised Land.

When this information is brought back through the medical language, we make note that this humming sound is the beginning of the ringing in the ears; named tinnitus; this disease represents that we are not paying enough attention or hearing the learned self! We are then busily creating more excuses, which will become our future difficulties in both hearing and accepting our inner truth when it is presented to us.

During these so-called Wars, that are repeatedly mentioned; the ark was housed in a tent to protect the people from the power of it. To protect our genes until we had earned the responsibility of accepting the power of our mind. The word 'tent' in the Latin language is interpreted as 'tabernaculum' or the tabernacle. Throughout the medical association this word 'tent' is situated at the back of our throat, where our spoken word come through.

If you place your fingers into your mouth and search for the section where the lower jaw connects to the upper jaw near your ear and press that section, you will find that in most people there is a tremendous amount of pain stored in that soft fleshy area and we need to release it. The reason being is that most people, who have this pain, have yet to release their truth to themselves! While we are learning to speak our truth our mouth widens naturally, which autonomically tunes our sonic sound into a greater expansion of the collective inheritance; which creates change and adds to our alphabet! I am explaining to you the opening of the mouth ceremony, as hieroglyphically explained throughout the Egyptian Philosophies. I manipulate this section of the skull for healing deaf children, also those who stutter or who have inherited or created difficulties in accepting their own sexuality. We find cause to over protect this section which has become a safety haven for our fear, when we can't release the confidence to speak our truth through finding solace in holding onto the security of our past.

This section is the doorway of our unconscious mind and metaphorically, is where the twelve Tribes in the old language of the Testaments, or Disciples in the New Testaments live and call home. I relate to them as the Postulates who desire to know, and through earning their genetic inheritance; they evolve and become the 'Divine Apostles' where they live in their heavenly home for ever more.

There were those who wanted to receive the glory of the ark without mastering themselves. Also, there are many stories of the ark lifting itself up off the ground and hurling itself at the opposition and destroying those who did not allow God his dues. We can understand how these stories were created by others as to why it supposedly did this, when we read the previous paragraphs.

*

As it is with every story of the bible; until we understand the codes to this hidden language, we will keep on surmising what these stories are trying to interpret back to us. The point I am endeavouring to make to you here, is that every story of the Bible is written in this hidden language; it is not an historical explanation of the lands? It is an evolution of you releasing your inner story you were born with as to how you correlate to the words you think! You are your land! The army is an explanation of your thoughts; your personalities; striving for their own contentment. All of these s called wars that are mentioned in the bible, did not happen to the lands, they are explaining the internal revenue of our self being educated. It is where we pay our dues. Please, once again, take your time to hear the story that is written, not just listen.

Do you believe that God impregnated us genetically with all of his wisdom for us to destroy one another?

The ark that was carried by the high priests (Pri-Ests decoded interprets as the **P**ower **R**eleasing the **I**ntelligence of the **Est**ablishment or Estate) of the inner self; it is representing the highest evolution of attainment up to this point; these priests are supposedly always one step ahead of us, until we learn to balance our mind from within. It is not necessarily your deeds! Symbolically these High Priests are the introduction into the six areas where the upper glands or lymph nodes are situated around the throat area.

They begin with the thymus gland and come up through the thyroid gland and release up into the neck area and into the lower brain; now we can understand medically why the thymus gland shrinks as we evolve up into the higher levels of our mind, before we come home to the pyramids where we are able to see the alchemy of the brain collating on our behalf. This is further explained in my book *Decoding The Sacred Alphabet and Numerology,* recently updated.

Once the autonomic responses have collected enough mathematics to set the scene for the opening of the heart to self, we become aware of the spirals of energy it creates in its own circulatory system; as the energy travels up to connect to both the superior and inferior sections of the Medulla Oblongata; the superior is already open to assist our intellect reaching its own acclaim. For us to open up and become more attuned into the right hemisphere, we must earn mathematically the right to open the closed inferior section of the Medulla, which is where we mirror the unconscious recognition of self, back in to remind our logic self of its soul's purpose.

Through the Egyptian Philosophies, we are given the hieroglyph of the Ibis headed God Thoth, holding the scales of the heart and the feather, where we note that they weigh the same, all of which is symbolically representing the divine value of the new language we earn; through opening the heart to self!

Some say that it was the heart of Anubis that was tested. We now realize that he is the sentinel of the doorway into the unconscious mind and represents the ancient loyalty to self. I suggest that he is symbolically representing the sentinel, for us to accept his position for being there, while we are the ones being tested. Once we learn to revise and rebalance ourself mathematically, Thoth can weigh our heart. If a feather and our heart could balance and weigh the same, then we know our heart is open for eternity. What a symbol we are given through Egyptology. We are beginning to understand how the angelic realm came into our being. Through understanding the symbolism explaining these philosophies, we become more aware of how the heart became more important than the brain, as we step up into the journey to explore our next life, right here in this lifetime.

The God Thoth was also known as IB; symbolically representing the journey of our internal balance to us earning our five free days, where we are free to reside permanently in the unconscious mind, which is equivalent to our soul. Through the teachings of Catholicism, it is announced as the five virgin births!

Therefore, the Thymus gland has earned its freedom, once it is opened; where it becomes a member of the Divine EA. Remember that the Thymus gland is in relationship to our ego; and once the ego is sustained through its own belief; we permanently remind ourselves that: "Thy must be true to thyself!"

Yes, you are also receiving an education into understanding that the Biblical records are also the life history of our medical inheritance. Once our truth begins to unfold, we realize that we have walked through our past, where we no longer inherit our previous generation's diseases, or create new diseases for the next generation to inherit on your behalf. Let your light reflect through you. Let's bring the 'Science of Religion' and the 'Religion of Science' together; as it is all explaining the one and the same story!

CHAPTER FOUR

The Hidden Collection Seal Of Conscious Recognition

May I again remind you that the Bible is written to the coded recognition of the language of the unconscious mind. It is collected through the eternal language of the DNA which is habituating within us through familiarising itself with the ultra-mathematics of the advanced levels of the collective consciousness. It is all numerically induced through the sanctification of numerology, which is brought through the Soul's essence during humanities gestation. The stories correlate through the thoughts of others and are collected up into the sacred alphabet where they become available for everyone to telepathically hear these words where they are available for everyone's benefit; we call this form of recognition Mythology; my theology, my way of life.

Amazing, isn't it, that we as humans must accept that we had nothing at all to do with this language? It has always been present on this planet, carried through the previous species that evolved before us—trees, animals, the bird kingdoms, and the ocean—all functioning every moment of our lives. As previously written in this book, this forms the basic structure of the human brain. Our ability to use these codes depended entirely on our levels of intellect.

We are becoming more aware of how each species that has evolved is connected to it, as we realise the importance of becoming accountable for our own actions; and more importantly live it, through their mathematics reaching their own velocity of light, which means they cannot evolve beyond themselves. Throughout my teachings, I like to refer to it as the 'Cosmic Speed Limit'.

Once their antenna has been struck through their achievements of each thought coming into its own fruition, it becomes each species eternal light. This family of species then begins to recede, which allows the next species to move through their fields towards refining these Cosmic Laws which become the ultra-language of the Universal law. All of which is available for every human's inheritance. It is here always to serve us and in return we are able to nourish ourselves with what has been placed before us.

This intellect once unfolded, allows us to nurture others for them to reflect their light out to others. It all depends on what you attract to you. You release your levels of intellect, according to what is placed in front of you. We are all born with this specific genetic code in the brain, which has been collected together from the energetic species of every development that has already reached its peak of perfection and has collected its own antenna. All of which is attracted to the electromagnetic fields of the human strain, through the deliverance of our pineal gland; which is the Amon Re or Rah energy, correctly explained through the Egyptian Codes. We refer to this gland, as the energetic saver, or saviour of self; which becomes our everlasting life. The genes connected to our pineal, are hidden and protected in our folds, until we learn to reach in to search for ourselves.

The hymen which protects this gland will shred itself automatically the more our belief in self-accrues. And when we have suffered enough emotionally through our ego refusing to understand this God given moment; we become open to suggestion.

Automatically the matters of our physics are collecting for us to reach up for tomorrow's inheritance, where we begin to communicate only in the religious language of Metaphysics, where we are earning the privilege of linking back to the truth of ourself.

Goodness, once again I have led you into another parallel world of your own gestation; where you are free to support and add value to yourself.

CHAPTER FIVE

Stringing Ourselves Together

Remember that Moses' father, was supposedly named Amram as there was no pronunciation for the letter (I) in the ancient Arabic Language; we have named him through the codes of the metaphysical language as 'I Am the Ram'. Another point to remember is that when explaining this ancient language, when speaking to others, if he felt a sense of responsibility for what he was about to announce, the orator of that time always touched his heart with his right hand, then his mouth and finally moved up to the forehead to the gene above the pineal gland that we are finally opening up, known in the northern hemispheres as the God head, or the head of God, in the southern hemispheres. This movement represented that I am speaking my inner truth to you, therefore Amram was referred to as, I am the ram of my family tribe. This sacred sign is still being used today in many of the ancient cultures. Why the right hand? This ancient symbol is the ultimate moment of one's truth, (which hand do we put out to shake when introduced to somebody) where we are giving of our inner self, where we are tuned to our inner God to continue our conversation, and nurture ourselves with the words we are about to speak.

It is through our innocence that the lamb grows up to release his inner strength to become the ram. The word 'Ram' is also represented in the name of the Pharaoh called Rameses or Ram-Isis, where the stories are explaining how the ram is emotionally birthing itself. We are aware of the steles and temples informing us of Ramses, I, II, and III, presenting a story of you climbing your own ladder to open up these three Gods, reaching higher levels through the attainment of your own intellect, to become your own Kingdom.

Continuing on with this story I could take you further to explain the unconscious journey where he began to continue up to Kadesh or referred to in the past as Qadiash in Syria, which represents the supreme divine inner knowledge; where the last of his three-dimensional mind had sojourned up into the heavenly realm for him to accept his entry in the Kingdom of God to become the EA.

During the battle of Kadesh or the Kha Di Ash (the inner knowledge of the divine ash) as it is explained through the codes, also another interpretation is the resurrection of one's self; we have assumed that his armies deserted him when he was supposed to be fighting the Hittites. Not so! Let's bring forth the next level of understanding! Through the codes we find that Rameses or Isis, took responsibility for winning his own battle against his so-called enemies of Egypt. His enemies were his own egotistical personalities of his ego, that were still refusing to change their old ways and would not conform to the new. The stories change throughout history to also include his four armies that supported him which were named Amon, Re, Ptah, and Seth. Let's look closer at these four names? Amon Re, is decoded as the hidden one! Ptah is representing the right hemisphere of the brain and Seth is representing the left hemisphere of his brain. Therefore, our ego and emotions and the light of God within, all join forces to become the divine inheritance of Rameses or Isis, where the ego joined forces with the emotional aspect of himself!

His armies grouped together to become his inner strength and were there to support him, as you will notice when viewing the carvings on the temple walls explaining this so-called battle. There is one view of him with many heads with arms raised, which are representing his twelve apostles or twelve strands of his DNA (or to take this story even further back through the codes to say his armies) are assisting him to release his inner strength.

History denotes that the sea people came and absorbed Ramses and of course these people represent the ultra-consciousness. All of which is identical to how we evolve today. These wars that Ramses was supposed to have fought, are identical, as to how you reply to the inner wars your ego creates, through it not wanting to lose its own control of you or to conform to the position he is here to fulfil. All of these stories are explaining to our personalities, how we connect to our inner relationship for us to release our truth!

It all sounds similar to the evolution of Abraham, Isaac, and Jacob, doesn't it? Just like the stories of Eli—becoming Elijah, then becoming Elisha. You are living all three, having embodied both Eli's and Ramses' kingdoms, which began with Abu Simbel at the lower end of Egypt.

The God EL, began by extending his journey up to Luxor to explore the codes and teachings of the temples to complete his education which is through the university of the God AN; and then continuing up through the opening of the heart which is the ancient city of Amanea which Akhenaton built, to replace and eradicate all of the lesser Gods, and he declared that there was only one God, with the message that when we had opened our heart through understanding our new self, we were at the doorway of the heavenly realms; then we can all ascend ourselves to continue towards Cairo.

Once we had completed the journey of the three-dimensional earth, we then continued up into the fourth Dimension, we were then given the go-ahead that finally we were on our way through travelling up through the seven vertebrae of our neck towards the heavenly realms by opening up each of the seven seals on the back of the book of our DNA, that had been closed at birth. I thank you for reading my explanations to these important facts of how Egyptology is still misunderstood, until you begin to understand the journey of our inner language which is embedded in our cells through the process of every humans gestation before we were born, we find that we have opened up our inner strength to lead ourselves up into the metaphysical interpretation of numerology which leads us up into the sacredness of the Metaphysical Gematria, where we are able to oblige, coerce and work with the upper alphabetical language and beyond.

*

I would like to explain the information regarding the metaphysical language in greater depth, to the codes of the battle of Jericho. They become more interesting in the story which is explained more fully in chapter 6, verse 2: *"I have given into thine hand Jericho, and the king thereof, and the mighty men of valour"*.

"And ye shall compass the city, all ye men of war, and go roundabout the city once. Thus, shalt thou do six days".

This is where they were collecting and advancing those six seals as they marched forwards towards the seventh.

"And seven priests shall bear before the ark, seven trumpets of rams horns and the seventh day ye shall compass the city seven times and the priests shall blow with the trumpet".

These seven priests are the united strength that has been ignited intellectually, through the advancement of self. Through them blowing the seven ram's horns; which represent the honing in to the unconscious mind, we can understand how the Lamb is growing up to become the Ram.

We are being introduced to the sacred numbers through the codes of the number seven. Every seventh year, our body has been coded with the opportunity to reinvest in its self! Do you remember the story I spoke in my previous works of the Olive tree. How it reseeds itself through one of its fruit burrowing under the trunk of the original tree to fortify itself every seven years? For us to inherit in the first of our seven years on the earth; it is through the genetic inheritance of the mothers thinking, as she has autonomically passed her intellect on to the child. She represents the emotional mind of the next generation.

The second cycle of seven is up to the age of fourteen, the teenager; where the child begins to use the genetic inheritance of the Father's thinking, which represents the ego. The teenager then has the opportunity to work with their countering from the father, or move through as the warrior where they will learn to collect their own inner strength to sustain themselves.

The third cycle is the adult section of becoming twenty-one, where we are given the key of the door, which represents the three levels of our personalities being educated into understanding the divine equation.

Then comes the last one; which is where we are becoming

at one with the self, four times seven, 4 x 7= 28, through us being in conformity with the unconscious mind, or Temple mind. The number seven relates to the inner teacher, which we have Biblically named the Christ communicator. Now you can understand more fully why the Armed forces regale us with the 21-gun salute, as the highest honour they can endow to special occasions.

"And it shall come to pass, that when they make a long blast with the rams horn and when ye hear the sound of the trumpets, all the people shall shout with a great shout, and the wall of the city shall fall down flat and the people shall ascend up every man straight before him".

"And Joshua, the son of Nun, called the priests, and said unto them, Take up the Ark of the Covenant, and let seven priests bear seven trumpets of rams' horns before the ark of the lord".

"And he said unto the people Pass on, and compass the city, and let him that is armed, pass on before the ark of the lord".

Through the explanation of the Biblical connotation; being armed does not mean with a weapon. We have two of them one on each side of the upper half of the body. It means to release the accumulated results of your own action. *"And he said unto the people Pass on, and compass the city, and let him that is armed, pass on before the ark of the lord".*

The word 'armed' means being prepared, in other words they are living the inner truth of their intelligence. They had no need of weapons to fend for themselves; this word weapon also needs transforming through the sacred language; **W**isdom of **EA** becomes the **P**ower of my inner **O**rder **N**ourishing me. It is all to do with the inner Divine language; it has nothing at all to do with harming another member of humanity.

Once again, I remind you; do you think that the written word of the Lord, which is embedded in every gene; (and is also the mathematical equation to the laws of the universe) are so stupidly defined; that our ego thinks we have to create a war with one another? We seem to be hell bent on trying to divert these codes and destroying what comes naturally!

And so, we move on; the next interesting section is in verse 10, where Joshua commanded to the people, not to make any noise or speak one word, until they were told to do so and were told to wait six days. The number 6 through the codes is to gather one's self together, through earning the freedom (number 5) of understanding, to be master of one's self, and through our stillness becoming our silence, we are automatically releasing the past and stepping up into our higher mind.

"And then the walls came tumbling down". This is where our genetics evolved to create the human strain where we learned to collect our speech that is already embedded within; or is similar to the beginning in Genesis where it took seven days to create these seven seals to build our world.

Now, continuing on to explain the recognition of these sacred codes; we are looking at the city of Jericho, (through the codes this city denotes as, your riches that you have earned, taking you higher) towards the intellectual light above; just as every city mentioned in the Bible is being foretold to us. Through the explanations of the Egyptian philosophies the language of the soul or inner language; is sometimes mistaken as the afterlife, I like to refer to it as the next step of your life.

The word they used was 'REAN'; pronounced 'REN' or 'RA'AN' today. This word was referred to as the name of one of your personality's that was opening itself up to a greater degree. It had to be earned! It could not be acclaimed under false pretences.

And as this personality evolved, the next personality could move into its place and the earnings began again. These codes are our inheritance, which becomes a language of self-endowment that we can all live up to; before we can alter and change the collective of our consciousness. Through my education of earning the coded language of Shamanism, my name changed every time I had completed a quandary of the inner or unknowing. When my name had changed, I knew that I had passed my previous exams.

History is now informing us that these cities that we have claimed to be; have been created from the stories of the mythical collection. In the Temple of Luxor, (which is the temple of the light, where the oracle releases our education) there are the two rows of eight columns in the centre and there is only one name carved into the base of these columns that is known in any of today's languages and that is the word 'Israel'.

Remember that the word 'Israel' is the entrance or the doorway into the unconscious mind. Through the codes this word denotes as my **Intelligence** is my **Soul, I Release** and **Ascend** to my **Everlasting Life.**

The Temple in Luxor was renowned as the 'Centre' of both the Political and the Religious power, where it served and shared its responsibility throughout the whole of the Egyptian Empire. As each Priest climbed their own inheritance, they advanced up into the city which was previously referred to as Cornubia.

*

The book of Revelations in chapter 1, verse 4, explains it to us as the seven churches of Asia. These seven churches are the ultimate aim that we are able to open up within ourselves! They are symbolically represented as the information that is stored in our seven seals which follow one step after the other. These seals open up through the freedom we attain into the knowing that both on an inner, and an outer level, how we can attain the next step of our learned intellect. This is the last journey we attune to as we leave the third dimensional world behind to live eternally up into the fourth dimension or the temple of the heavenly kingdom.

The number seven wherever it is mentioned in the bible; all relates to the same explanation. We have seven layers of skin which is the first garment we wear. The number seven is decoded as Christ consciousness, meaning our ever-lasting light when we have discovered and accepted what we have already earned. It is also the number that equates to the angelic resonance.

Remember when the Lord told Joshua that the city of Jericho was in his hands and the King and the mighty men of valour. This gave Joshua the understanding that the city awaited on him to find the strength to create and add to the next level of his intelligence. Remember in verse 7, when Joshua said to his people: *"Pass on and compass the city, and let him that is armed pass on before the ark of the Lord"*. No, the Lord was not talking about a war between two lands; he was talking about the war one has, within oneself, when we do not want to listen for our highest good. This is also the symbol of the double headed serpent that was placed on the pharaoh's head in the hieroglyphs of Egypt. Also, it represents the symbol of the medical hierarchy as the ego finally found the courage to transfer its self over to the right hemisphere of the brain.

Move on and surround yourself with this light that is waiting for you and when you are ready to accept the divine teachings, that you are releasing throughout yourself, you can walk before your ark and carry it with you as your own covenant with God. In other words, you become your own church! Sounds absolute, doesn't it?

Now remember, to make all of this intellectual light release and become Joshua's, (the word 'Joshua' is denoted as JO meaning YOU, SHUA, or shwa, are tuning yourself into the direction of where you are willing yourself to be) the Levi Priests had to walk around the outer walls of the city, once a day for six days and on the seventh day they were to walk around the walls seven times. In other words, the seventh seal of Divinity had been opened, and the city of intellectual light was his. Do you remember in verse 10, regarding the silencing of the mind, throughout those six days and then the shouting on the seventh? The more silent we are in the mind, the more information is collected on our behalf and released back to us through the unconscious mind. We begin to see through the inner eye, which of course you remember, is reflected back to us through the eye of God.

If everyone could create half an hour of silence every day, they would be amazed how they are reclaiming their own existence. It could be through prayer as we know it to be; and please remember the word 'prayer' through the Latin language is decoded as 'orare' or more commonly pronounced as 'aura', which is the energy field that surrounds the human body and this we know, is the energy that vibrates from the divinity of our soul's life force. Through us achieving a sense of stillness autonomically follows a silence of the mind that has no continuation of thought. It then becomes a meditative experience.

Can you imagine how this relaxes the pressure in the brain or more colloquially, do you understand the importance of how the body then has the go ahead to repair itself? Remember our cells are full of exemplified consciousness. My mind opens up as I write these words to so many other examples that have been foretold to us.

Another reminder is in regards to Noah who was asked by God to collect the clean beasts, times seven to take into the ark, one pair for each of the layers of skin to keep them fortified, also to create the seven seals. The unclean he had to collect only two; one male and one female of each species. All of these animals are representing the personalities that we need to sustain ourselves.

This is the evolution of our second section of the brain; and on the seventh day we rested. Of course we could, we had earned our own teachings and this supplied us with the freedom to inherit more of our mind. Again, another reference springs to mind where I recall the Greek mythical story of Cyclops, as it relates to the same rendition. Now back to the Ark.

Then the ark disappeared for 300 years, so the story is told. It abandoned the Israelites when the Priest's ignored and sacrificed their obligations to the Ark in a battle against the Philistines (who are our personalities that refuse to digest their highest good). Supposedly 30,000 (Their temple mind had succumbed) Israelites died and the Philistines took the Ark back to their homeland. Within seven months it was returned back to the Israelites owing to every illness, also the plagues, that had succumbed to the Philistines land. Again, we are becoming aware of how important this number seven is through the codes of the mathematical mind.

The sacredness of numbers is written in my revised book of *Decoding the Sacred Alphabet and Numerology,* so let me refresh your mind here to the codes of this previous paragraph. The 300 missing years is decoded as my mind's relationship to my soul, (The number three represents the mind and the zero is the number of the soul, there are two zero's which relate to the relationship of self). Now if these numbers relate to the missing years, then we are being informed through the unconscious mind, that we are depleting our own self-worth.

This allowed the Philistines to take the ark back to their land. The battle is occurring within you, the Israelites are your positive acceptance of self and the Philistines are representing the doubt still trapped within you.

Of course they are representing both hemispheres of the brain. Instead of looking after their own positive thinking; the Israelites allowed their ego to try and create a dysfunctional unity of self, hence the death of 30,000 of them dying. We are viewing the number 3 with 0,000. The four zeros represent the 'Temple of our soul's mind'. So, once again we are being reminded that the collective mind is losing the inheritance that it has earned.

Leaving the Ark to the Philistines, who took it back to their homeland and through their own doubtful behaviour; they found that their seven seals were still closed down. Through misrepresenting these codes, they created their own plagues and illnesses. Can you see more clearly how the Holy Books were written? Do you realize that this is still being explained to us today, exactly what we have not yet understood, where there are still many of us who are blindly repeating yesterday's thinking!

*

Digressing here a moment; the Chinese people relate to the number four as the symbol of death where we understand their language perfectly through the metaphysical language; as it interprets to us that the past is finished and they die to their old ways. In this way they are not recalling yesterday's thinking to deter today's outcome! The mind recycles all by itself! Now this previous sentence is very important for us all to remember, isn't it? No sin! Please also recall, that they have already evolved up into the unconscious energy and applicate themselves accordingly to the language of cuneiform, where a symbol announces the complete story. We have a long way to go to inherit ourselves; before we can fully understand and comprehend the intellect of their divine language.

A reminder is that they were in Egypt for over three hundred years, deciphering and discovering the codes to the hieroglyphs, 3,500 years ago. That is 1,500 years before the Bible was created or had entered our mind. I know I have seen the scrolls, written in both the Egyptian hieroglyphs and language and on the same scroll, also in the Chinese cuneiforms, which gave me confirmation that I was on the right track and to keep going forward.

*

King David (remember in previous books I have explained that the word 'Davidea' represents the forehead; the inner screen) then took over Jerusalem and announced that his son Solomon would build a Temple on Mount Moriah, which would be twenty stories high and to pay for this, Solomon had to relinquish twenty villages to a neighbouring Kingdom. Now we can see how it all came together. The twenty story, high building is representing the relationship that Solomon had with his own soul. Therefore, to create this temple, he had to release the same number of his past; to balance his mind.

Only the Holy of Holies, were allowed into the centre of the Temple, who had to be smoked in incense to protect themselves from the brilliance of the light and then the story disappeared and was no longer mentioned. Please refer to the end of the book to realize the stature of the seventh seal.

The Temple was overrun by the Babylonians led by King Nebuchadnezzar who tried to destroy the Temple to take the Ark, as the Talmud quotes 'The Ark was hidden in its place', which means that it was in its rightful place and could not be destroyed.

Another interesting little parable is the story of a man named Ouzar, (You-Zar, denoted as 'you are the Tzar') who was supposedly struck dead when he tried to balance the Ark during traveling. We will look at the codes again to realize the hidden meaning. The ark was so pure that it did not need to be balanced. It was the gene or the man Ouzar who needed his mind balanced.

The Bible stories are a collection of the mythical stories which were brought back into the current language of the day to attract our attention, they have been released over time and were revisited by the High Priests who were placed into a seminary dialect of their own solitude, so that they could create a story according to that myth, revealing the hidden language to us in a metaphorical form.

Throughout my education, many times I had to wait for up to twenty years to fully understand one of my questions. One of my questions to my teacher was, "Who wrote the Bible?" It was quite a shock to be told that the majority of the current works came from Ancient Egyptian Empire, where the Jewish brought it into their religion, then from the Ethiopia and Sudan regions right through to Turkey and across to India and up into the land of China, as at that time they arrived there by boat to learn and understand for themselves as they had evolved at a faster rate, than other lands. These countries have placed an incredible amount of their wisdom to attaining their language through their understanding of the evolution of man and their stories were repeated as they met with other members of different tribes at the crossroads through traveling along the 'Old Silk Roads or Routes'. These resting places are still standing on the earth and have been there for thousands of years; they are tourist viewing points today. These Sahrai's or resting places are where they stayed to barter and exchange their goods and once the bartering had ceased for the day, they were given the opportunity to share their intellectual inheritance with one another. Now we can see more clearly how those ancient stories from China, Israel, India, Persia, Turkey, Syria, Somalia, Arabia, Egypt and many other lands were exchanged.

Those stories released in us the opportunity to broaden our

horizons, which gave us the possibilities of collecting and bringing a story together into our current evolution that is spoken to this day.

The alphabet has been brought forward as one new word releases itself from our inner library; it triggers a response in the middle ear which rearranges our thinking. This project is carried forward through the responsibility of the pituitary gland where this new word travels forward and opens up into the right brain to release the codes of the divine consciousness, which autonomically advances our educational language. It's all up to the cells! If they are in their own abeyance, they are more than ready to be introduced into their next step!

This is how the consciousness collects itself and the unconscious mind advances upon itself for us all to inherit. There is no interference up here in this realm. We are becoming more aware of how our mind can heal itself when we are at peace within.

Is this the true explanation that I have mentioned previously in the last book of our Bible, which is named 'The Revelation'? How once we turn within, we have the opportunity to 'Reveal to Ourself the importance of our Inner Nations'. We inherited them before we were born. Throughout your life you are given the opportunity to delve deeper within yourself to know who you truly are! We again read in chapter 1, verse 4: *"John to the seven churches which are in Asia: Grace be unto you, and peace from him which is, and which was, and which is to come; and from the seven Spirits which are before his throne".*

*

I would like to bring more of the divine science of religion, or maybe it is the divine religion of science, into the picture that we are all forming within our mind, as we read these words and bring this information up to the present moment.

We can also bring this understanding into the string theories that are all the fashion in conversation around the table at this time. I became interested in the word, when one of my students mentioned them to me and asked me how to understand this theory and asked 'could we use it to our benefit'.

I began by using examples of my teachings that are explained in my book 'Fung Schwa' as it is pronounced in the Chinese language by the learned ones. Also, the word is now spoken as Feng Shui, as it is being pronounced in the western tongue. Let us get the interpretation correct before we begin to view the word on an inner level; as to how much tension we place on each string when we tune in the violin to its correct scale to make ready for us to play.

To bring these theories back to us I explained how much tension we place on the double helix of our DNA when we are choked off through over exerting the self. We try to reach a peak of perfection for the purity of the note or thought to come through and this all depends on the focus of our mind in relationship to the acclaim and attention we give to the note or thought, we are aiming for. I remember when I was a member of a choir when there was someone singing in the group who was out of tune with the rest of the company! The others have a tendency to sing louder in the hope that they are drowning the other one out!

We repeat the sound over and over again until we hear the pitch in the right ear which automatically tunes us in to the pituitary gland where we balance our mind up into the mathematics of the unconscious mind. Or we continuously think the same thought over and over again and our DNA begins to stagger with its heavy load, where each coincidence remains the same.

It is also explaining how we enter up into our Temple area of the Divine intelligence. This makes our home much more compatible, in regards to our thoughts and creates a peaceful resonance to the mind.

Through some of your personalities, the sound may differ to others through the disturbance you are creating through too much inner chatter. This interferes with our matter or the mathematics of the mind. The strength of this matter will depend on how pure we create the note or thought; in other words, which one of our personality's substances is in the forefront, so try to take note of how many of our personalities are tuning into this vibration and listening. When enough of them collect to listen, only then will we begin to hear. The sound is then registered with the inner ear and as I have previously stated this opens up the divinity of self where the pitch and the vibrations create a tone of the note that we are searching for, is registered up into the unconscious mind.

If we speak in our purity which is motivated by us releasing our truth; we are automatically honing back into our self! This creates the tone of Aum, Om, Oum or these three sounds are all alike, only they are pronounced through different stages of our dialects. Sounds nice, doesn't it? All of this action is happening through the ultrasonic waves of time which is collecting into its own time capsule, all in a split second.

String theories are also created moment by moment. They are created if there is one personality that is not in alliance with the rest; then through their inner strength they must collectively bring this one up to the standard of the group force. This is exactly how our inner strength builds upon itself.

Or we can look at the other side of this equation and see how just one negative thought can pull the rest down, if they have their attention outside their own boundaries and are focusing on others therefore, they are no longer focusing on themselves. This rebel outlaw is back in its own control. Now we know that this thinking is the creation of all disease, in the human form. It all depends on the power of one. Either one is positive or one is doubtful of its capabilities. The electromagnetic fields are always collecting and working in a positive outcome. Therefore, for us to understand our inner quandary, what attention must we realign to ourselves to create our constant reality? Do you remember that old saying, "To thine own self, be true!"

String theories can separate or live in a complete harmonic convergence, that is, to stay within its own circle. Now we can understand why the weakest circle, which stems from not being satisfied and is wanting its own control, has to disassociate from itself so that it can search for its own contentment. Then it becomes its wholeness once again through searching for its beginning to support its own strength.

So, it is with the understanding of this magnificent Book of Revelation. It must be read over and over again with a honed mind to understand the magnificence of who you are able to truthfully become.

*

I feel exhilarated to have fulfilled my life up to this point, where I have only to ask and I receive. Now if this can happen for me; then so it can happen for you. The stories handed down throughout our history are all explaining to us, exactly the original blueprint of how we all began to Babylon or Babble On, in the first time.

Can you hear me when I say unto you, that your responsibility relies totally within yourselves for you to become your own ark, where you can become the 'Knower of Ways'. This can only occur through your space and time earning its mathematical right to release your Ark; you are arcing your mind up through your own recorded history, which is referred to as your DNA.

This wonderful inner library or Bible has every answer known to man! It does not need changing to suffice an ego. Let us understand the original story relating to the numbers written in the first time! You are missing the other half of the story! It is a coded recognition of every cell in your body. Our cells hold every prefix of what we have earned, which is the mathematics collating to a precise alignment; once registered they are held in abeyance until we require them. We are the ones who need to re-educate ourselves up into raising our awareness, where we begin to feel our self, change through what we did not previously understand.

These feelings rearrange and balance our heart and through this we learn to harmonically balance our thinking. To be able to feel one's thoughts; starts to set the healing process of our body.

The Bible is not to be read literally. That is for the beginner. Once it is understood in its correctness, we find the stories are explaining the next journey of us unfolding our intellect. There are many people who have said to me that they have no idea how to understand it! It is a recorded journal for the rest of us to accept the responsibility one must have for one's self. As the book of Revelations in chapter 14, verse 1, explains to us that 144,000 people will be saved, and of course they are the familiarity of the twelve tribes or the twelve disciplines or disciples, also the big one, they are explaining the twelve strands of our DNA, earning their rights of passage through multiplying themselves, for each one of us to find an inner contentment within ourself.

Another more important explanation is that it is the awakening of the twelve strands of our DNA (our store house of our previous generations) through their thoughts, which are threaded throughout our own genetics assisting us into multiplying our inner dictionary in context to give us the confidence to continue on. Symbolically these numbers 144,000 also relate to your emotional responsibilities that you can accomplish for self. Remember the two kings with these same numbers carved in their forehead?

I would like to refresh your mind and explain once again the story of Noah's Ark as to why the species had to be gathered the way God asked Noah, in Genesis, chapter 7, verse 1: *"And the lord said unto Noah, come thou and all thy house into the ark; for thee I have seen righteous before me in this generation"*. Remember that the ark is your body and we are shown how it collects intellectually to embed your genetic inheritance throughout your brain. In other words, God was asking Noah to commit to himself to allow his truth to release from his DNA, which is the blood lines and the store house of memories of the 64 generations of our previous grandparents and to step up into his next positive moment with much more conviction, to advance his thinking. Verse 2*: "Of every clean beast thou shalt take to thee by sevens, the male and his female":* (these seven clean beasts are symbolically representing our inner strength and one of each being placed into each one of our seven seals) *"and of beasts that are not clean by two, the male and his female. Verse 3: "Of the fowls* *also of the air by sevens, the male and his female; to keep seed alive upon the face of all the earth".*

Of course, the fowls of the air are the emotional feelings that one releases when we open our heart to our self, and through our feelings, we become more aware and alive. They stimulate our ego for it to take its next step forward which relaxes our emotions. Remember that the fowls represent the higher rendition of the Biblical angel and our angel is collected through us releasing positive emotions, towards our next thought. We can begin to see how this ark, is symbolically informing us of the intellectual awareness that is already in our body and is filled with the entire species that evolved before we were born, to evolve into becoming the desire (left hemisphere) and divine (right hemisphere) unity of the human brain?

Please don't expect to understand these works in the first read. It will take time for you to accept the written word and many of you may have to read this section of the book over and over again. If the book becomes too heavy, then put it down and walk away to ease the pressure of your mind. When you pick it up again, please find the time to read the previous page to allow what you have already read and heard through your thoughts, to ignite and remind your intellect how you have accepted the words in regards to yourself. It has taken me over 45 years to bring the story of our evolution together. And when I look back over this time, it all seems like yesterday!

Now that we are more aware of the ancient language to understand the 'Ark of the Covenant' and how it is with you every breath you take, we can begin to understand this next section which will lift you up and ignite you into your heavenly kingdoms. My heart-felt thanks go out to those of you who are reading this last paragraph and a giant 'thank you' for taking the time to rebalance your mind through reading my explanations to these stories.

SERIES THREE: REVELATIONS

CHAPTER ONE

Revealing The Inner Knowledge

Finally, we are coming to the title of the book. Hopefully the previous information is enough for you to begin to understand and connect to this ancient numerology and language, that I am reintroducing back to you. I can now move you in to revealing the inner knowledge regarding this hidden God, this powerful gene, which some have named Ein Sof or as it was written and explained in the ancient chronicles of Greece where it was pronounced as Ein Tzorph and then changed to Sophia, which represented the energy releasing from our feminine emotional right hemisphere of our brain, which is the emotional aspect of the highest pinnacle we can earn and achieve through the codes in connection to the God EA, before we journey on towards our next education, which becomes the ET Connection. All of which, when fully understood is interpreted as the **Truth** of **Zeus** through our **Oracle Releasing** the **Purpose** of **Heaven.** Now take the first letter to the words of the previous sentence for you to better understand this word Ein Tzorph. All in relationship to humanity becoming the 'One God'. In other words, we are all a member of the **G**reatest **O**rder of the **D**ivine, explaining our inner language to us that we are all connected to our inner divinity that we are born with. These cells are sealed at the time of our birth, and as we learn to take control of our thinking, they will open up to assist us as to how we think to take our next step forward, this rearranges our thoughts, through the downloading of our cellular structure during our gestation.

We have our own individual aura surrounding our body, and then we have our soul, which is the intellectual light that manifests from within, as we open up our mind for us to tune into our inner sanctum, this inner library we have named our DNA that we were born with. The more intellectually aware we become, the more our inner communication is stimulated into assisting us to invest more attentively into understanding our own inner strength through opening up our outer perspective, supplying us with a more important view in relationship to our inner and our outer thoughts combining and becoming balanced, where they are measured as one. It is the light that manifests from this endeavour of our inner self combining with our outer perspective, harmonising and balancing as one. This effort releases and creates our inner strength combining with our outer perspective, which creates the balance of our mind through the assistance of our soul. As my visions appear they are highlighting the sun shining on the earth which is the soul or in previous languages the Sol, of the planet.

Now, let us move forward in understanding the written word of St. John as presented in this book. Please have your Bible beside you, so you can follow along as we refer to each chapter. My education has been based on the King James Bible, the version my father and I consulted when referencing scripture. Throughout my early childhood, this was our primary source for the information I sought.

Let us begin to explore the significance of the seven seals that St. John the Divine reveals to us, and what he conveys regarding the seven-headed, ten-horned beast.

As history informs us, I have often wondered how St. John the Divine, while isolated on the island of Patmos, arrived at his conclusions to write this magnificent book. He explained the spiritual realm for us to decode and piece together—not merely through myths and legends, but through revelations that ultimately shaped the Bible. My spiritual journey, guided by the assistance of my Masters of Time, has led me to understand how this sacred text came to be. Many years of training were required for me to uncover the sacred codes of the matrix—the 'All That Is'.

Now, that I have climbed my way out of the bottomless pit, I know I have earned my own testament as I felt my inner peace and interpretation explaining them relax over the years, to understand the codes through earning the rites of the 'sacred alphabet' and also to open up the 'sacred language' from many thousands of years ago as to how I can explain my version to you. We know that the seals are not mentioned at all, throughout the other stories of the Bible; and yet when we read the Bible backwards, from Revelations back to Matthew we can better understand how the stories in Revelations are collected from the information written throughout the New Testament. In the beginning my first thought was that we have seven layers of skin that surround and protect our body and the word 'Revelations' is decoded as; through releasing our intellect we open up our inner library to reveal to ourselves the Gospels of our inner nations. Now I can accept my education to know that it was right for me and yet there is much more to explain. Over the years I just had to bring the stories together one by one, before I could interpret this inner or heavenly language to you correctly.

I had finished decoding the information in the early nineties where I had finalized the readings of the opening of the Ark of the Covenant. It was at this stage where I could understand what the Beast with the seven heads and ten horns had in relationship to me and how it presented itself, to my mind. I had finally come to the conclusion that the fear that we inherit from our forefathers and mothers was re-embedded in each forthcoming generation until we got it right, and the more we invested in ourselves; the less stress was seeded on to the next generation.

I remember the day that I had finally accomplished and understood my covenant with God and as I looked outside my window, I noticed that it was getting dark very quickly and I glanced at the clock and it was 3:33pm. Immediately, the heavens opened up and the rain poured down from the sky.

The wind picked up and shook the house and as the house seemed to twist around like a spiral with what I first thought was an earthquake, I ran from my office and hid under my bed; while the storm raged outside, I heard this voice yell out to me through the scream of the howling winds, "READ THE BOOK OF REVELATIONS, CHAPTER 11, VERSE 19." I was so frightened and was wondering what the dickens, I had done wrong! I was so proud of my achievements that day. Why was God anointing me with the Baptism in such a vicious way?

I crawled out from under my bed and grabbed the torch that was on my bedside table and my Bible and quickly returned to the safety underneath my bed again and read the verse. *"And the temple of God was opened in heaven and there was seen in his temple the ark of his testament; and there were lightnings, and voices, and thunderings, and an earthquake, and great hail"*. Well, I had just been given them all, ten times over.

I lay there waiting for the house to stop shaking and the scream of the winds to abate and when I was able to hear my own heart beating, I crawled out from under the bed and went outside to view the land. The red earth was covered in white from the hail, which were as big as teacups. Throughout this storm, twenty-one large eucalypt trees were uprooted and crashed around my house. Some of them missed the house by up to 15 centimetres where they were brought to the ground through the wind. I then came to recognize that there was one tree uprooted for every seal, times three; I remembered that PHI equated to the number three which alerted me to the fact that the mind of God or these universal laws do not work in small measures.

My thoughts returned to the voice that called out to me. I thought to myself, 'I know that voice who called out to me, why did it sound so familiar?' I went back into my mind and I replayed the movement over again and realized that the voice was my Uncle Edwin, who had passed away a few years previously. Both he and my father had realized before they passed over the commitment I had made to the journey, to see it through. What a relief for me to know that they were both still with me!

Hopefully by what I have previously written; you have a basic structure regarding these areas connected to the language which comes through our heart to chelate with the neural pathways of our brain. In the beginning of the Ancient Egyptian Language the 'Nephesh' explains to us that we are a living being, when brought forth into today's language this 'Seal' is presented to us as the seven steps we need to take to completely unfurl the layers of our Soul, which opens us up to walk up into the kingdom of God. Metaphorically all is explaining that our skin has seven layers, there are seven vertebrae which create the cervical section of our spine. What part did they have to play in our mosaic of bringing ourselves together? Read on to see how the story completes itself!

We learn to understand through reading the Book of Revelations, how we can open up to earn our intellectual light embedded in each cell. Symbolically it is explained that these seals release and open up automatically as our intellect unfolds which re-energizes and re-chelates our inner nervous system, where the results are passed on to the responsibility of our mathematical injection through our glandular inheritance as we urge ourselves up to release the next phase in regards to the sacredness of our inner alphabet. Watch how the information releases as I write the following words to create this book.

I will rearrange that last sentence, so that we may balance the sound of the words that I have just explained. We have the first seal, which is explaining the first layer of the soul, so the sound of the seal, becomes the cell of the soul, all of which is pronounced with an 'S' at the beginning of the word.

All four explanations are announcing exactly the same thing; it all depends on how your emotional stability organizes itself; as to how you pronounce your words. We do not pronounce the cell, as a 'Kell' as in cat. Once the first layer has lifted all by itself, you are then faced with lifting each layer off the next step of your education. The third step then appears before you as to how you understand more of your inner self, and so on until all of the seven clasps are opened at the back of the book. Which allows your soul to be free of the restrictions you have had wrapped around you through your DNA for your own protection.

Are you more aware of how you see the similarities between the stories of Jesus who wore a crown of thorns to announce to us that his ego had finally released its control over himself to allow the emotional right hemisphere, to be accepted once its fear had relinquished itself! Do you recall the story of sleeping beauty that we were told as children of the Princess who was cursed for 100 years and became trapped in a glass case in the middle of the thorny briars? And one day the handsome Prince came and released her. Well, it's the same story!

Now we can understand how the evolution of the Egyptian Empire explained the scribing on the walls, where they first designed the seven sacred steps that we must walk up to earn our right to exalt ourselves up into the heavenly kingdoms or what is termed as the 'after life'. The picture is explained to us in the seven steps which are before we enter into the grand gallery in the largest pyramid just outside Cairo. Much more to come on this subject.

And when this inner language has accomplished itself; is when your inner sound reverberates through every cell and clears the blocked energy that you have already created and used as an excuse for yourselves in the past; and only then will you begin to realize that your mind is cleansing and releasing the tension of your past all on behalf of itself.

You will learn to understand this inner language of your own DNA, or DNS which previously is referred to as the Bibliotech as it is now pronounced in the German language or inner Biblical library, which journeys all the way up to Alexandria or taken back even further through the Aramaic language, was pronounced as **EL**-ex-**AN**-dri-**EA**, (decoded this word means: 'through the mystical expansion of our intelligence; is where the PHI of each of the three Gods earn each right, to come home together, EL-AN-EA'. When this word is brought together it is explaining to us that we have now entered up into to the Mind of God). History informs us that this area is in the north of Egypt, which was supposed to have housed the largest library on the earth; also, these stories throughout the previous Aramaic language are explaining to us that this area had the largest lighthouse that could be seen right around the earth, which we now understand is the trunk of your body. Now with this information taken forward I would like to reveal to you, that this light is our auric field which surrounds and expands around our body, as we open up the continuation of our inner self.

Remember the earth is your body and these seven seals on

the back of the book of life, are situated above the heart area, they begin at the base of our neck! They are represented by the seven vertebrae in the neck area, these seven pyramids in what is known as the road to you discovering your eternal peace, as we journey up into the heavenly kingdoms. Which is known throughout Egyptology as the seven bands of peace. These bands release as we release each clasp on the back of the book, of our internal DNA. We see how the stories of our past explain the inner story to the best of their intelligence; are we beginning to get the gist, where we begin to sense on an inner level, how we have interpreted this wonderful story? Each following generation heard these stories from their forefathers where this road less travelled, found the inner strength to release their intelligence up into us all, where we could take our next step up the rungs of our own internal ladder.

Many hundreds of years ago, we used our energy the same way, when a letter was sealed in wax and our stamp that represented the self was placed into the wax. It was our own personal seal and at that time of our belief, no one dared to open it. Why? The unconscious mind of every human automatically protects the power of the greater source. It is only when the first God EL, interpreted as the ego's journey to understand the meaning of ever-lasting life, which in the beginning represents our innocence and as we become more aware of our knowledge, is when our sexual energy wants to try and take control and interferes, through it refusing to bow down to its greater good (which I like to refer to it, as the ego's ignorance). We find that we very easily create more excuses to deter us along the way.

My intellect since that time has moved on over the last thirty-five years and now, I know with strong conviction and belief that these seals have to do with this next journey of humanities earnings, that is in its own sacred space beyond our every day, recognition.

This has been through my acceptance to receive from God also referred to as the Universal Law, the inner strength that I had to find within my own mind, regarding the understanding of this wonder, as to how my ego kept on leading me astray, which is interpreting the seven headed Beast. I had walked the stony path for years and was not going to give in to an insubordinate excuse again. I refer to this beast as my greatest challenge that is presented to me. This is mine and your program! Throughout the Egyptian Principles we have named it 'the journey into the afterlife through our underworld or the nether world'. Throughout my genetic inheritance, my previous family's fear created a place for them to hide, when things became too difficult for them to understand and overcome; we find that this fear or innocence is autonomically passed on to the next generation for them to pick up from the previous generation.

Let us return back to the book! Is it one head of the beast for each layer that looks for protection around our soul; maybe it feels comfortable to know that the soul is in its clutches? Is this the reason for the seven layers which becomes our skin? Are these the first of our 'Royal Garments' that we all wear? Let us return to Genesis chapter 3, verse 21: *"Unto Adam also and to his wife did the LORD God make coats of skins, and clothed them"*. Layer by layer of discovering and releasing our intellect, we have all inherited this Royal garment.

To begin to understand this wondrous book we read in, verse 1: *"The Revelation of Jesus Christ, which God gave unto him, to shew unto his servants, things which must shortly come to pass; and he sent and signified it by his angel unto his servant John"*.

Verse 2: *"Who bare record of the word of God, and of the testimony of Jesus Christ, and of all things that he saw"*.

Verse 3: *"Blessed is he that readeth, and they that hear the words of his prophecy, and keep those things which are written therein: for the time is at hand"*.

We are being informed from God above (*unto*) that all of our genes are our servants also, that they must be prepared for their future which will happen when we hear the angels speak. Our angels are our next positive emotional thought and as they speak through us, our genes recognize that things are on the move.

We know that the word 'John', 'Johannes', 'Shaun', 'Shon', or 'Shone', throughout the languages of the past represents our collective intellectual light, which is the brightest servant of God.

Every human bares a record of the word of God as this is the make-up of our genetic inheritance. We call this the written word, which is embedded in every gene where we learn to read our bodily functions, when and if we can take responsibility to believe in ourselves. Remember that we listen only through our left ear; and when we hear our thoughts through our right ear is when we hear the words of his prophecy, where we are being absorbed into our cellular recognition with each thought we think. These thoughts then become a reflection of one another; therefore, our inner light is becoming brighter and lighter.

Please remember that the information in this book was written for the education of the Priests and Monks; they had to live alone to be able to absorb this unconscious level of endowment, which I perfectly understand, as this has been a major extension of my own earnings. And when they had evolved up into the book of Revelations, (revealing our inner nations) they had accepted themselves, where verse 3: is asking us to remember that every word God speaks; is also written and transcribed within each gene. We can also understand why many of us feel we must take the journey to the Vatican in Italy, as it is reflecting back to us the complete book of Revelations. There are millions of us around the planet who have now evolved up into this Divine area of consciousness and if we have understood these words correctly up to this point, then time learns to work for us. Instead of us working for and through time.

*

This next verse could take a while to interpret, so please bear with me. St. John's writings in chapter 1, verse 4: *"John, to the seven churches which are in Asia; Grace be unto you and peace from him which is and which was and is to come; and from the seven spirits which are before his throne".* Here is the beginning of the explanation of these seals that are closed when we are born and is where our soul is reflecting back to us these garments of skin that we are born with, in an arrangement of colours that create the rainbow effect. It is this effect that arcs itself the more we expand our intellect, they release themselves and are free to comfort and surround us. Joseph's coat of many colours! As previously written the word 'Joseph' is decoded as yourself, Thank God for Sir Isaac Newton! The explanation of the biblical Asia ends in the Mesopotamia fringe in the land of Turkey, where the large heads are buried and being unearthed all the way back, including many other nations into the land to where it first began of Iraq to Ur, known previously as Asia Minor.

This area now is known in today's language as the Anunnaki, please allow me to interpret this word through the sacred alphabet. <u>Anu</u> through the ancient languages is decoded as the seed of creation, this area is known as our kidney area, as we ascend through the <u>nurturing</u> and <u>nourishing,</u> we receive as we extol our self (praise enthusiastically) through how we are accepting our understanding and decoding of our inner metaphysical belief, as we <u>ascend</u> up into our inner <u>knowledge</u> and <u>intelligence</u>.

I thank my Masters of Time for their explanations into the decoding of this word. Let us start at the heads of animals and birds, which are explaining to us the species that are placed in the base of our brain in the pons area, which is also explaining to us the power of our oracle nourishing our soul. We note that this class consciousness is explaining that Eagles fly higher as we broaden our view with much more colloquialism, as we continue climbing our inner ladder or DNA as it releases itself rather than the animals, who represent the ego which represents the forthrightness of our power and inner strength. Then we come to the outstretched wings as to how we are entering up into us becoming the angelic species, right here on the planet. This occurs through our heart area as our temperance changes where it rearranges our thinking, as to how it switches in to our inner growth and the conversation of our thoughts. We birth the knuckles that project through the 4th to the 7th vertebrae of our upper spine, which are where our wings begin to manifest and expand. I call this area, the doorway up into the heavenly abode.

Many of the Chinese Nation lived in Egypt for hundreds of years nearly two thousand years before the Bible was collected for the rest of us, and they understood the hieroglyphs long before Christianity had even begun to evolve. They took back to their land their interpretation of the information as to how they understood the Divine Language of the Egyptian hieroglyphs and from their knowing, they created their own stories and recorded it into their language.

I spent many hours with learned fellows of the University of Languages in Beijing and listened intently, as each one explained their version to me. When I had brought all of the information together, I could understand their interpretation more clearly. They are so much more advanced in their spiritual understanding than we are; and through time they have already absorbed and released their intellectual awareness, in regards to the unconscious energy of the planet. The Asian Philosophies begin to write from the right-hand side of the page; where we are still trapped in our left hemisphere of the brain. Our right hand, is their left and their right hand, is our left. They have always been our mirror. And this will stay that way, until you have released yourself up into the unconscious recognition of yourself! Once you have released the image of yourself you will know that you and your soul have attained their freedom, through understanding and equalizing with and through one another.

A symbol of recognition of the seven churches of Asia is placed on top of the dome of the 'Duomo Di Milano' Cathedral, right in the middle of the Business Capital in Northern Italy. The word 'Milan' is decoded as My Land. There we see the seven spires in all their glory. If you slip across the road for a meal, you have the pleasure of dining on the balcony with this Cathedral in view to attain all of its glory. There are many wonderful stories written as to how they brought this magnificent Cathedral together. Take the time to investigate it in all of its glory.

The journey for the majority of us is still ahead, where one day, we will also reach the same heights as they have. So maybe now we can accept that our journey of understanding ourselves, is of course a major distraction for this rebellious child within, known as our ego. If we can control our ego and hold it by the hand, until we are qualified to know and extend our self, we will continue to allow this beast to keep control over us; once it has surrendered to its higher realms, it has then rebirthed into the dragon where it assists with the emotional mind and is where the spoken languages of Asia celebrate and dance with it. We can now understand and see how their medication works, as they are replacing each emotional species that has been depleted within themselves and are always repairing and replacing their spent energy. Shades of Homeopathy.

John is informing us that he is our brother, he is the power of our light, in verse 10 - 20: *"I was in the spirit of the Lord's day and heard behind me a great voice as of a trumpet Saying, I am the Alpha and Omega, the first and the last: and what thou seest write in a book, and send it unto the seven churches which are in Asia; unto Ephesus, and unto Smyrna, and unto Pergamos, and unto Thyatira, and unto Sardis, and unto Philadelphia and unto Laodicea".*

It is these seven churches that are identical to the same relationship as the seven chakras of the Indo Asian Principles. They each represent one of our seven layers of skin which helps and assists us into accepting ourselves.

They are also explaining the seven layers of the soul and as we intellectually earn each church, each layer ascends up to reveal the next. The first layer is the church of Ephesus, the second layer is Smyrna, and so on, right up to the seventh layer which is the first layer of skin that surrounds our body and is named the church of Laodicea.

Through the Asian mathematics this layer is also representing the eternal mast or master named Lao Tzuea. In their language it is pronounced as ELAH-O-TZU-EA... which means that through understanding the mind of God, you and your inner order of these genes that were presented to us during our gestation become one.

These seven churches which are in the south-west of Turkey, we earn and become, as each seal is released on the back of the book for us to attain our everlasting life!

"And I turned to see the voice that spake with me. And being turned, I saw seven golden candlesticks; And in the midst of the seven candlesticks one like unto the son of man clothed with a garment down to the foot, and girt about the breasts with a golden girdle.

His head and his hair were white like wool as white as snow and his eyes were like flames of fire; and his feet like unto fine brass, as if they burned in a furnace; and his voice as the sound of many waters.

And he had in his right hand seven stars: and out of his mouth went a sharp two-edged sword: and his countenance was as the sun shineth in his strength".

The old man symbolically represents the head of the family, he is the one who keeps tabs on us, making sure we do things right! Take your mind back to your own grandfather when you were a child and relive those old experiences, he expected us to do the right thing, and he speaks to us with the double-edged sword. Both sides of the blade are as sharp as one another! Therefore, the mind of your grandfather had become balanced; now let's take another step forward to look at the word 'sword'? This is explaining to us that he is representing to you his soul's word!

There are two sides to every experience and then we realise that we are so busy trying to evolve, that we sometimes wonder how the dickens we ever created those negative experiences that we have had to live; until we learned to understand ourselves, that same mistake is presenting itself to us over and over again, until one day we finally wake up! Enough is enough! This reasoning is why my teachings are so difficult to understand and accept, to many of you, as I am explaining both sides of the same coin. He had lived his life through his own resurrection and as he had learned through his mistakes, he would like his tribe to inherit his wisdom.

His intelligence had shone through to give him the right to teach, and this is what the seven stars in his right hand represent. They are also in relationship to us releasing the clasps on the back of our inner book or throughout Egyptology, of removing the bands (previous restrictions) of us accomplishing to finalize our inner peace. Our right hand is the result of our emotional intelligence and our left hand is our logic. Do you recall the mythical story of Merlin who had released his inner strength to encompass his own power, for him to be able to accomplish everything?

"And when I saw him, I fell at his feet as dead. And he laid his right hand upon me saying unto me, Fear not; I am the first and the last:

I am he that liveth and was dead; and behold I am alive for evermore, Amen; and have the keys of hell and of death.

Write the things which thou hast seen and the things which are; and the things which shall be hereafter; the mystery of the seven stars which thou sawest in my right hand, and the seven golden candlesticks".

So now we understand how the seven stars in his right hand represent the seven seals clasped on the back of the book, which are the results of him discovering his divine spiritual action. The seven candlesticks represent the resurrection of his past, which allows his divinity to have the confidence to release itself. To write these things, means to act upon, to release them throughout your cellular inheritance.

"The seven stars are the angels of the seven churches; and the seven golden candlesticks which thou sawest are the seven churches".

These ten verses were written for us to fully comprehend the meaning of what these seven churches of Asia, are informing us about ourselves. Again, I come back to my first thought many years ago, that they are the garments that were placed around each one of us in the beginning. They represent our sixth sense which is the embedded messages of the written word in each layer of our skin. So let us begin to read these verses, metaphysically to understand the importance of these wondrous codes.

We move on to chapter 2, verse 7: *"He that hath an ear let him hear what the Spirit saith unto the churches; to him that over-cometh, will I give to eat of the tree of life, which is in the midst of the paradise of God"*. We then move on to verse 17: *"He that hath an ear let him hear what the spirit saith to the churches; to him that over-cometh will I give to eat the hidden manna and will give him a white stone, and in the stone a new name written, which no man knoweth saving he that receiveth it"*.

And in verse 29, we again hear the words: *"He that hath an ear, let him hear what the spirit saith unto the churches"*. Throughout the teachings explained in my books, you will have read many times what the creation of our church is and how it is through our own belief that releases from within the marrow of our spinal column or the eclectic fluid (our religious experiences that we achieve for ourselves) of our DNA. The word 'CH-UR-CH' ('ch' represents the word 'life force', or the 'creation of heaven', the two middle letters 'ur' denotes the words 'understanding and releasing', both 'ch' represent the outer casing on the double spiral of our DNA) hence the idea of the mythical stories of Ur being the first City on or in the earth; and once more the first two letters are repeated. Therefore, the word 'church' is in relationship to our life force understanding and releasing us up onto the next rung of our internal ladder.

This is how we evolve up into our etheric wisdom of the mind, and we begin to understand the story of the three Gods who earn their own PHI (power of our heavenly intelligence) through their own experiences, as to how they collected themselves together to become one God. Our churches then are free to represent the knowledge that we receive, through each one of us overcoming our own fear. Now we can accept the knowing that we are all our own church.

Let us return back to verse 17: *"to him that over-cometh will I give to eat the hidden manna and will I give him a white stone and, in the stone a new name written which no man knoweth saving he that receiveth it"*.

We know that the word 'manna' (nourishment from above

or heaven) and the word 'bread', (nourishment within) both interpret to the same thing. Manna represents how we begin to nourish ourselves with the hidden knowledge that comes down from above and this we become more aware of through our understanding and acceptance of the restrictions of our fear. It gives us food for thought! The word 'Manna' means we have the opportunity to re-educate the self to release the information within our genes that are still held up in their own abeyance, until the right brain has earned its freedom from the entanglement of the ego, always trying to control it. It is interesting to note how the word 'bread' began; the word was first used by the Egyptians and pronounced as Braid. When they began to combine water to the flour and bring it together, they created the braid pattern and rolled out the mixture into three separate lengths. One roll was for each of the three Gods within, where they were being anointed and thanked for their service. This word informs us to keep on nourishing the left brain for the journey, it must overcome.

The next gift that we receive is the white stone and this denotes to us how we are receiving the spiritual purity of our brain. Once our fear has re-educated itself, it blends into us in a positive way, then all is white. Remember the story of Levi who searched for his own garment and collected the fabric of many colours and placed them in the vat of boiling water to cleanse them and purify them; when they were finished, they all came out white. Remember this one, as it comes to you towards the end of the book as we bring the story together. The results of self, begin to expose themselves to us to become our inner light, they are instilled within us as we arch and then ark ourselves intellectually up into the world of the divine or what we have earned, which is already instilled within self.

Go back to King Arthur and the story of removing the sword (the soul's word) from the stone, which is the unopened or innocent inherited mind. Our journey is to release our inner Bible through beginning with the Artists Door or Arthur (Art-Hur) where for the rest of our lives we speak our language through the Divine Wisdom of opening up our intelligence which has now become our learned truth? Now you can understand why I was given all of those names throughout my journey, which have been explained in my previous books. As I understood and earned each message that was presented to me, I had to evolve up into the next level of the sacred codes, and when I had accomplished each layer; then the next exalted name was released in front of me. These over the years, I kept to myself, as I knew that my journey had not yet fully attained itself. With each new name; a new learning to understand the sacred language of the Bible was revealed to me.

And now let us return to chapter 3, verse 6, the final explanations are repeated, and again in verse 13, and again in verse 22, as in chapter 2, verse 29: *"He that hath an ear, let him hear what the spirit saith unto the churches"*. And we see that they are repeated and given to us three more times. The reason for the three times is to anoint each level of the bodily mind. And here it is given to us, regarding us all becoming our own church. That church that you attend is there for you to learn the mystery of your life; until you have birthed the confidence to open up your own.

The codes denote this passage for us to understand that our hearing is where our thoughts are collected; in what is known as the mastoid area behind the ear; we listen and look at things when it is passed through our left ear and we hear within and look through things, when it is passed through our right ear. It all depends on where your thinking is, as to which one walks in front of the other in the moment!

This thought then begins the journey of traversing into the middle ear which is collected through its own vibrations; through the belief you have in yourself and then it is forwarded on to the pituitary gland. The pituitary gland then measures each thought to see how we are balancing and harmonizing our thoughts and more importantly, in which way the mathematics are collecting in the mind. If we are not moving forward then the energy is submitted into the left brain where we must repeat and relive the same experience again. In other words, our ego is still trying to reclaim each situation. If it is a positive movement forward; the energy is transferred into the right brain where we are able to release the thought and move on from that internal quandary that your own ego keeps on pulling you to walk backwards on yourself, all through it refusing to let go the hold it has over you.

These repetitious sentences are repeated four times in total, one for each level of opening up into our God-ness and once for the Royal Attainment, which is when we have accomplished our enlightenment and are more than willing to take on the responsibility of moving up into the higher vibrations that are available to us, through the gift that is given to us from that amazing gene, that sits under the fontanel of our inner head of God, who holds the keys to our ultra-conscious mind. Now you can understand the reason the pineal gland has that tiny eye on top of it as it looks up to the eye of our God Head or the Head of God.

St. John is explaining the hidden codes that we can all earn. He is explaining the life of Jesus as his ego learned to succumb to his God within, as it is explaining to us the previously written philosophies of the Aramaic language and also of Greece, over 5000-7000 years ago, which were at that time, originally known to us as 'Ye Zeus'. As their language evolved through their new found intelligence as it released itself over the years, the Y became the H, pronounced as He Zeus. Now we have become aware that fifteen hundred years ago, the H became the J, so now we can perfectly understand the interpretation of Jesus. This information was first given to me when I was interviewing an Assyrian Priest in 1996 as he explained through their language of their first knowing, of a man referred to as Yesus, pronounced Ye-Zoos. I remembered the conversation that we had with one another and I had to put the information on hold as I was preparing for a trip to Germany for six weeks to speak with two Universities in regards to my interpretation of how I had earned my training to extol my teachings. The students wanted more information and asked me to stay and teach all of my earnings. As the years sped by, after being an invited guest to speak in over eighty countries and renovating three Castles and turning them into Teaching Academies, where my many thousands of students travelled from all over Europe, Sweden, Norway, Finland, Russia, and then came the Asian countries, ending up in China. They came and were taught of my findings, and

took them back home to explain my teachings and over the years they then with confidence started their own groups.
Fifteen years later I returned home, to start writing my books. It was when I was trying to join these fifteen years of my exalted life, with my previous life that had been kept in storage that I found this piece of paper with the Assyrian Priest's conversation we had previously shared so many years ago. I filed it away with my ten thousand notes collected in Europe, and thought to myself, "I must go through this carton and sort things out".

This was a momentous task that took many months, when I found a piece of paper where I spent my time with a high member of the Coptic religion in Egypt named George, who opened my eyes to me unravelling the inner codes of the statues, as to how they stood, facing right or left, the clothing they wore, which God was in charge, where the stars were situated in the relief etc; my favourite subject of explaining the truth to me became much simpler where I could see through each phase as to why the land of Egypt was created in the first place. This was between Greece, Egypt and other African Nations when China entered the scene for around 300 years learning to understanding these hieroglyphic codes for the benefit of its own language. On my last trip to Egypt, I was shown a scroll of camel skin wrapped in the most delicate Chinese gold silk with the hieroglyphs on the left side and the Chinese language on the right that they had left behind when they ventured back home. The ink had never smudged over thousands of years, as they added salt to their ink.

This was around 12-1500 years before Christianity began to surface and assemble. They were working together to give us a coded blue print on the evolution of how we can understand the make-up for us to realize how our inner language is communicating every second of our life to us through our telepathic inheritance realigning through our mathematics approving and authorizing our cells and genes through co-habiting with one another to retain a balance in our mind. George was also explaining his understanding of Christianity through their earnings 4000-4500 thousand years ago where the letter 'Y' was changed to 'H' and then fifteen hundred years ago the 'H' was changed to 'J' as the new languages were correlated to be connected systematically to bring through the original story. Just as I had been given over the previous 25 years. Now let us return back to the original story!

Both of whom were known as: *"the first begotten of the dead and the Prince of the Kings of the earth. Unto him that loved us, and washed us from our sins in his own blood, And, hath made us Kings and Priests unto God and his father; to him be glory and dominion forever and ever. Amen"*.

Please bare, with me. This is becoming an exceedingly long chapter for me to explain to you in the beginning of the book. The more you are informed of the truth of Revelations, the easier it will be for you to comprehend the following information. Therefore, it is time for you to place in your book mark, put the book down and get up and walk around the room and think about what you have just read, go get a note pad and pen to jot down your thoughts of this moment and the page you are reading for future reference for you to realise how your inner truth will set you free, as I am receiving many irritations of ego's that are flaring up through finding this information hard to digest!

Right, it is time to get back into the book again! A glass of water would help wash down the information and also to cleanse and release the pressure from our inner genetic inheritance, so that it can mirror itself throughout your genes to correctly allow your mucus to flow. Remember that our genes are the recorded value of the last 64 generations of our united family inheritance which is downloaded into our DNA, just as the Books of the Bible have tried to connect the story of our religious inheritance, where we link back into our own source, which are then passed on to our cells. They are our inner device, where their responsibilities are to equate this information through your biological induced earnings that you have already earned that are passed on from our genes.

Allow my information to explain to you this wonderful scripture, through the interpretation of your next language; the metaphysical (the measurement of your inner physics) language, which begins with Geometry, the geometrical tree, the trunk of our spine as the energetic information connects to the branches that we have created through understanding this sacred language, which opens up our inner language to connect to our lymph nodes to advance our inner mathematics to equate to our cellular memories.

This opens up many doorways to our cellular structure, where our genes then collect the information more colloquially, which automatically lifts our intelligence up into our next step of our inner hereditary conditioning, which lifts us up higher into our inner light for us to become more aware of the reverberation to our energy which you become aware of autonomically that you now understand is self-governed, as it rearranges and makes the appropriate changes to our inner dictionary.

*

Remember that the two words 'unto' and 'upon' come from our heavenly realm on high; it is an explanation that we use in our conversations only when we have connected up into the hierarchical mind where we are looking and refracting the information, back down through the earth (now known to you as your own body).

Through the next exalted level of intellect; it is explaining that we are looking back inside ourselves, by reminding our egotistical personalities they are to accept and believe in themselves and not shy away; where they have continuously relied on others to work on their behalf. When we use these words in our teachings, we are unconsciously reminding our students to sustain and endure this new found knowledge, which will become their new freedom and more importantly their future strength. Just by them hearing the word, they can accept that changes for the betterment of all concerned to both the writer as well as the growth the reader adheres to, that they are well on their way.

Now we begin to understand why both 'Jesus' and 'Ye Zeus' were known as the first begotten of the dead, as we had not realized this important information. So many of their stories are identical to one another. Both of them represent the next generation of their father. The God Cronus (or Crown) that we can all accomplish and the one God are symbolically both one and the same. Remember the story that you may have read previously in my books regarding the story of Zeus? Once they had both made an excuse for their thinking through their emotional mind; the next generation came through and took over from their father; then their father was pronounced as dead. Are you beginning to see how the mystery of metaphysics begins to come alive? We are talking about our life force and how it collects. This encoded force of energy releases from our DNA which are heralding the thoughts of our previous generations; where they can begin to assist us into how we are creating our new reality.

This story infers to us that every thought we think is the most important announcement to one's self. The 'EA' (Everlasting Ascension) is the resting place of God and this cannot eventuate until we have brought the collection of our intellect, or the height of man, unto or in today's language into his home. I remember as my own enlightenment opened up, I became calm and exuded a serene gentleness to myself as I watched the aspects of my personalities grow quieter. I found that I could walk upon the waters, (consciousness) also that all of my desires were defining themselves as I entered towards the divine. I was no longer calling myself Virgil; the woman who was caught and trapped in the depths of her own hell. I had endowed upon myself the new name of Vimana to add strength to my new truth as I was contributing to the intelligence my new ship of light (my body and mind) would become. Remember that the ancient ones, spoke of these ships as a gift from those upon high. Through the Tibetan and Asian Philosophies dating back four thousand years or more ago, the Vimana had the power of the ten thousand suns. Therefore, it was time for me to boost my mind up to where I belonged. Hence why today they salute the ten thousand Buddhas in their Universities and Temples.

I remind you once again of the codes within the word 'El-ex-An-dri-Ea,' which housed the largest library and lighthouse on the planet—Alexandria. It is known as the three minds of God. The first God **EL** is being **EX**ecuted through its education, evolving into the **AN**, which represents our inner university (our universal city) where we complete our education as to who we are. Through this journey, we gain the ability to read from our own oracle within. This tutorial of information is collected throughout our mind, and is where we learn to open our heart to ourself. Once the heart has been defibrillated through the soul's energy, (a word my Masters of Time used throughout the ancient languages) through the changes it has earned through its tenure of its new official capacity is where the heart now directs the brain up into its official capacity which over-rides the old ways of the past inheritance. In today's language, I liken this word/process to our inner fibre optics, strengthening our character as it is collected through a transmission of light—a positive step forward through our Sacred Geometry, Numerology and Alphabet. The **Dri**, or the three Gods, earn the right to merge as one, releasing the pressure of control exerted by our left hemisphere (ego) of our brain. As the heart earns the right to stay open forever, these two Gods ascend into the **EA**, where all three are becoming as one with the God Head. Additionally, this is the crown (or Cron-us denoted as our crown understanding our soul or seals) we wear. It represents the moment when we attain the royalty of self-worth.

We move on with this next important discovery of self, to verse 7, to bring this story together we read the *words "Behold he cometh with clouds; and every eye shall see him, and they also which pierced him: and all kindred of the earth shall wail because of him"*. The clouds represent through the ancient language of the Universal Law, the gathering of matter which collects all of the available knowledge that you have at your disposal, to discover your future.

The mist of the clouds is announced to you, when you are in doubt of self. You are being informed that if you step up into the higher heavenly mind, you will have the opportunity to understand the language of the visions you receive. Throughout the Chinese and other Asiatic lands of their hierarchical mind, the totem energy or life force represents the heavenly home. Their totem is the clouds situated two thirds up the pole. The ancient cultures used the animals and bird tribes to place in the centre of their villages for protection. Each one represented a different emotion that the tribe needed to sustain them and keep them in balance.

Both species are correct, the animal is the beginning of our evolution to help us understand ourselves on an earthly level and the birds represent the heart area which is representing our angelic principles which become our emotional action. Are you with me on this sentence? Now can you understand, what I have written and explained in other books; that many of the Asiatic cultures have already evolved up into the intelligence of the unconscious mind, thousands of years before the rest of us?

Take a look around Tiananmen Square in Beijing in China for example; which is right in front of the Forbidden City; it is all explaining their interpretation of the journey of mankind. Take note of their symbolic totem poles or columns, which is denoted with the clouds on either side four fifths up from the ground. They are announcing to the world that you are entering into their sacred heart area, which is explaining metaphorically their Heavenly Home.

The codes to the Geometric Alphabet are extremely frustrating in the beginning, but as you become more familiar with them, they begin to roll off your tongue and very quickly you are decoding the sacred sound of the language of the collective DNA. I am hoping by now that my introduction into you discovering the codes and realising them at the start of this book is becoming easier, for you to click your mind up into this ancient geometrical metaphorical language that is already embedded in every one of your genes.

We move on to the next word of the verse. *"And every eye shall see him and they also which pierced him: and all kindreds of the earth shall wail because of him. We begin to see how this verse is coming together"*. Every eye is the light of every cell in your body *"and they which pierced him,"* represents your ego's disbelief in your higher self. *"And all kindreds of the earth shall wail because of him"*. The kindreds represent your innocent thoughts. It is not a nice thought for the young and innocent, to know that there is always an eye watching them. How can they continue to create an excuse for their own innocence and insecurities?

Verse 8 and 9 inform us of John's words, *"I am Alpha and*

Omega the beginning and the ending, saith the Lord. Which is and which was, and which is to come, the Almighty. I John who also am your brother and companion in tribulation, and in the kingdom and patience of Jesus Christ, was in the Isle that is called Patmos, (decoded, is informing us of our inner **P**ower **A**scending to our **T**ruth as we **M**aster the **O**racle or **O**rder of our **S**oul) *for the word of God and for the testimony of Jesus Christ".* Patmos through the Greek Philosophies is the home where Zeus was supposedly born.

When we understand this word through the sacred language, we see how it relates to the ancient words 'Pat-ha', which evolved into 'father' and 'Mos', representing 'Moses' or 'Mosque'. The old word for 'Mosque' was pronounced 'Mo-Che' or 'Chi', reflecting our mastery of inner energy. Over time, this understanding transformed into 'Moses'—the one true thought that journeyed through every experience to lead his family of genes, evolving through his own personalities, toward the Promised Land. Now, we can more clearly recognize how this island was named to reveal the story. Are you becoming more aware that all the myths of creation are converging, honing in on the original story? And yes, I must agree with St. John the Divine, who teaches us that we must walk alone to release this knowledge, allowing us to take the next step in our educational journey toward the future. It all comes down to how we begin to embrace and believe in our inner thoughts.

Take notice of how the sky transforms itself just before the rain falls. The clouds collect and gather and then the baptism begins. Fears where you are holding yourself back through your innocence, need to be anointed. You have earned this gift from God. The rain which is pure consciousness, has come to wash away your inferior signs. You understand through reading my previous material that the sins have created themselves through you living and relying on your past thoughts, therefore search your genes for your inner dictionary, to release the word you wish to uphold for yourself. If you've been baptized by the rain, you're cleansed, now begin again. Hopefully now, you can see how these universal laws rains or reigns pronounced the same, (different spelling, different meaning which is explaining the inner Royalty each one of us have already been endowed with) over us.

As Plato's words from thousands of years ago, still keep on reminding us of, "We can easily forgive a child who is afraid of the dark; the real tragedy of life is when men are afraid of their inner light". And my next one is "The first and greatest victory is to conquer yourself; to be conquered by yourself (ego) is of all things most shameful and vile".

*

For ten long years I screamed my way to find my place with these ancient laws. Many is the time my road disappeared from my view until I straightened my spine and found the faith to reinvest in myself again. I had to release all of those fears that I had hidden inside through my innocence and then to realize why I allowed that to be. I had to search for the inner strength that was hidden within to bring them out to face up to the responsibility that I had placed on and around myself; to earn my freedom. I could release those personalities that I had inherited their opportunity to search within, to live in their own light. This is the ancient stories of the Greek Gods, also Jesus explaining the oracles or the ancient orders of the past!

When we view something that is around us, the first thought instigated through our ego is to have a tendency to judge the motion at the same time. It is only interested in the 2nd person definition; it is definitely not interested in understanding itself! When we view a DVD or a movie on TV, we are attracted into the scenes through the frame that surrounds our viewing. The frame creates a world that we have the opportunity to view through. Just like when we are at the Ballet; watching the corps de ballet where we see a group of dancers on both sides of the stage, and the two Principal Dancers, are in the centre of the stage, these two groups on the perimeter bring our mind up to viewing the whole picture through the unconscious mind, where we become at one with the ballet. In other words, we are on stage participating in the dance and yet, we represent the audience at the same time!

It is that frame that enhances our mind. I remember when I

spoke at my father's funeral and I asked the thirteen hundred people who were in attendance; for them to anoint the presence of my father, as to how they could paint their own picture of him in their mind; to choose their colours of how he had endowed himself to them and place it on a canvas. And to be very careful of the frame that they used to surround it, as it was the frame that brought the picture together, not the picture itself. Thirty odd years later many still talk to me about that day as those words changed their lives forever, as to how they view their own world, through understanding the eyes of others.

*

We move on to reveal more of the information that we are given in this everlasting gift of knowledge. John is reminding us that he is there to hold our hand; as we take this journey into what we refer to as the unknown and will accompany us through our pain as we come to realize that all of this information is known to us on an inner level. We can read through the verses one at a time and we see how these seven churches came into being. We move on to verse 11: "*Saying, I am Alpha and Omega, the first and the last: and, what thou seest write in a book and send it unto the seven churches which are in Asia; unto Ephesus, and unto Smyrna, and unto Pergamos, and unto Thyatira, and unto Sardis, and unto Philadelphia, and unto Laodicea*".

We realize now, that these seven names are related to the emotional stability that supports us, as we awaken within. They are explaining how we collected through the alphabetical resonance of the collective of all, these seven sacred layers of our skin; also to how we removed the clasps on the back of the book, which are in relationship to the seven vertebrae of our neck, as we leave the earth, (our body) to journey up into our heavenly abode, as these layers are in relationship to the seven candlesticks, as it is the responsibility that we must uphold, as these layers hold the DNA together. More information is on its way.

Now we move on to verse 12: "*And I turned to see the voice that spoke to me. And being turned, I saw the seven golden candlesticks".*

Verse 13: *"And in the midst of the seven candlesticks one like unto the son of man clothed with a garment down to the foot and girt about the breasts with a golden girdle."* Verse 14: *"His head and hairs were white as wool as white as snow and his eyes were as a flame of fire".*

Verse 15 and 16 go on to explain: *"And his feet like unto fine brass as if they burned in a furnace; and his voice as the sound of many waters. And he had in his right hand seven stars: and out of his mouth went a sharp two-edged sword: and his countenance was as the sun shineth in his strength".*

Verse 17 through to verse 20, the words explain to us where we can hear the reply given to John:

"And when I saw him, I fell at his feet as dead. And he laid his right hand upon me saying unto me, Fear not I am the first and the last: I am he that liveth and was dead; and behold I am alive for evermore, Amen; and have the keys to hell and of death.

Write the things which though hast seen and the things which are and the things which shall be hereafter; The mystery of the seven stars which though sawest in my right hand and the seven golden candlesticks. The seven stars are the angels of the seven churches and the seven candlesticks which thou sawest are the seven churches".

These seven stars are the intellectual light that is produced in our next positive thought. One for each of the seven seals that we will unfurl through constantly believing in our self.

The seven candlesticks remind me of the menorah used in Jewish worship, that I have here in my office as it meant much to me when on my journey in the outback, once I had decoded the word. I realized that they read from left to right so I went back into my syllables to decode the word. Through the **Men** Our genes, my **O**racle **R**eleases through me **A**scending **H**eavenly.

Do you understand the importance of this first chapter more clearly now, as to how it is reframing your judgment of yourself? I thank you most sincerely for taking the time to read to the end of the chapter. So how do you feel now? It is a nice view up here in the upper most branches of your tree, where you can rest a while in your own garden of Eden. Or would you prefer that I mentioned you are rearranging your truth into the wisdom you are becoming from you understanding the codex of the sacred language and also the sacred numerology from the beginning of the book, as you learn to fully understand each layer as to how the Bible was officially collected.

You have climbed your first mountain, where you can view a greater perspective of all, in this moment; your peripheral vision has broadened, where you see a greater expanse of firstly yourself and then your view of others, through you attaining your new found freedom of self. Now take the time to turn around and look back into yourself to see how far your earnings have opened up new doorways for you to be free to walk on. This is why the eagle builds its eerie or nest so high, as it can view over all there is to know as it can see further into the distance and set its path for the next moment to autonomically appear before it. Now a sip of water to baptise yourself through honouring your inner self, which will bring an added sense and peace and contentment to both your inner vocabulary and your outer collective mind. Now finally, we move on to chapter 2.

CHAPTER TWO

Explaining The Angelic Vibration Of The First Four Seals

When reading this second chapter we become aware that it is explaining the Angelic vibration of the first four seals. The intellectual light, the freedom of mind, the emotional learning's that in time will release, only as we begin to open our heart to ourself.

All of which reminds us of not understanding the sins that we have already created, through our own innocence of self; please remember our sins are just our own repetitious thoughts and experiences that we all hang on to for our own security. Until we begin to earn our inner rites of passage, we all do the same. You have done nothing wrong!

The first church is Ephesus, which is the innocence that we have all inherited at birth; it is the journey of the inner child. We have no idea how things work or understand how to love ourselves as yet; we act pious towards society and become judgmental. I have seen the hardest heart melt through the coercion of a small child, reaching out to offer to assist them.

The second church is Smyrna, this is where we feel the need to deprive ourselves; we allow our poverty thinking to over-ride the good; it is a message for us not to stumble and recollect our fear. We are caught up in our past which is no longer applicable to the living moment. We are being introduced to our innocence and fear through the eyes of the child, or our innocent mind through these two churches.

The third church is Pergamos; verse 13 ends with: *"these things saith he which hath the sharp sword with two edges"*. This is in relationship to the two hemispheres of the brain. I feel the answer is in verse 14: *"But I have a few things against thee because thou hast there them that hold the doctrine of Ba-laam who taught Balac to cast a stumbling block before the children of Israel to eat things sacrificed unto idols and to commit fornication"*.

In this area is where in our mind through how we are living, is in the deprivation of self. Also, through the ancient language it is referred to as the ancient land of purgatory. May I remind you that this is in connection to the martyring of self; which is where we look for the attention of others and this my friends will get you nowhere! We have refused to eradicate the thoughts, which control other personalities from learning to find their own inner strength. We have allowed our ego or egotistical beast within to control us and through this suppression; these personalities will grow up to become our future excuses.

The fourth church is Thyatira and is the first room that we open to traverse our thinking up to our inner crown. In verse 20: we hear of Jezebel who represents the emotional blackmail that we use to cover and protect our self and in verse 23: God informs us that our next thoughts are explained to us, *"as our children will be destroyed"* as we cannot keep continuing on in this way. When we read on in verse 26, the words speak to us of: *"And he that overcometh and keepeth my works unto the end, to him will I give power over the nations."*

Our nations are the individual personalities that we have created for our self to nourish our intellect; these genes that have already been downloaded into our cells collect and gather their strength through grouping and supporting one another where they become our nations and are also on their path of learning to become our future positive thoughts. These personalities represent our children and must be brought up to the best of our knowledge.

Just the same as the many wars that are happening in the world today; whoever created each one did so as they need the support of others, so that they can obtain their strength to overcome their foe through their beliefs. There is safety in numbers and the higher the numbers we think, the greater the rebound and the reward. If our thinking can become righteous and be delivered from the unconscious mind; there is no need to war with anyone! Our **W**isdom **A**scends and **R**eleases when there is no war. We are unnecessarily destroying our own domain as to what we have already earned; through an over bearing attitude of self.

In verse *27*: "*And he shall rule them with a rod of iron; as the vessels of a potter shall they be broken to shivers; even as I received from my father*". This story is in regards to our sexuality. The deprived sexual emotions are used as a sacrifice. We sometimes refuse to step beyond our sexual behaviour, (through the mind of our ego) which has a source of control that is all under the command of the uninitiated self.

Verse 28 is short and straight to the point. "*And I will give him the morning star*". There we are then; we have earned the first level of our Tiara, which in time will become our crown.

The writing's keep on reminding us of our responsibilities to the highest attainment that we have accomplished regarding our thinking. God is informing John, or our inner light, that we are failing within ourselves, through us not allowing ourselves to manifest the inner faith to move on. Now we can see more clearly how our hereditary experiences are autonomically passed on down generation by generation; not up, as it should be, to allow the next generation to walk tall into their own future.

The deceiving thoughts that we innocently hide behind are those who work against us, as to how they try to keep our mind retarded, until we can see ourself from within.

CHAPTER THREE

Continuing The Seven Seals

We can slowly bring the information together to see how the last three of the seven seals are aligning with the inner language for you to become the future Prophet to inherit your own wisdom.

The fifth church of Sardis, is where we lay claim to its priorities as we see how God asked for our personalities to reunite and come together, which will initiate a perpetual balance of freedom in our mind. I would also like to add to those readers who are not spiritually inclined to understand that these words equate with the laws of the universe in the same intellectual light! Even the planet earth does not do it to itself! It is a reminder for us to be more spiritually aware, as to how our inner thoughts are collecting, which when decoded is explaining to the self, that our inner light is bringing a sense of freedom through the results of our thoughts to our collective mind; the code is in the first verse. *"These things saith he that hath the seven spirits of God and the seven stars; I know thy works that thou hast a name that thou livest, and art dead".*

When the word 'dead' is mentioned in the bible it means that you have evolved from your previous existence and have advanced forward to begin the next level of unravelling your intellect. You cannot keep on holding yourself back, no matter how comfortable you feel. Your past is no longer applicable to your life. That is why the name change. I mentioned this experience in my first Book which has recently been separated into nine small books and revised and brought up to date with my teachings.

As we evolve intellectually the human brain keeps on advancing; it improves upon itself with age. And when one reaches the end of their antenna; they are free to die to this experience and return home, back to the source of all things created from whence they evolved, back to the source of what we truthfully know. Here we note the three Gods working in unison with one another through balance and harmony. Which is showing you an advancement of your personalities all coming together for the freedom of self!

I would like to give you an example of one story of the Bible and that is the gathering of ELI, who was tested by God to become Elijah; tested again to become Elisha; and then tested finally to become Elias. There are many examples of this story becoming a saga. The code to the word 'Eli', is denoted as '**E**verlasting **L**ife's **I**ntelligence'. Each time this story ended; it portended a death for the name to change so that it could go on to inherit the next education of self-worth. Each added value to the original name climbed up the double helix, to improve again and again.

The sixth church is Philadelphia; which is spoken to us here to remind us of our inner vision, where we learn to always release our truth first, "*he that hath earned the key of David.*" We are aware that David through the ancient Sanskrit language represents the third eye, Davidea our inner teacher, or the wisdom that we can perceive through understanding the language of our visions.

The explanation in verse 7 says it all. It pertains to having earned your inner strength to support your earnings of the freedom that is available to your mind; therefore, not one person on the earth can interfere with your mind, once you have achieved this sixth church, as you have earned the right to master yourself. This person can never be harmed again. Why? We have entered up into the doorways of heaven and are protected in God's name and arms. We have earned the right to receive the keys to our own countenance. Once your inner eye has opened up and you are now well on your way of understanding this hidden language; you have earned the opportunity to see through every person who stands before you. The image inside your nation, your divine intelligence, is mirroring them back to you.

God has made us a pillar in the temple to become a continuous light for all to see. We become a beam where those who are still trapped in their darkness, can search for us; or a lighthouse that reflects out to others so that they may see us on an inner level through their unconscious mind. Do you recall the story of Alexandria and see how you are seen right around this wonderful planet, also the availability of your inner library is always at your disposal? There is never a mistake; you are always in the right place at the right time.

My mind opens up to recall a thousand people who all said that they had met me in their dream world, before I arrived in Germany. And also, when I was conducting my seminars, I would see a face in the audience and could recall talking to that person regarding their illness, before I left my homeland. Our telepathic inheritance is so astounding between one another and is heard right around the planet.

And now we come to my favourite church and that is the Laodiceans; in the Chinese philosophies, this word is pronounced and revered as the Eternal Master, Lao Tzu-Ean, informing us that Tzu; meaning you, are EA. This eternal master through his ultimate aim of becoming the seventh church represents the world of healing the self from within and he stands as another interpretation through his knowledge and teachings of the faithful and true witness.

This intellectual level of intelligence is never hot or cold; it is always luke warm, (Remember that the book of Luke in the New Testament is another reference to the stories of the inner physician). This power and strength have a balanced mind and always speaks the truth to become the exalted crown that you wear for the rest of your life; that no man can put asunder. It represents your Holy Temple of the seven golden lights.

And so, we now understand with more clarity that these seven seals are your future investment in yourself. In all the Asian cultures and religions, we can now understand that the triple seven is representing the world of the Avatar; the 'Ave' throughout Christianity, of our truth **A**scending **V**ictoriously through releasing our inner **E**nergy. Wear your white robes with honour and know who you are.

CHAPTER FOUR

The Entrance Into The Throne Of God

This chapter informs us of the entrance into the Throne of God where we meet with the four and twenty elders.

To reveal this chapter to myself, through me learning to understand that I was opening up my inner ministry in the early nineties, was an extremely powerful time in my life, as those voices that I continuously heard, seemed to yell out to me, none of them spoke quietly to begin with, until I could realize that they had to carry me beyond the last temptations of my earthly third dimensional mind. I had come to realize that these were my Apostles or Disciples or Disciplines working on my behalf, as there were still a few little niggling fears within me, as to whether or not they were really speaking their truth, or was there a part of me trying to confuse the verb (my, doing word) of my old language in me.

I kept on repeating to myself a lesson that I learned many years before where I had understood my Teacher Swami-Dharma-Videananda, when she explained to me how we participate to help release the twelve disciplines of the Tibetan Philosophies in relationship to the twelve metals that created the strength of our crown. When these twelve metals were melted down and brought together, they were shaped into a bowl and the Priests were trained to gently rub their fingers around the edge of the bowl to release the harmonic sound of the voice of God. This sound when played releases the pressure points that collect in our DNA and the more the Priests played their instrument, the purer their energy or essence grew. There was a cassette that she played constantly at that time during our meditation classes titled Tibetan Bells which is created by Klaus Wiese, which is absolutely brilliant to centre one's self to calm the mind.

Being just over five feet tall, of course I never forgot this story. I had to reinvest in the word 'imagination' to realize that they were trying to commute to me regarding the inner strength I needed, for me to produce my next thought.

My inner language was replacing itself into my day-to-day vocabulary; and I found that my inner dictionary of words, were advantageously pronouncing and speaking new words every day. My voice had changed and was resonating much deeper whilst communicating with others; I had a tendency to speak the Biblical language while I was thinking to myself; which was then directed out to others. I seemed to be echoing the ancient language of metaphysics unknown to me at that time. I was permanently walking on the tip of my toes and was stressed out to such an extent, that I had difficulties to hear anything on an inner level. These voices I began to register within me, as beings of light which were always dressed in white with gold flashes around their heads and there was lightning and thunder and flashes of flames shooting around the inside of my head and maybe this is why they were so difficult to understand at first. I never realized that they were the intuitive sections of my Akashic records that every human has inherited; all through the enfoldment of my DNA being handed down to me.

Over time, I had to find the courage to accept that this was part of my new education, as I was learning to marry my mind as one; this stage when interpreted through the metaphysical language, begins to be explained with the marriage of Canaan where Jesus turned the water into wine; which allowed me the privilege to evolve into accepting this next inner region, of my learned intellect. We can understand how we thought of the word 'religion' as we added the L-I – (Life's Intelligence) into the word 'region'.

My words had a mind of their own and I seem to be talking in parables; as I spoke to others, I noticed that I delivered my words out to others in reverse. Little did I realize that I was being brought up into the crossover point which is situated around the medullar oblongata in the brain, where we have evolved up into entering deeper into the security of our inner strength and power, which I am now more aware of, became the doorway to our unconscious mind?

Please allow me to introduce you to the next step of your intellectual ascension. We begin to understand these following words initiating us into the throne in heaven; as it is explaining to us, that we can envisage this scene of a throne in the centre of a room with an elder who looked like jasper and also sardine stone, which in the ancient times, symbolically represents an opal, where all the colours of the rainbow shine through. Both of these stones are a companion of one another, and where you find one, you will certainly find the other.

The jasper is the soft stone that manifests beside the opal to harmonize and protect it. The opal is much harder as it is produced over thousands of years as each drip of water which is condensed through the earth mixing with the elements to create the colours of the rainbow. What a sacrifice to produce such a gem!! We can see how it has earned and opened its seven seals. That is why there was a rainbow around the throne, coloured in green. Green is the colour we release into our aura, when we are speaking through our heart, which also represents the colour that releases from the alchemy of our brain when we step up into releasing our extra-terrestrial intelligence. This colour is created through the gold of the Soul-ha-plexus area and the blue of the throat area and represents the educational voice that each one of us has inherited.

Both the jasper and opal supplement one another and live happily side by side, out there in the dry arid areas of the outback. Once again, they are balancing one another just as the two brains have finally melded as one. I use them symbolically as the jasper, representing the left hemisphere of the brain and the opal is representing the right hemisphere, as our ego earns the right to stand and balance itself with our emotional self.

We are now being introduced to the twenty-four elders who surround the throne and are dressed in white and are wearing girths around their waist and crowns of gold. These twenty-four elders represent the double helix of our DNA as they represent the twelve Lords of Light and the twelve Lords of Dark throughout the stories of the myths. This is where up in this realm of our learned intellect the ego begins to submit to itself, in other words it staggers, it pulls itself up. To take its next step of surrendering to itself, for its greater good, it now understands that this marriage of the mind, has brought both hemispheres of its brain up into a unison, which over time will become a oneness, where they could both earn the right for their inner strength to mature into becoming as one.

Verse 5: informs us of the power that was collecting and connecting with lightning and thunderous voices and amongst all of this furore, the seven lamps were still brightly burning as they represented the seven spirits of God. Surrounding all of this grand vision were the four beasts full of eyes above, before and behind; in other words, they had a view of 360 degrees, where they could see in every direction. Each of these beasts had six wings about them as they were being initiated into the membership of the upper inner realms of consciousness.

Through the interpretation of the Shamanic language, the insects that are born with six wings, have evolved through the moth, butterfly and dragonfly species. The moth species represents our inner tension which when ignored could become our worries, to abate this feeling they look for the light to free their mind. The dragonfly represents our ego's illusions, reminding it of its false attitude, go back to the thought you have in the moment and correct your thinking, and finally, the butterfly represents our transformation, you are asked to take a step forward as your next step is waiting for you to guide you into your next education. The six wings represent mastering of the inner self. These four beasts had the head of a Lion, our ego and pride, an Ox, the contentment we receive through our inner strength, a Man understanding the capabilities of himself, and an Eagle who lives on top of the mountain, with outstretched wings, for him to soar above the heights, which widens his peripheral vision. In other words, they had to overcome their own iniquities.

This explanation is also scribed on the outer casing of the smallest of the three pyramids, above Cairo in Egypt, many thousands of years ago long before Christianity was released to us. The outside casing has now crumbled through time, although you can still see where they originally gouged this message into the wall, along with many other messages. This area is now fenced off for fear of accidents and closed to the general public, as this small pyramid is crumbling and dissolving owing to its size. Through my understanding as I explain my message to you many years later, this reminds me of the people who are yet to realise the importance of their inner quest, as we walk along the road less travelled. In other words, they still need their insecurities and aberrations to support their ego and as yet, have not suffered long enough to walk out of their world of doubt, and I bless them, for they know not they do.

Now back to my story and revised edition from my e-book, where I was to understand at this point of the ceremony, that through the ancient languages of the Mauri Culture, that my Elder explained that they are representing the first four books of the New Testament. This appearance happened to me while I was being initiated into the Mauri Tribes on top of a mountain in the North Island of New Zealand, in the early nineties, all in cloud formation as they came together in a circle over my head. They were so precise and clear.

The man had a broad smile on his face as the Elder gave me my tribal name of 'Toui Toui Papa' which when the name was converted into the English language the Elder informed me that my name meant that I was from the 'Blood of the Earth, the Blueprint of the Earth', that took me a while to digest this information as to why he could not change Papa to Mama. Over time I realised that Papa meant power, whereas Mama meant the wisdom of mastering. Up here it interpreted to me that they are both of the same difference! That information kept me quiet.

A similar interpretation is given to us in the book of Ezekial, chapter 1, verse 10, gives us an explanation of the four beasts as in Revelations, chapter 4, verse 7. This being on the throne is you and symbolically you are accepting your inner personalities with an added responsibility and respect throughout the wholeness of you accepting the awakening of these seven sacred seals.

CHAPTER FIVE

The Book Sealed With Seven Seals

This chapter is an important lesson as it reveals to us the book that is sealed on the back with seven seals.

Verse 1: begins with *"And I saw in the right hand of him that sat on the throne a book written within and on the back side sealed with seven seals".*

Verse 2: *"And I saw a strong angel proclaiming with a loud voice, Who, is worthy to open the book, and to loosen the seals thereof?"*

Verse 3: *"And no man in heaven, nor in earth, neither under the earth, was able to open the book, neither to look thereon".*

And John representing our inner light, wept. Now for the explanations, our right hand is symbolically representing the hand of our inner testimonials, our inner character, which autonomously tunes in to the mathematics of the gene above our pineal gland where it becomes our God within. We are finitely measured through this endeavour, all through the results of our action when we think or speak from our emotional inner mind. (Why do we always place out our right hand when we are introduced to someone else; the automatic reaction comes from within us as this brings an equality to both of our minds which are clear of the judgement of one another). It is the culmination of our intellect. We are acting and talking about the recorded history of our DNA, that is placed within during our gestation. The book also known as our inner Bibliography was written within, before we drew our first breath as I have explained previously, this is what the written word is explaining to us.

Allow me to explain this sentence to you in another way. When the Bible explains the written word, it is informing us that everything there is to know is already recorded in our genes. It is up to us to earn the information, as our mathematics align with one another throughout our positive behaviour.

We cannot confuse the collective if we don't accept our own responsibility for us to release our own truth, the mathematics are passed on to the rest of humanity. There is no escape!

Through the examples of the Egyptian hieroglyphs, the scribe as we know it to be is seen kneeling or standing in so many of them; we think it refers to the tally keeper, the one who took care of the records.

Yes, it does in the beginning of our understanding. Now allow me to introduce you to the next level; it is a metaphor explaining and reminding us of the inner strength of our genes that is already embedded in our bones, as do all of the hieroglyphs that have been scribed on the walls. They are representing a metaphorical tutorial explaining your thoughts back to your genes. You are your own scribe, it is you keeping tabs on yourself, as everything you do is already recorded for you to live. Shades of Daniel, Chapter 5—where Bel-Shaz-Zar (Belshazzar) was feasting with his entourage and the writing appeared on the wall. In verse 25, we read the meaning of the words: ME-NE, ME-NE, TE-KEL, U-PHA-SIN; isn't it? Briefly explained, we are informed that God has numbered our kingdom and brought it to an end, having weighed us in the balances and found us wanting. In other words, through His judgment of ourselves, we were needed to continue on.

When the scribe wrote down the records of so many cattle and grains etc; he was referring to the emotional responses each species represented, not what they ate! The cattle are an example of how we are nourishing ourselves. 'Cattle' is decoded as the contentment that one is able to achieve; grains represent our thoughts and ideas. And so, it is with all of the stories written in the Bible. It is not scribed in the language of the third dimensional reality. Each word is a code of the metaphysical language, which is the exalted crown, we are here on the planet to earn and have the opportunity to wear.

That is why for so many of you it has been difficult to understand the written word in its totality. It is amazing; there are so many religions on this planet and yet every one of them, are all trying to explain exactly the same stories. No matter what race colour or creed we are, there is only one story that created this planet! It all depends on the personality in charge of each person as to which one of their personalities or strands of their DNA is reigning supreme and controlling the others. And more to the point; every one of these regions or religions are right, according to their spoken language. So how many of you are going to understand my story; only those of you, who are hearing the words I have written! While you are listening to my words, you are still measuring my words with the knowledge you are in this moment. Therefore, you are autonomically prepared to put up a defensive barrier as this information is sounding new to you. Up here in this language, there is only one God, one religion; it is the whole trunk, branches and leaves of the original tree of knowledge, or our three Gods accomplishing what they are here to explain and teach us within, wearing and sharing the one crown. Remember we live in a three-dimensional mind.

In verse 4, John speaks through his tears as he explains to us: *"that no man was found worthy to open and to read the book, neither to look thereon"*. In other words, John is referring to the person who has yet to understand how to open his mind to himself.

We move on to verse 5: Metaphysically we are being asked to proclaim our self to move up into the next level of inner intelligence; through preparing ourselves to relinquish our pride *"The lion of the tribe of Juda"* we come to the inner mind or what is known as the forehead, where it is explained to us as: *"the Root of David hath prevailed (*he has earned the right to become his own master*) to open the book and to loosen the seven seals thereof"*. All of which is explaining the closed mind through each individual person or personality within, is still containing too much pride and ego! Once the ego has forsaken itself, we become aware of how the root of David is the energy that stems from our pineal gland, which is explaining to us the awakening of our third eye. We have earned the balancing of our thoughts and found us desiring to step forward, which releases the tension throughout the neural pathways that pass the information on and throughout our brain, where it becomes our imagination; the image inside our nations, all of which can assist us into releasing the seals for us to abide by. In other words, the consequences we are responsible for, must be now upheld and lived up to, as we earn and take our next positive step forward.

"And in the midst of the elders, stood a lamb as it had been slain having seven horns and seven eyes, which are the seven spirits of God, sent forth into all of the earth". We are being introduced to the next step from chapter 4, where the four beasts were in attendance surrounding the twenty-four elders. We read that there was: *"a lamb as it had been slain, having seven horns and seven eyes which are the seven spirits of God, which are sent forth into all of the earth".* In other words, every cell in our body has inherited exactly the same information. We are all one! Through these ancient codes, the lamb symbolizes our innocence of the unknown or the in-known; it has seven horns which represent our inner sonar, one for each seal that is clasped on the back of our inner book we have named our DNA, which is for our ego, until it resurrects itself, as it cannot enter up into the Kingdom of God, through its own innocence, for its own higher good. We are then informed that the lamb also has seven eyes; again, one for each seal; where we are able to see through our innocence for the rest of our earthly life.

The only species on the planet that has seven eyes is the spider. It can view 360 degrees completely surrounding both above and below itself. This species is one who has ascended up into the unconscious mind or better still, into its own planetary consciousness where it is able to weave its own web, which is manifested from the silky substance that its thinking has created from inside its own body! Long live the spider, after reading this section you will never look at one the same again! Shamanically explained, when spider enters your vision world, you are being asked to weave that thought you have in your mind, right now and bring it closer to your attention, in other words, if it is positive, work on that thought you are manifesting to attract spider into your energy. If it is negative, rearrange your mind by apologizing to the combined thought.

This information applies to the genetic inheritance of the whole of humanity. I recognized that the essence of God is the intuition that each one of us has available for us to honour (not inhibit) the thought we release in the moment.

We are being given the codes, which explain the beginning of our conquest as we reach intellectually up into the next phase; which is why the lamb appears to have been slain. One horn and eye, introduces you to the antenna that is created through the inner sight of each seal. We are viewing how the beginning of our Oracle collected itself!

Again, the image is explaining to us a metaphor of you reaching beyond your own expectations and boundaries to enhance your intellect, which autonomically rearranges and increases your genetic light: also remember, our DNA rearranges itself from this enhancement, as it is busily alerting the cells towards combining with one another into attracting its next positive endeavour.

"And so, the lamb stepped forward to take the book from the right hand of the one who sat on the throne and the four and twenty elders bowed as they began to release the music, and the essence of God which are the prayers of the saints and they sung a new song". This is regarding the redemption of self, to allow your mind to be free. It is in these next few verses that we understand where we have earned this evolution of self, as these four and twenty elders and beasts are available to us as Kings and High Priests and that they would reign on the earth, or what we now know, has already been impregnated in our body for evermore. The rest of the verses 11- 14, explain to us the announcement of entering into this new world of conversing to self and our conversation to others.

Verse 11, begins with: *"And I beheld and I heard the voice of many angels round about the throne and the beasts and the elders; and the number of them was ten thousand times ten thousand, and thousands of thousands".*

These numbers are explaining the mathematical codes in relationship to how we converse with the inner mind of God. It is explaining every thought we think! I will repeat what is already written regarding the sacred coding of the numbers

1 and 0. The number 1, is the 'I am' and the 0, relates to the soul. Therefore, the number ten thousand is interpreting to us as; I AM, through my soul, the mind of God. Once again, I take us back to the Principles of the Chinese interpretation to the knowledge of the Lord Buddha, who in their Temple, has ten thousand Buddha's which are placed around the circular walls in little niches to support those who have entered up into the afterlife; as you begin your new walk into the 'Temple of Death' to release from your third dimensional reality. Another explanation through the Egyptian Principles is the cloak that is worn by the Goddess Sekhmet and created from the ten thousand eyes taken from the peacock's tail. The Goddess wears it to announce to us how she ark's her colours which are collected and released through the vagina to connect to her ego and pride in regards to her sexuality; which is again informing us that we are all connected to the never-ending story.

Verses 12,13,14: *"Saying with a loud voice, Worthy is the lamb that was slain to receive power, and riches, and wisdom and strength, and honour, and glory and blessing.* (Please note that there are seven of them) *And every creature which is in heaven, and on the earth and such are in the sea, and all that are in them, heard I saying. Blessing and honour and glory and power be unto him that sitteth upon the throne and unto the lamb forever and ever. And the four beasts said, Amen. And the four and twenty elders fell down and worshipped him that liveth forever and ever".* Now do you understand the meaning of your innocence more clearly?

It was at this stage that I began to understand how my education into my Shamanic journey was releasing itself in me to reveal my inner truth. These codes were explaining everything that my teachers had explained to me. Through my own innocence at that time, I needed verification and as always, as I evolved, the answers to my questions were released to me, only if I had understood each parable in its mathematical correctness. I began to realize that all of the stories in the Bible were explaining my evolution to me. If these messages were for me through releasing my inner truth, then they were the same stories for the rest of humanity. And over the following years, I delved into the teachings of most religions and metaphysically I came through at the end to know that there is only one story! It all depended on me.

CHAPTER SIX

Opening Six Of The Seals

Please remember the Book of Revelations is explaining to us how we ark our self, up into the divineness of self. The Old Testament has explained how we came into being. The New Testament has explained the journey of our ego learning to sacrifice itself to its emotional inheritance and here we are at the doorway to where we begin our walk as an anointed one. We are about to leave the earth and take these seven sacred steps into the afterlife or the heavenly realms as the Egyptians explain it to us. No, we don't physically die, we die to our past thinking, as our brain has come together as one unit instead of two separate units, for the first time in our life. Now you can understand how the number seven is in relationship to us making contact with our inner teacher. The light communicator; adeptly named don't you think? We have reached the stage of opening six of the seals, therefore let us continue.

"And I saw when the lamb opened one of the seals as it were the noise of thunder, one of the four beasts saying, come and see. And I saw a white horse; and he that sat on him had a bow; and a crown was given unto him; and he went forth conquering, and to conquer". The white horse through the upper echelons of the shamanistic language represents the spiritual strength that we have all inherited genetically. You are being prepared to become the church of Ephesus. Allow me to also explain this word through the codes E-P-Hesus, does this sound familiar? As I introduced to you previously, the codes are revealing to you, the eternal or energetic power of the story of Yesus, and then around 1,500 years ago when the Greeks stepped in to take over Egyptology, they realised that so many of the stories were identical to their own myths through their stories of Zeus, who was thousands of years before Christianity came to our attention. As time stepped forward these myths combined with one another where they became the heavenly energy of Hesus, or in today's language and understanding became Jesus. Have you noticed that it is explaining to us, again the three, the inner mind. Does

this sentence remind you of the Christmas Carol: "We three kings of orient are, bearing gifts we've travelled so far." When we open up our inner dictionary, we realise it explains how to orient oneself to get one's bearings; when we become accustomed to a new situation.

"And when he had opened up the second seal, I heard the second beast say, Come and see. And there went out another horse that was red: and power was given to him that sat thereon to take peace from the earth, and that they should kill one another; and there was given unto him a great sword".

The red horse denotes new beginnings; when using your inner spiritual strength, you have the offer from the universe to advance your mind through releasing your sexual energy which produces an inner surge of power to urge you forward; this hidden strength will oblige and compliment you to eradicate those thoughts that are no longer applicable to your old intelligence; that is how we can interpret the word 'kill' as it is written. It does not mean that we go out and kill others; it means that we eradicate those thoughts that are hindering our state of mind. This is why the colour red is so prevalent in China in all of the Temples. Once we have acknowledged each thought we begin again! Again, I would like to reiterate to you that the sword is you speaking through your soul's word. We must remember that the Egyptian and the Greek nations combined, introduced this story to us as they explained the BJA (pronounced BYA) as the iron or strength of the earth, which is explaining a very strong metal. So, it is with us being human; it is our inner strength that allows and creates the two-edged sword, which can only come through both hemispheres of our brain being harmonized and balanced with one another. It is here where we are earning our second church named Smyrna.

"And when he had opened the third seal, I heard the third beast say, Come and see. And I beheld, and lo a black horse; and he that sat on him had a pair of balances in his hand."

The black horse represents our source of power that releases itself through the confidence we have created within, through us balancing our past and our current moment in each thought, before we commit ourselves to speak! Hence the balances in his hand.

"And I heard a voice in the midst of the four beasts say, A measure of wheat for a penny, and three measures of barley for a penny, and see thou hurt not the oil and the wine". Throughout my many seminars around the world I loved explaining this verse; these two grains have been around and eaten for thousands of years, right up until today. Wheat is one of the oldest strains of grain to sprout on the planet. Once boiled the grain is still in its original form. Our inner strength comes from wheat, that has been heralded down from our past, therefore it nourishes our DNA. Through grinding the wheat we create bread, also referred to as the manna from heaven. Once the substance of Barley is boiled, it breaks down the solid matter and becomes more fluidic, which flows throughout the body.

They flush and cleanse our muscles, unclog our veins and clear the arteries of the heart. Barley harmonizes the body. All grains should be eaten as they regulate the blood pressure and realign the temperature of the body. Each grain has a different vibration and they all stimulate our immune system and supplement our lymphatic system at many different levels. A good old barley broth has been eaten for centuries to ease the pressure we allow to build up, when we have difficulties to make the correct decision in the moment!

Remember, the grains denote ideas we are able to use to benefit our thoughts. The lymphatic system which is threaded completely throughout our body, we know is the umbrella that God symbolically holds over us. The oil and wine of course are the fluids and mucus that flows throughout our system. Don't allow them to choke you up, use them cautiously. We are earning the third church named Pergamos.

"And when he had opened the fourth seal, I heard the voice of the fourth beast say, Come and see. And I looked and behold a pale horse; and his name that sat on him was Death, and hell followed him. And power was given unto them over the fourth part of the earth, to kill with sword and with hunger, and with death, and with the beasts of the earth".

My mind takes me back many years ago, to where I was working this verse out metaphysically, as to how I could interpret it correctly and explain it to you. Remember that every species that has evolved on this planet has its own emotional outlet, therefore it is accountable for its own actions. Also remember that humanity has inherited their attributes since the beginning of our gestation as this seance is embedded in the pons section in the base of our brain. Each species follows its own DNA for them to evolve up into the antenna of their mind to earn the right to evolve up into the telepathic inheritance for their thoughts to transfer to the rest of their own species, as does the whale of the ocean and the elephant on the land. The word 'Sciential' comes to mind as it represents my first logo that I began with. Interpreted this word is decoded as, 'To Know the Knowing'.

We know by now that symbolically the horse is representing our spiritual strength. The pale horse is representing our inner spiritual divinity. This is the last of the four horses; now to decode what this pale horse represents. We have the white, the red, the black, and then the pale horse was the last. Again, I refer to the story of Levi where he washed the different coloured garments all together in the same vat and they all came out exactly the same pale colour. More on this subject as the story unfolds. This verse alerts us to the fact, that as we empty our mind of old thoughts; we are finishing previous experiences that we have already lived. We then die metaphorically to these thoughts where we can prepare our mind to take its next step forward for us to move on. That is the interpretation of the word 'death'.

"And hell followed him". Yes, it does, as people living in their own hell need to search for the light, as they cannot find their own. Hell is all of your thoughts that have not been digested correctly, chasing you around looking for someone to lead them out of their murky existence, as they have no inner light to guide them. The next codes to decipher are the words? *"And power was given unto them over the fourth part of the earth, to kill with sword and with hunger and with death, and with the beasts of the earth"*. Allow me to explain these words through the shamanic language.

You are more aware now, that this hidden language is embedded in every human gene where you will allow each thought to bring itself to your attention, as you are being prepared to step up to anoint yourselves. This is how your thoughts become an earning, through your learning.

The next part of the sentence mentions *"to kill with the sword"*. Kill what? The sword represents our soul's word! Therefore, we must confront our negative thoughts—killing them will eradicate them. *"And with hunger"* means starving these thoughts out of our mind. In other words, we must eradicate them of attention, ignoring their constant chattering. This way, they will surrender and die, as there will be no energy left to sustain them.

By now, you understand that we are referring to the ego—there is no nourishment for it to cling to. Now, onto the final section of this verse: *"and with the beasts of the earth"*. These beasts symbolize the primal part of our mind, where the roots of our fears spring to our attention. Remember, these fears are layered throughout our gestation and embedded in the foundation of the ego's brain. They like to think that they can hide beneath the garment of God, represented by the hypothalamus gland. The fourth part of the earth refers to our body, and these beasts live in its lower half—the legs and thighs. In other words, we are to tame our sexual connotations before they deter us and become rampant.

The eternal mathematical language is threaded right throughout your inner universe; as well as reflected outside of you, where they become the never—ending story or everlasting life which is always placed in front of you; constantly watching over you; repeating itself, until you get it right!

These natural Laws of the Universe are permanently attached to us as each one of us autonomically think when we request attention or release a thought; it is the collective consciousness at work. This symbolic structure requires a balance to equate throughout our sympathetic nervous system.

Once each spark has produced its own light, our body

naturally releases the right chemical analysis, which is sent through our genes to our DNA. If it is not the correct thought, then the universal law claims the priority right, to slam dunk you into producing your own inherent disease. This is God at work! You have earned what you have sown! The DNA begins its work as to how the correct alphabetical formula is released. As we bring forth our intelligence, it delivers itself up into the thyroid gland and from here, it is taken over by the upper glandular system, which as previously explained is where we note, that it becomes the responsibility of the pituitary gland where the information is then converted over into the fourth dimension or the unconscious recognition of self. You will understand this easier when you have read my book on *Decoding Disease*.

Our sonic sound or heavenly kingdom is at work here, as this hidden language releases from the mastoid area behind our ears and traverses with the mind into producing the next thought up into the neural pathways of our brain. Therefore, we can see more clearly how we evolved into a three-dimensional species and are well on the way to inheriting the information of the fourth dimension.

You have entered up into the energy of the unconscious mind. The Bible refers to this place as Israel. (Through the **I**ntelligence of the **S**oul, you have **R**eleased and **A**scended into **E**verlasting **L**ife.

Now, to verse 8. This verse is informing us of our Passover from the third-dimension reality, up into the fourth, and if that is too hard to understand; I will write it a different way. We have understood that the pale horse is our combined spiritual strength; or could this colour be a strain of grey, through the black, the red and the white all mixing to produce this pale colour? Our spiritual strength is the energetic force that releases from within our mind, which we have named, our aura. Our aura is our field of condensed light that surrounds our body just as every living thing on this planet also has surrounding it. And this positive energy has climbed its way up through our DNA or inner library to knock on the door. This door is autonomically wide open through the mathematics of our central nervous system; which is highlighted through the sympathetic nervous system. It takes a considerable strength for one to find, the courage to walk into this unheard-of world of thought. Maybe now you can understand the potent words regarding this previous paragraph. Now we are earning the right to accept our fourth church named Thyatira or as sometimes written as Thyatirea.

"And when he had opened the fifth seal, I saw under the altar the souls of them that were slain for the word of God, and for the testimony which they held". Again, we are being reminded of those egotistical personalities or thoughts that were refusing to change and were working against us through their fear, as we extend our intellect up into the power of the higher realms. They were placed under the altar, not in front to release themselves into their truth.

"And they cried with a loud voice saying, 'How long O Lord, holy and true dost thou not judge and avenge our blood on them that dwell on the earth". God, this greatest order of our inner divinity, never judges, we avenge ourselves.

"And white robes were given unto every one of them; and it was said unto them that they should rest yet for a little season, until their fellow servants, also and their brethren that should be killed as they were, should be fulfilled".

Through resting the mind; we are giving those personalities which are still in abeyance to rearrange themselves and think positive, as we learn to bring our attitude together to feel at peace with our self. Not long to go now as we learn to earn our fifth church named Sardis.

"And I beheld when he had opened the sixth seal and lo there was a great earthquake, and the sun became as sackcloth of hair and the moon became as blood".

Hair represents worry in the metaphysical. It is amazing how just one strand of hair falling on your clothes or body can show you exactly how each strand of hair magnetizes, to where you have created a blockage in your own energy. It portends the temperature of the body that is collecting where ideas have not been fully digested. The message is for you to allow your worries to cease for tomorrow to be better than today.

"And the stars of heaven fell unto the earth, even as a fig tree casteth her untimely figs when she is shaken of a mighty wind".

Unto the earth is the code. Therefore, we understand that the message is coming from the heavenly realms of our brain. When we rearrange our thoughts, we have the opportunity to plant new seeds or ideas. Remember that the stars of heaven, is your intellectual light being flushed throughout your system. We are well on the way to becoming our sixth church named Philadelphia.

We are realizing how the stories are repeating themselves over and over again, each time gently bringing up our intellect to understand these words which are harmonizing and balancing each other, as we perpetually move towards our pinnacle to reach and attain our Divine truth.

I am so looking forward to you reading on to the last chapter as there are many of you who are beginning to view the language of the hieroglyphic empire or inner self much more eloquently. I feel your light becoming stronger as you see how the Masters of the Divine Mind of yesteryear have explained and released this gift of knowledge for us to understand more eloquently the hidden language scribed in the Temples all around the planet that they have left for us to earn the real reason for us being present here.

CHAPTER SEVEN

The Original Story

We begin in Verse 1: *"And after these things I saw four angels standing on the four corners of the earth, holding the four winds of the earth, that the wind should not blow on the earth, nor on the sea, nor on any tree"*.

Verse 2: *"And I saw another angel ascending from the east, having the seal of the living God: and he cried with a loud voice to the four angels, to whom it was given to hurt the earth and the sea"*.

Verse 3: *"Saying, Hurt not the earth, neither the sea, nor the trees, till we have sealed the servants of our God in their foreheads"*.

Verse 4: *"And I heard the number of them which were sealed: and there were sealed an hundred and forty and four thousand of all the tribes of the children of Israel"*.

So here we are, right back at the beginning of the Old Testament again; where we were first told the stories of the twelve tribes of Israel. By now you have begun to understand how your personalities are continually multiplying themselves, as the written word is being accepted by each one of them. Please remember your personalities add to the experiences you have the opportunity of living and through their new found belief in themselves we see how the tribes are fortifying one another and coming together. All of which becomes our innate strength.

The original story is explaining to us that we are the earth. The wind is our breath. The sea is our consciousness. The trees represent our understanding. The east is the results of our inner spiritual action; it is the expedition we are taking on to understand what is already scribed within our genetic inheritance, this is our own family inheritance which was downloaded in the beginning of our own personal gestation, before we were born. The four angels who were standing on the four corners or directions of the earth, represent the future thoughts that are out there supporting you as you search for your positive outcome, which becomes your new belief in yourself; in other words, it is through the faith you find and release within yourself, that you can overcome for you to release your inner fear, also the support of your inner strength in knowing that you will succeed to become the elder of your inner tribe. Now we understand more fully the gift that was left to us in Egypt. The Golden Pharaoh is you becoming your city of light. Hence the twelve times twelve, $12 \times 12 = 144,000$. Can you recall the numbers carved into the foreheads of the two Principle-Kings of the Mayan and Egyptian philosophies? Now we move on.

Verse 5: *"Of the tribe of Juda were sealed twelve thousand. Of the tribe of Reuben were sealed twelve thousand. Of the tribe of Gad were sealed twelve thousand".*

Verse 6: *"Of the tribe of Aser were sealed twelve thousand. Of the tribe of Nephthalim were sealed twelve thousand. Of the tribe of Manasses were sealed twelve thousand".*

Verse 7: *"Of the tribe of Simeon were sealed twelve thousand. Of the tribe of Levi were sealed twelve thousand. Of the tribe of Issachar were sealed twelve thousand".*

Verse 8: *"Of the tribe of Zabulon were sealed twelve thousand. Of the tribe of Joseph were sealed twelve thousand. Of the tribe of Benjamin were sealed twelve thousand".*

And now we can take note of how our mind is being re-educated for us to become each tribe, through the unfolding of our cellular memory we have earned of our new found belief in self.

Verse 9: *"After this I beheld, and, lo, a great multitude, which no man could number, of all nations, and kindreds, and people, and tongues, stood before the throne, and before the Lamb, clothed with white robes, and palms in their hands".*

Here we see how the results of your action honour you through the whole collection of your personalities joining forces to support you into becoming one another! Your inner dictionary has every language that is spoken and more importantly you are representing all of these words. I use the word 'important' quite often in my writings and some have suggested that I change the word. Why, is it abrasive to your ego? The word begins with 'import' and what does this word mean? Having great authority or influence; now are you sick of hearing it? Also, it interprets as coming from across the waters, now that explanation I like! One explanation is for the left hemisphere and the other is for the right hemisphere; when they are harmoniously brought together, there is the balance of a job well done.

Verse 10: "*And cried with a loud voice, saying, Salvation to our God which sitteth upon the throne, and unto the Lamb*".

Verse 11: "*And all the angels stood round about the throne, and about the elders and the four beasts, and fell before the throne on their faces, and worshipped God*".

Verse 12: "*Saying, Amen: Blessing, and glory, and wisdom, and thanksgiving, and honour, and power, and might, be unto our God for ever and ever. Amen*".

Verse 13: "*And one of the elders answered, saying unto me, What are these which are arrayed in white robes? and whence came they?*"

Verse 14: "*And I said unto him, Sir, thou knowest. And he said to me, These are they which came out of great tribulation, and have washed their robes, and made them white in the blood of the Lamb*".

Remember that the lamb represents the sacrifice we make to ourself, which is through our innocence learning to release its fear.

Verse 15: "*Therefore are they before the throne of God, and serve him day and night in his temple: and he that sitteth on the throne shall dwell among them*".

Your intellect has taken a step up towards your temple mind

to become your ever-lasting life. It is always with you and through you.

Verse 16: "They shall hunger no more, neither thirst anymore; neither shall the sun light on them, nor any heat".

Verse 17: *"For the Lamb which is in the midst of the throne shall feed them, and shall lead them unto living fountains of waters: and God shall wipe away all tears from their eyes"*.

The frustration that was in our life is beginning to diminish and our innocence is earning the right to be educated through our new found trust into a form of gentleness, where it has taken supremacy in our mind, and our life continues on as we have earned the right to live through our spoken words.

We see how the numbers carved into the skull of (note the spelling) Tut-Ankh-Amen of Egypt, as well as the Mayan King, reveal their significance—explaining why they were placed in their tombs for us to inherit the truth of the original sacred language. Through our belief in self, we continue to earn our next evolutionary step. In verse 4 of the codex formula of numbers 144,000, we are shown that these numbers are symbolically presented as sacred codes, allowing us to truly understand our inner consciousness. As we begin to release or unearth ourselves—in today's terms, to unravel our own intellect—we move towards deeper awareness.

Through sacred numerology, we recognise that the number 1 signifies 'I am'. The number 4 represents an area we have earned—where we embody both our past and our present moment—as we set out to create our temple and reach our divine self. The number 4 signifies 'my temple'; it is where we begin to see our shadow self and where we become the cross we bare. There are two 4s. The number 2 represents our relationship to our Temple, while 0 represents the soul. There are three zeroes, and the number 3 represents PI as well as the mind of God.

The more we evolve into own relationship and move away from allowing others to control us, the more we evolve through the twelve tribes of Israel, as referred to in the Old Testament.

As we continue onward, these tribes multiply our intelligence through their own wisdom, unravelling themselves.

Over time, these tribes who were representing the history and energetic responses of the last 64 generations of our DNA. All of which created the purification of our blood lines and also the story of how our bone marrow is rethreaded throughout the generations, which is embedded in our bones as it has the information that is already scribed in our genetic inheritance where through our step by step walk into our transformed future we could accept the conversion into us all becoming the twelve Apostles of the New Testament, formally known to us as the Lesser Gods. Now we understand how important they are to us.

The New Testament is now introducing us up into our Royal Chambers which is where we are able to reach the doorway to the divinity, the divine unity of our self. Now we can understand more intellectually how each one of these Tribes of Israel had released their 12,000 servants who were available to serve, or be of service to you, as well as to how we look, see and finally view one another. 12 x 12 = 144,000 people or personalities of self, who will be saved.

All of these earlier tribes spoke through their own tongues, their written word was genetically carried through to one another, that is why they could all speak the same language; in other words, they have magnetically attracted and created their own hologram, where each gene could mirror through to one another this holographic imprint to create the three-dimensional image, to become equal to the summarization of our soul! Hopefully now you can begin to understand how the conductivity of our inner mathematical mind first began to inherit itself.

I will also explain to you that the higher we open up to extend our emotional intellect, the more we unravel what is metaphysically known as the spiritual scribe within; as previously explained the scribe is referred to through the Egyptian Philosophies as the author, this little figure that is down on their knees writing their next thought on a tablet of clay.

We also understand that the clay is in reference to the image that was made in the book of Daniel, in chapter 2, where Daniel was asked to interpret King Nebuchadnezzar's dream. Our clay is the lower section of our body and is situated around the feet and toe area; through the Ancient Shamanic Principles, it is symbolically referred to us as our understanding; we release our own written word, also known as the Sanskrit language; where we scribed in the sand. Allow me to explain another rendition of the word 'Sanskrit'. If I break this word up into syllables through the ancient language it is pronounced as Sha-An-Skrit. These syllables are informing us that as we move up into our Academic education just above our navel, which is the home of the second God AN, the **S**oul's **K**nowledge **R**eleases our **I**ntellectual **T**ruth. Nice interpretation, don't you think?

All of which is genetically passed on to each following generation where it is recorded for each one of us to inherit, you will understand more clearly, as you read further into the writings of St. John the Divine. The written word, or 'scribe' as it was known at that time, comes from the everlasting energy that is embedded in our cells. This embedment is also responsible for creating the bone matter of the body. It is magnetically accepted through its own positive enhancement as it develops throughout our bone tissue. Additionally, it surrounds us through the electromagnetic fields of the universe and is responsible for keeping us gravitated. This allows us, along with every species that has evolved, to stand upright and walk on the planet. Our own cosmic force, or field of force, solidifies and strengthens us as we learn to earn, honour, and protect ourselves.

Our cells become adherent, which creates the density in our bones, as it becomes the core of the body, just the same as the planet has its own core. The Egyptians referred to this same energy as the Bja. And if we take this pronunciation back into its Arabian beginning; we pronounce this word as Bea, which is decoded as the place where we have earned the right to 'Balance with EA'. In other lands close by, it is referred to as the Rean and when interpreted this word decodes as Releasing the Energy of AN. We see this symbolic reference thousands of times; when we read the hieroglyphs correctly, they explain to us a different interpretation as to what we think is the original story.

Let us take a look at the new born child, until the child begins to learn to walk, our babies crawl or shuffle along on all fours, just like a loyal little animal. At this stage they are relying on their second dimensional brain, and they learn to empower themselves through their little ego's enquiring attention which allows them to urge themselves forward.

*

I have received a message that I have to pause your minds as the previous paragraphs need time for you to equate and digest the information that you have previously read. Therefore, the paragraphs ahead lead you into a parking area on your new super highway for you to pause and rest, while I write a short essay in regards to the species of the planet. This will allow your imagination to relax and unwind the pressure that has collected, and when you have the opportunity to either re-read or think about what you have previously read, you will find that the story that releases from your inner vocabulary, will sound and become much more harmonious to your mind.

This portends to those who walked before us, as explained in Genesis, per se' every living animal, fish, bird as well as the magic carpet that was spread across the earth which relayed the rivers to meander so they could oblige the earth to accommodate for the species in dry areas for the grasses to grow where they could absorb the nourishment from the rain as well, right up to the trees to ensure that those less fortunate than ourselves could find a safe haven to build their home in a cave or the trunk of an elderly tree, as well as forage for their food and water to sustain them. Through thousands of years of their evolution, they have reached their inner antenna of their DNA, where they can magnetically read and understand our thoughts long before we realise the direction we are leading ourselves into, especially if we have taken on the responsibility to domestically claim them as our own. They then dedicate their life to take on our illnesses and our thoughts through harmonising and protecting us.

*

The fish species of the oceans and rivers who can change their sex to mathematically ensue through the multiplication of their own species when they began to realise that they are depleting within their own families from keeping their entire species up into a perpetual balance, where there is safety in numbers. This mass energy becomes a school of fish of same species, as they earn the right to become one mind, through them living in the consciousness of water, which still holds every combustible thought since the beginning of time. Does this remind you of when you first began your schooling through your learning to remember your mathematical tables, through the whole class repeating over and over again each table, where it became familiar to you? It then became a repetitious tune the more familiar it sounded, which led you on to your next progressive step. Your progress had made an indelible imprint into the upper sections of our brain that was metaphysically registered with the unconscious mind that we were to remember always.

*

The birds to whom I previously referred to throughout my shamanic journey of isolation in the outback, as the angelic realm of the earth, as they have taught me over and over again, that we are all one; they were born with wings to lift themselves high above the earth to view and broaden their expansion and elevation, which opened them up into their inner sonar where they could travel further into their terrain, as they are situated up into a higher elevation to be responsible for the upper echelons of their telepathic area of their brain, where they are permanently in contact with our thinking here on the earth, as we prepare our mind for our next thought. Each species of bird relates to a level of intellectual compatibility of the human mind, no matter how we speak or pronounce our language, which is through their inner sonar connecting with us on an etheric level of telepathic enhancement. Now you can understand more clearly that these sentences also refer to us who are living in the metaphysical areas of our mind.

When they appear in our terrain they sound their call to us through the language of the sacredness of the ancient numerology. Not the alphabet, we have to use ours as there are many languages on this planet; the numbers of the whole universe, all relate to the same word we speak. They pause at the end of the numbers of each word that equate to the language of the sacred alphabet, where they announce to us by informing us of our own iniquities, which are those of our personalities that are walking backwards through a repetitive congestive thought that we have anchored ourselves into, which is forcing us to rescind our thinking, for us to repair the damage we are creating. The moment we have acknowledged their message, they fly on to the next house that is ready to receive their message. They have already earned their inner sonar to fly in the direction they are aiming for, as they have become their own arrows, where they have the knowing how to sonically point themselves in any direction that they measure through the energy statically being shown to them to arrive at their destination to inform us. My training came in the beginning through Crow, who represents and is renowned through time as the 'Keeper of the Sacred Law', as he trained me through the sacred numerology which I had to concur with to become of same mind to understand these messages he was transferring onto me, as well as through all of the birds who were coloured black and grey with a touch of white, as they are layered differently where they can represent to us how to become responsible to accept and represent the combined inner and outer power and strength that we are collecting through the metaphysical pathway, to bring it to our attention, where we are able to use to assist us as we journey further into the unknown, which I now refer to what has already been relayed to our cellular inheritance through our gestation, that we unfurl when we can accept the power and order of the in-known, or this **G**reatest **O**rder of the **D**ivine. Further information is explained through my book *Decoding the Sacred Alphabet and Numerology*.

We return to the grasses that grow in the earth, where many species can begin to grown their seed heads from seven days after their gestation, and then the winds come to scatter their tiny seeds as the magic carpet spreads across the land, to create the food for those animals to nourish themselves.

Larger grasses take a longer time to reach maturity as their seeds have turned to grains which takes time for them to build up their substance which are used for us and many other varieties of the animal kingdom as well. And then comes the trees who communicate to one another, through their underground root systems, which explains to us why they can stand in the same position through the totality of their royal existence. Remember the story of the olive tree that can live for a thousand years and still bare its own fruit, as it is fed from its own nourishment every seven years from one of its fruit burrowing under the ground to renourish its own trunk! I thank you for your tolerance in reading these last few paragraphs, I was asked to lighten your load as the pressure was disturbing many of you, through the temperance of your ego demanding attention as it was realising that it was again being replaced by added information that it had no control over and was totally unaware of. Now that we have brought you back into a sense of balance, you have learned to understand something differently, therefore I can return back to the story and move on.

Yes, there are new words and information being mentioned in these paragraphs, as I explain to you the importance of the mathematical resonance that created these ancient words. Again, may I remind you that we are autonomically (self-governed on an inner level) as to how we are sized up mathematically, through each layer we accomplish regarding the laws of the universe, as we are now beginning to hone in on how we are reflecting our inner strength through every word that our family has previously inherited, as we earn the right to accept that all is recorded in our DNA. Our DNA is a mirror that reflects an illusion to our written word, which we now know, stems from our bone matter. Remember that the roots of our brain begin in the lower section of our spine, as we birthed up into the third dimension of reality and as we travel throughout our life with every positive move forward, we climb each rung of our inner ladder of our DNA to reach the end of the three dimensional earth, as our inner body now understands that we are out of the ego's clutches, for us to face this Book of Life with the seven seals that we must learn to unclasp on the back of the book, for us to continue our journey up into the higher dimensions of our mind accomplishing for ever more, our everlasting life.

We are beginning to understand more as we read and hear how these Tribes and Apostles evolved symbolically to represent the twelve strands of our DNA. Each strand is being explained to us as a tribe which has inherited their antenna through reaching their PI or PHI. It is where the tribes come together again; as explained to us in the book of Matthew in the New Testament. Remember the book of Matthew is representing the mythical story of the God Prometheus from the Greek philosophies. (PRO-MA'AT-HAUS, this word decoded, is informing us of the promotion we have earned to be delegated up into the house of our mathematical resonance which is represented through the codes as the angelic vibration). Through the Greek interpretation of this version, this God was renowned for giving man the gift of fire, which of course represents the resurrection in Christianity's teachings or the golden phoenix rising from the ashes, throughout the Asiatic and Shamanic Principles.

We see a new announcement to herald our new beginnings, as we notice how the story has been collected, and through the Greek Philosophies we are informed that Zeus was not too happy about this gift that Prometheus had, and he chained Prometheus to a rock (his mind) and sent an eagle to peck out his liver by day, where at night it grew back again, only to be eaten out again the following day. We see the same story in the Bible. Metaphysically this was to remove his frustration, which became his anger, which built up into bitterness, where the Eagle could show him the steps he could take for his own purification. Therefore, we can see how he ventured up into the adult mind, where we could understand much more colloquially, how the New Testament is the resurrection of the Old Testament.

From the twelve Tribes of Israel, came the twelve Disciples or Disciplines to work on behalf of and for Jesus all clothed in white, which came out of great tribulation. And this wonderful book of Revelations is showing us our next level of intelligence. The final verse speaks to us: *"For the Lamb which is in the midst of the Throne shall feed them and shall lead them unto living fountains of waters: and God shall wipe away all tears from their eyes".*

So, what have we understood so far; the seals are opening through each person learning to believe and trust in themselves; as they take their next step to earning their freedom? The fears that have kept us trapped in our past are no longer applicable, in our new way of life. Our inner strength is becoming more direct to our thinking, fewer mistakes are being made; our body is becoming more subtle, diseases are terminating and eradicating all by themselves. We are growing up and accepting moment by moment our inner wisdom. There are no more tears of frustration. Please remember that tears are just a repose for your ego. You are no longer the innocent child. You are now learning how to honour your inner Royalty and serve yourself for the first time in your life. Your personalities will grow into a fruition of knowledge never acknowledged to you before, as they have been furled until you could understand who you are, for you to experience these new ideas where they will come into a finalization of understanding that you and God (this **G**reatest **O**rder of the **D**ivine) are becoming as one.

You are about to step into taking part in the first of the 'finale' where the ego is about to exonerate itself and accept the consequences ahead. Please remember that this will happen three times as we learn to ease our way up into our divine equation. This we have named heaven.

CHAPTER EIGHT

The Opening Of The Seventh Seal That Created The Great Plagues

In this chapter we are introduced to the codes to awaken the seventh seal; as it begins to open, we find that we still have the opportunity to release the basic irritations that may be still trapped and caught up in our personalities which up to now, some of them have not yet had the opportunity to be corrected; or more importantly we see how the old thoughts that are still trapped must now turn around and mirror themselves to their inner self.

Those lower worlds are starting to release their own pressure to empty themselves where they are finally able to diminish; there is more room for those old fears to breathe their own breath to allow their light to glow. They are beginning to resurrect themselves as they journey up towards their heavenly abode.

Regarding the underworld; our fear does not like to be left alone when it is trapped in its own darkness; insecurity takes over where it is permanently searching for the company of someone else to step in and take over! It is all hell and brim fire down here and until you can lift yourself up and out of this pit, you will be continually choked down. Throughout my rendition of decoding the ancient language of Egyptology, all of the myths explain this seventh seal as the smoking apparatus which purifies the mind as to why the seventh seal must always be permanently kept opened. This is the last cleansing station before your entry into stepping up into everlasting life.

As you are now becoming more aware of, when we create another blunder in our thoughts, these thoughts tend to hang on to one another and embed themselves deeper within our memories. They need to resurrect through sacrificing to themselves. And that is the responsibility of the seventh seal.

"*Again, the seven angels with the seven trumpets return to our eyes, the incense was burnt and the blessings came from all of the saints".*

We begin with the first of the four angels, just like we began with the awakening of the previous seals. Remember that seal number four is connected to our heart, through the explanation of the Egyptian God Thoth, is where we learn to open the heart to our self; once we have executed the opening of the heart ceremony, we become aware of our angelic resonance where the feather and the heart both weigh the same. One cannot become an angel until the heart has executed the ego! In other words, we look upon everyone else as to how we would treat ourself. We also note that Anubis, who is the keeper of the gateway to the underworld, represents the ancient loyalty one has with oneself! He is there to assist us as we atone ourselves to our innate Lord, into re-harmonizing and rebalancing our mind.

Verse 7: "*The first angel sounded and there followed hail and fire mingled with blood and they were cast upon the earth: and the third part of trees was burnt up and all green grass was burnt up".*

We are becoming aware of the fire and ice syndrome; the upper and the lower sections of self, which is mingled with blood, while there is a fire down below, we cast ice in the heavenly home to create the waters to put the fire out, also to flush out the irritations of our mind; which through the art of symbolism, is our life force, that was cast or rated by God from above; which is now referred to us as our heavenly home. And the third part of the trees is interpreted as the first section of our lower God, named EL (Ever-Lasting) throughout the mythical agenda, or the first doorway of our Royal Order to begin this education of stepping into the next world, we have named as us stepping into the Metaphysical journey. It is in this next section for us to understand that our spiritual life begins to awaken in our upper inner thighs, at the mouth of the vagina in women and at the back and between the testes of men, that every human must abide by, as this the home base to our ego. This section is our base chakra as explained in many others culture.

Throughout my journey with my Master's, it was explained to me as to how we earn the right to birth into the first doorway of the home of the Kundalini Empire, there is a gland situated up high near the mouth of the womb, which when we are ready, realigns the base of our DNA as it traverses up through our bone marrow to our heart. Once this next section of our DNA has been stimulated this allows for the heart to re-fibrillate these small fibres to expel the old to allow for our new inner fibre optics, that is endowed upon us from the God Head above, which is an advancement of light to shepherd us up into our next advanced step of our journey. All of which releases the heart from its past thinking into the base of our skull, known as the Kingdom of God. This keeps us on the straight and narrow!

The tree section of our body, is our feet and represents our lower legs up to the knees, which has been embedded with the memories of the species, trees, grass and the waters of the ultimate consciousness. Now maybe you can understand why we have named a group of trees a stand? We have also had to learn to stand upright!

Through our evolution into becoming the human species, we have been energetically impregnated with the memory of every living species into the base of our brain, that has ever evolved on this planet. Why? We are the last to evolve and therefore we must accept the consequences of those who have evolved before us.

We know that the first dimension to evolve, through the creation of our brain, is medically known to us as the Pons; which relays signals from the cortex, where it supports the storehouse of every thought that our previous generations had the experience of thinking and using. The next section to gestate is, in the middle section known to us as the olive. So here we are aware of the waters and the trees as they were created on the planet from the beginning of time. Read it again if you doubt what I have explained to you, and take your time in digesting the information. Once understood, you will be amazed at your growth for you to accept the next positive step of your journey, as your miracles begin to rearrange your thinking appear before you.

Verse 8: *"And the second angel sounded and as it were a great mountain burning with fire was cast into the sea and the third part of the sea became blood. And the third part of the creatures which were in the sea and had life, died and the third part of the ships were destroyed."*

My interpretation to this verse begins to explain to you how your old thinking must make way for the new. We can see that this is the beginning of us accepting the resurrection of self. A mountain is symbolically referred to as a huge section of our energy that has collected through it becoming insecure to begin with, which has condensed our mind; just the same as a fat cell creates itself in the body. This mountain burning with fire was cast into the sea, which means for us to cast our mountains of trouble out into the ultra-consciousness of all that is; so that we are able to face our inner truth as we resurrect our thoughts. The next evolutionary truth we earn comes in a warning for us to release this blocked energy and return back into our inner consciousness, that we have already evolved into. In other words, this makes us accountable for our own actions.

"And the third part of the sea became blood". Again, I mention that this is all in the delivery, to explain the inner language to teach the first God EL. Now we can understand that our life force is building and creating. It is not mingled with blood; it has become blood, which gives it the confidence to flow completely around our inner body. *"And the third part of the creatures which were in the sea and had life, died"*. Here we are learning to accept that these creatures were those who devoured one another. They represent personalities of self that could not or refused to evolve up into accepting their higher wisdom. *"And the third part of the ships, were destroyed"*. What do these ships represent in us? How do we metaphorically create this sentence? Remember that the ships symbolically represent our mind-body that rides through the consciousness, so if a third part were destroyed, we can see that once again we are being reminded of the first sector of God, as it is being transferred up into the next level of its educational learning.

If you are having difficulties with this section then please put the book down and walk away for a little while; have a glass of water and then come back and reread from the beginning of the chapter and slowly over time with you reading and repeating the words often enough; you will find that you release your inner mathematics autonomically, which will open your mind up to where you will be able to read it again and all will be revealed to you. Once again, slowly, slowly, rings the bell.

"And the third angel sounded and there fell a great star from heaven burning as it were a lamp and it fell upon a third part of the rivers and upon the fountains of waters.

And the name of the star is Wormwood. And the third part of the waters became wormwood and many men died of the waters because they were made bitter".

This verse has been spoken or written by millions of you and each one of you have come to your own conclusions as to what is its interpretation. We now understand that the star that falls from heaven, means that your intelligence has been awakened and the intellectual light from your learning and earnings has been flushed down through your waters, which we know interprets as your consciousness or body, to filter throughout your genes. And as you have been exalted up into the higher realms by your God within, the old thoughts that created their own bitterness, must deteriorate to make way for the new. Once again, I remind you that symbolically through the ancient Sanskrit language, the men who died, represent your genes, which you now understand represent the last 64 generations of your own personal tribal laws.

Through earning my years of education into the Shamanic Principles, my teachers explained to me that there is nothing we do not know! We as human, have the ability to answer to everything there is to know; never give up and walk away, just take a deep breath and rest or resist the inner chattering of your mind; you will learn to release your mind to your highest of high, which lives in heaven, as we become more aware that heaven is within and begins to manifest itself around the throat area at the base of your head.

When we understand the stories of the Egyptian Empire correctly as it was originally created and scribed for us to decode; over the years I came to realize that the whole story of Egypt was explaining to me the evolution of the human body, from Lower Egypt to our navel and once we had opened up our universal city, our inner university, our educational centre, which became an extension of our already in-known knowledge, where we were given a new and added language to combine with our intelligence, as we stepped up into the second Master known as AN, or Ang throughout the Asian Principles. Have you ever realized that there are over 100,000 plus myths written on this story?

It took many years of isolation for me to open up these codes one step at a time, for me to end up with understanding Egyptology explaining itself to me, as the inner evolution of the human being, human. To study more of Egypt, I journeyed many times to the country; I realized that each time I attended, I was autonomically shown my next educated step, no matter which temple I walked into. I was able to read more into the story. I was adding to what I had already understood previously, until it dawned on me that I was being shown the evolution of the human body. More importantly, I came to realise that I was being informed that I was viewing the make-up of our central nervous system.

Back to the drawing board I went for three long and tedious years for me to file the story together, as to the map of Egypt, the position of the temples, the obelisks the pyramids etc; as to our inner glandular system and their responsibilities to our liver, kidneys, gallbladder, pancreas, spleen, heart and lungs, again we are reminded of the number seven! Please remember through the sacred alphabet the number seven relates to our 'Christ Consciousness' as to how our inner light manifests itself as to how these seven regions were accepting their responsibility which was explaining to me of the utmost importance of ourselves.

We become aware of this doorway of time, where these seven steps of pyramids that relate to these seals, can be seen in an alignment with one another as they lead us up into the unconscious mind. Hence the Pons and the Olive that began in the brain. Another point for you to remember also, is that the olive tree can reproduce itself for a thousand plus years if the branch is severed where the previous olive has grown; if it is not pruned correctly, you deter its life force and denounce its age. Also remember that every seven years this magnificent tree, fosters its own growth, through one olive dropping onto the ground close by the trunk of the tree for it to burrow under the ground to come up through its own root system and refurbish its own trunk for its own sustenance to strengthen and reinvest in itself. My goodness, shades of our own life force, isn't it? Ours is through us releasing a positive thought, the olive tree is through what it has already produced, its own fruit of labours. Now do you understand the Olive named at the base of our brain?

Don't bother reaching up and out for the stars right now. It is our unconscious mind that is our exalted mind, which is connected to the soul of our gravity fields as well as the cosmic force field or the collective of our own consciousness. It is referred to as the east through the teachings of the bible. Remember the three wise men, who came from the east, now recall that the east is within to bring gifts of Frankincense and Myrrh to celebrate the birth of Jesus. This is the myth of your genetic inheritance.

Our unconscious mind knows all; 'it sits within and lovingly waits for our ego to fall' is a parable that has stood by me over the years. It sounds similar to the Biblical verse "*Suffer little children to come unto me and forbid them not, for of such is the kingdom of heaven*".

When I began to read these passages metaphysically, my training led me up and through my education, step by step. If I had difficulties understanding something, I had to reverse the words back to its point of conception to find the answer, as that is how the system of the metaphysical language or unconscious mind replies to our questions. It is known to us as the 'Divine Language' or the Great Memoriam. That is why some of you still have difficulties interpreting your dreams as you do not understand the language that the unconscious mind is delivering back to you. Never think that you have had a stupid dream, as so many thousands of you have told me.

It is just that you have not yet understood where you are still allowing your ego to over control your mind. If it is off the beaten track; then you will be reminded through your inner vision world. Once my students understood the interpretation of the Divine Language, they were free to sail the heavens. Always reverse your dreams to find the answer!

When we reverse the word 'Wormwood', it becomes 'woodworm'. The herb wormwood is bitter and is a purgative. It is a very toxic herb, which eradicates parasites and must be taken very sparingly. As a child we had a perimeter of wormwood planted around the homestead, so we always felt protected. As the sun shone throughout the day, it emitted a silver hue and always sparkled with light, as children we knew our boundary protected us as God was looking after us and all was good.

So now you are beginning to understand why this star was given this name, it is eradicating the parasitical thinking that always wants to control your old ways and deliberately stays trapped in your old tree of knowledge. A good dose of wormwood thinking, definitely not taken internally through the mouth, will help it make up its mind to move on.

The positive intellectual light is what the stars represent in Egypt. Symbolism is the innate truth that releases and realigns the mathematics of the mind, for us to be able to create our reality. Remember that the whole planet is under the jurisdiction of the Numbers, Geometry and Alphabet and where the ultimate aim is for us to understand the creation of how our mathematics works permanently on our behalf.

As you can see, we are reaching up into the heavenly area where we now deal with the sun, the moon and the stars, which are the heavenly heights to explain verses 12 and 13. Again we see the same announcements regarding the one third of each, as we notice the darkness being brought to our attention to see how the first God EL, is no longer applicable to control the wholeness of self. It has been executed as we evolve up into the next God AN to receive our university training! Now do you understand how the word 'EL-EX-AN-DRI-EA' where the three Gods become at one, with one another, or as is spelt in today's language Alexandria, which housed the largest library on the planet, which is situated in the crown of your head. The ego has had its first deliverance from God, all because you had an enquiring thought and you wanted to understand how to accept and acknowledge yourself!

You have finally opened the door for you to become the seventh church known to us as Laodicea, or the teachings of Lao Tzu through the principles of China. The old master steps forward into our life to remind us that there is nothing we cannot do to attain our belief, to heal our ultimate mind. If we have dis-ease in our body it is in this state of grace that we can repair the interrupted tissue to reinvest in its self again. We take the damaged thought that is trapped within, back to its original beginning. He is the teacher who always brings us back to where everything that starts at the beginning must end at the same point.

Also, this is where I realized that when society says that the largest pyramid was built for the Pharaoh Khufu, (Khu is interpreted as the inner knowledge gifted to us through the genetics of our gestation, which we are in the process of unfolding or unravelling, and Fu is interpreted as our freedom finally being understood) is where this pyramid is explaining to us the metaphysical journey of our evolution before we return home. where I could interpret this name back through the codes of the Chinese principles to reveal that if our thoughts and diseases are returned back into its gestation and blessed with the herbs and grains gifted to us, it has the power and strength to replace in us for us to eradicate the energy all by itself!

The little pyramid named Menkaure, I have previously mentioned as it explains our earlier childhood from birth to our teenage years.

The middle pyramid name Khafre is explaining the life we live until we have come to the end of our tether, where through desperation we are turning around and viewing ourself. Somewhere we have lost our inner freedom to think in a positive direction, where we are lost in our own branches, as our tree of knowledge has become forced, as it has become over-burdened and blocked. There is nowhere to run too. It is at this time where the universe place someone or maybe something across our path to lead us into the metaphysical announcement of discovering ourself, which is the requirement of our third dimensional mind. Remember that there are five levels of rooms and corridors that have recently been unearthed underneath Khafre (Kha, our inner knowledge free's our inner torment, to release our inner energy, this sacred part of ourself that was downloaded into our body before we were born.) Now what is the sacred version of number five? FREEDOM!

I hope you have inherited the information of how you have understood the inner codex of these seven churches as you now have the information, which will support and carry you through to understanding your inner journey through the miracles you will reveal to yourself right through to the end of this magnificent book. Let us read the Bible through the metaphysical understanding correctly. All of my books are explaining how I have had the opportunity and training to decode this inner language back to you!

CHAPTER NINE

Entering Up Into The Royal Chambers

"And the fifth angel sounded and I saw a star fall from heaven unto the earth. And to him was given the key to the bottomless pit. And the smoke came up out of the pit and the world darkened and out of the smoke came locusts upon the earth. And unto them was given power as the scorpions of the earth have power. And it was commanded them that should not hurt the grass of the earth neither any green thing, neither any tree. But only those men, which have not the seal of God in their foreheads". These are your inner personalities, who were not intellectually aware enough to keep up with the growth of progress you were trying to understand, in regards to your acceptance of this new information.

"And to them it was given that they should not kill them but that they should be tormented five months" (numerically this is interpreted as; until they had earned their freedom): *"and their torment was as the torment of the scorpion when he striketh a man"*.

The scorpion stems from your ego. It is the personality that becomes vindictive to the disciplinary action when it has to relinquish its control over the others and strikes out against the inner establishment.

"And in those days shall men seek death, and shall not find it; and shall desire to die and death shall flee from them".

This section is where so many of you who have committed yourselves to the supremacy of discovering your inner self, have so much trouble understanding this section of your mind and all want out of here. Death seems to be the way out and this cannot be so, through the codes of these stringent universal laws. You have made this commitment to yourself and now you must live through the pain that must release itself, for you to journey further into your future. Why cut short the experience of knowing yourself and create a huge excuse by dying?

"And the shapes of the locusts were like unto horses prepared unto battle; and on their heads were as it were crowns of gold, and their faces were as the faces of men.

And they had hair as the hair of women and their teeth were as the teeth of lions".

We are now aware that throughout the mythical stories, horses represent the spiritual strength that we earn for each of our personalities, which represent the faces of our genes, which are instilled with the information of the last 64 generations of our tribal law. Our hair represents the word 'worry', so long hair is alerting us to the fact that our worry is still embedded deep within us and we are carrying it along to support us. In the old days women were not allowed to cut their hair as it kept them locked into their sexual arena where they were here to serve their men. It serves to compliment the word 'sacrifice'. The locusts represent the irritations of the mind that you are afraid to let go, and are innocently hanging on to for support, which is the introduction into the medical term of tinnitus of the ears. Support for what? Yesterday's thinking! The sun has set and has risen again; your next challenge is waiting for you to begin your next positive thought; it is not for you to lay back and bask in yesterday! The teeth of lions are explaining that the locusts or irritated personalities spoke through their own vindictiveness owing to their ego and pride!

Verse 9: *"And their breast plates as it were breastplates of iron; and in the sound of their wings, was as the sound of chariots of many horses running to battle".*

Verse 10: *"And they had tails like unto scorpions and there were stings in their tails and their power was to hurt men for five months".*

Verse 11: *"And they had a king over them, which is the angel of the bottomless pit whose name in the Hebrew tongue is A-bad-don, but in the Greek tongue hath his name A-poly-on".*

Verse 12: *"One woe is past; and behold, there comes two woes more hereafter".*

Here is where you understand my verification regarding that the mind of God is delivered unto us in three sections, the EL-AN-EA which was released to you in the beginning pages of this book.

All of this drama is still informing us of the end of our old world of sorrow, which is the beginning of the end of our three-dimensional mind. The first God EL has now accepted and begun its new education and must move up into the second dimensional mind. Through the mythical stories we are being made aware of the God AN, who is in charge of our inner educational university.

Through understanding chapter 9, we have reached the end of our first antenna where we search for the need to refine our intellect. Your tests become much harder from here on in, as you have to release yourself up into the next evolutionary step. The suffering of the past has just about reached its peak of perfection and you are watching as your old worlds must crumble, to allow the new to begin.

Again, may I remind you that the angels symbolically represent your next thought? Your next thought is manifested from the Fibonacci sequence of your mathematics that is vibrated through your middle ear; it is your inner teacher, the one who is here to guide you into your next paradigm shift of you accepting the collective of the ultra-consciousness.

CHAPTER TEN

The Recorded History Of Your DNA

Your mind is slowly approving the information you have already earned, as you are invited to open yourself up to receive the book. This book is your written word, it is embedded in your bone matter; the recorded history of your DNA, which is your genetic inheritance that has been heralded down to you.

The more you release, you begin to realize that the written word exfoliates your past; your intellectual light can freely begin to expand your horizons. Your enlightenment is being prepared for endless waves of transformation which will lift you up into an etheric consultation through your innate God where the both of you become one. It is your memories releasing time, as you thought it to be.

Your fear is in abeyance as it seems to be walking on a tightrope and it stutters unto its own trepidations as it waits and allows itself, to receive and find the courage to do what automatically comes next. Are you now more aware that every human is issued with exactly the same codex of mathematics? Every word that I write, you are beginning to becoming more aware of; once you have read these words, most of you already have a sense of innate knowing that all is correct and accounted for! As I view into my vision world, the list of those who cannot understand my language are becoming fewer as I continually write my words. I eternally thank you for your trust in me as well as yourself!

Verse 1: *"And I saw another mighty angel come down from heaven clothed with a cloud; and a rainbow was upon his head and his face was at it were the sun and his feet as pillars of fire"*.

To explain this little parable, stay with me as I would like to do it justice. Again, I initiate you into your wisdom through the shamanic explanation. Remember that the cloud represents the future, therefore this angel is from the future and the moment as well. The next line informs us of the rainbow.

Remember, the Old Testament teaches us the story of Noah and the Ark. (This story is reimbursed in my book *Decoding the Sacred Alphabet and Numerology*). The ark we create is our body and as we grow up to become the adult mind, we release our intelligence step by step and our light expands. Through Einstein's explanation of his theories of relativity, we can view how our outer fields of energy change into their next equation where through this arching coinciding with its opposite, we begin to vibrate our colours, that automatically release as we blend our thoughts up into the responsibility of self and through our own force field, our seals are awakened and advanced over and over again; they can never close! And this precious gift continues each time we discover that we are ready for our next anointment from God. Again, I explain to you how the Indo-Asiatic Principles created their intelligence which they refer to as the chakras. When denoted interprets as our 'energy becoming knowledge where we release the Rah'.

This also explains the story of Joseph and his coat of many colours. So now symbolically we are viewing this parable from within as each story is written in Revelations. We can understand why the rainbow was upon his head and his intellectual light shone through his face and his feet were pillars of fire; his understanding of himself was permanently resurrecting. His intellectual light had arched itself up into his Divine Kingdom, to allow the colours of his seals to release out through his aura or fields of light. When this light is diminished you are no longer here, in your present condition. Do you recall reading a few pages back of the story of the mythical God Prometheus whose stories went on to become Matthew in the New Testament?

Verse 2: *"And he had in his hand a little book open: and he set his right foot upon the sea, and his left foot on the earth".*

Similar to the man standing in the sign of Aquarius in the tarot, the right foot upon the sea means that he has his spiritual understanding always ready and available to know himself. He is permanently connected to the collective of consciousness. And his left foot on the earth interprets to us that his ego is always grounded.

Verse 3: "*And he cried with a loud voice, as when a lion roareth; and when he had cried, seven thunders uttered their voices*".

These seven thunders are coming from the seven seals who have yet to conform into their truth. The lion, when he spoke, was with pride and truth; these are the confirmation of his open seals revealing to him his nations.

Verse 4: "*And when the seven thunders had uttered their voices, I was about to write: and I heard a voice from heaven saying unto me, Seal up those things that the seven thunders uttered and write them not*".

The lesson here is not to contradict yourself once you have spoken; always know that your first thought is the right thought.

Verse 5: "*And the angel which I saw upon the sea and upon the earth lifted up his hand to heaven*".

Verse 6: "*And sware by him that liveth forever and ever, who created heaven, and the things that therein are, and the sea, and the things which are therein, that there should be time no longer*".

I have great respect for this verse as it explains to us that we are continually earning our freedom, as we reinforce to our self that we are not out there in the wilderness, we are coming closer to connect to our eternal home; there are not too many more traumas that we can create; we find that our life force continues to evolve, as we continually anoint ourselves through the respect that we have earned where time becomes oblivious; we speak our God given right when we are at our peak of perfection. I find it a heavenly place to be, where, as I request, I know in my heart, I am given.

Verse 7: "*But in the days of the voice of the seventh angel, when he shall begin to sound, the mystery of God should be finished, as he hath declared to his servants and prophet*".

Here it is written as a salutation for our highest good when we know and accept that we now understand that we are made in the likeness of God. In other words, we are one and the same! Rejoice my precious readers, you're well and truly on your way.

Verse 8: *"And the voice which I heard from heaven spake unto me again, and said, Go and take the little book which is open in the hand of the angel which standeth upon the sea and upon the earth"*.

Verse 9: *"And I went unto the angel, and said unto him, Give me the little book. And he said unto me, Take it, and eat it up; and it shall make thy belly bitter, but it shall be in thy mouth sweet as honey"*.

Nourish yourself through releasing your innate truth, which your ego will not like, as it is losing control over you and yet the words that you will speak from now on, will be free to reign over you.

Verse 10: *"And I took the little book out of the angel's hand, and ate it up; and it was in my mouth sweet as honey: and as soon as I had eaten it, my belly was bitter"*.

Verse 11: *"And he said unto me, Thou must prophesy again before many peoples, and nations, and tongues, and kings"*.

The belly was made bitter and why? As you can see the words are explaining to us that they are an accompaniment to sweeten the soul for you to realise, your stomach is here to digest the results of your thinking. Please remember when we reach out to place something in our mouth, it is to nourish and create an inner solace to assist an excuse that we are thinking in that moment; hence why a fat cell is created through one of our cells creating the mucus to vibrate backwards. Therefore, if the food is replacing an excuse through our ego's thinking, then we can see how the belly tastes bitter.

We have been previously informed that slowly over time each personality will alter as it conforms into its own enlightenment; as long as you stand before your own alter, you will begin to accept your new growth. These are your people, nations, voice and kings, which must have confirmation from you to continually believing that these new thoughts are correct and accounted for. Again, I am reminding you of your genetic inheritance. Read on my precious wisdom warrior!

CHAPTER ELEVEN

Understanding The Differences In The Biblical Teachings

Verse 1: *"And there was given me a reed like unto a rod: and the angel stood saying, Rise and measure the temple of God and the alter and them that worship therein".*

Verse 2: *"But the court which is without the temple leave out, and measure it not; for it is given unto the gentiles; and the holy city shall they tread under foot, forty and two months".*

There is a difference in the biblical teachings between days, months and years to the thinking of today. Days relate to what we are thinking in the moment; they form a continuation of the educational program we are currently learning and understanding. Through the ancient language the word 'day' was pronounced as 'dea' or 'di-ea' denoting the words 'Divine EA'. Once decoded this word is explaining to us, that the inner divinity of self, is reminding us of our everlasting ascension. Each moment was referred to as your thinking releasing itself, which brought you forward. From sun up to sun up, where the darkness of that day, was where you turned over your thoughts to God to receive the right equation to these thoughts.

Why? It is in our state of sleep that the ego is unconsciously brought to rest. Therefore, it cannot interfere with your unconscious mind, which is how our dreams are manifested while the ego is at rest, to explain to us where we need to adjust our outer self with our inner thoughts to bring a harmonic balance into and through our thinking. The moment that the sun rose again you were expected to announce a new experience in your life, a new thought, to begin a new life! As you can view from within; it created time for us to adjust to our new way of thinking.

Hence our understanding of the earth was created in seven days! Those seven seals required time to evolve. Many animals and birds, have a gestation period of twenty-one days and of these days there are seven days where they are capable of becoming pregnant. The smaller the animal the quicker the pregnancy occurs. The larger the animal the longer the time frame between their cyclic evolutions. So it is, with the female of humanity when the cycle begins to count down to the twenty-eight days between each period of transformation, there are seven days in the middle of their cycle where if the thought that needs to be harmonized; is not brought into an equation, then the gestation will appear to surge forward. Remember that the child like mind, births the child. You receive a repetitious performance!

The explanation of months, are an extension of time for you to bring through this moment; it is Biblically written as times and a half, where there is given to you an extended allotted time for you to adjust to your new way of life. Throughout my training into the Principles of Shamanism, there was a number of years where I did not require sleep; there was no need, as I converted my mind through my education by learning to trust myself, to where I could release these bandages or layers that I had inherited.

These layers depicted my soul's experience, the inheritance of my DNA. I thanked God so many times for the strength to rent these old bandages away from me that I had duly accomplished; to allow for my soul to regenerate and take on the responsibility of carrying on in both of my parent's gentle footsteps.

Can you understand why the mummy was wrapped in bandages in Egypt? Their wrappings are the mathematical symbol that coincides with the vibrations of how our DNA releases itself. The curve of the layers is forming the arching of our intellect.

While their body was being prepared for the afterlife or the spiritual journey into the unconscious recognition of self, the Priests placed utensils and amulets between the layers of the wrappings. Again, the codes present themselves to inform us of the tools needed to assist this person on their journey. Each layer and additive explained a story of that person's mind. Throughout my training of the ancient arts, I was given a medicine pouch to place around my neck, which had to be in alignment with my thymus (thy must be true to myself) gland. In my pouch were a number of species containing certain bones, feathers leaves, grains, gems and nuts that I was offered by my teachers; also, I was asked to collect certain species myself that would suffice me when and if needed. This was to alert me to where I thought I still had a relationship to my own shortcomings. I was exceedingly grateful to have passed this journey as I climbed up and out of the bottomless pit.

Both the natural laws and God were the wisest of teachers and their patience was continually facing me, as I screamed, raved and ranted to them all when things did not go the way I had planned! Which one could I blame? There were times when I still had an old urge to create any excuse in the moment. Slowly over time, I realized that they were both one and the same. My urges finally surrendered through the lack of their own strength being diminished, where today, my strength in this moment walks before me and prepares the way for me to take my next step!

Your years are the final results of your earnings for you to complete your inner knowing; this beautiful word was pronounced as 'ye-ea', or 'yea-ea' as to how you have brought forth your inner strength to allow the three Gods which fortify your inner strength, as they become one with and through the mind of God, for you to become at one with yourself.

Verse 2, explains to us that the Court which is without the temple, to leave alone, as there is no substance available to you just yet! This temple is an initiation temple that is instilled within us until we learn to have the confidence to follow our intuition to initiate ourselves. We have named them the gentiles. These are the innocent ones who do not know themselves. God created an extension of time for them to earn their temple, forty and two months, we know that the numbers 4, relate to the Temple, and 2 is connected to the relationship. I was trained through these parables, that the gentiles were those who were still looking for Atlantis, their long-lost city. They were searching for their maps, to guide them into the fourth dimension. As you are becoming more aware, it all depends on each individual as to how they form a relationship internally with themself; as to how soon they will create or accept their temple to equate with their hierarchical mind.

Remember also, that through the numerology of the Asiatic nations the number 4 represents death. It is representing death to the thought of the moment; in other words, from sun up to sun up, or a day; not a habitual death of months or years. The flag that supports Japan is the rising sun! The gentiles of China were not allowed to enter the Gates of the Purple Forbidden City, until they had climbed up their own DNA to release their freedom, or to be accepted as a high priest where their energy or thoughts, would not pollute the temple. Hence the totem energy placed outside the compound of the city of the pole with the clouds two-thirds of the way up to the top. This amazing temple is known as the home of our higher mind, our spiritual heaven.

Through the Asian ideology this was created as a metaphysical explanation of the human mind. The number of rooms throughout this Temple of Wisdom, explaining their interpretation to these Laws of the Celestial Mechanics adds up to 9,999.5 rooms; not quite the magical number of 10,000. The half room that is missing of course is your left hemisphere of your brain. It is only after the heart has defibrillated itself through your constant recognition of self, which is now gaining and extending to its own momentum that it then informs the brain as to how it must now react. Again, I refer to the book of Daniel, as this book explains their teachings well. In other words, you have the opportunity to keep on re-investing in yourself.

Verse 3: *"And I will give power unto my two witnesses, and they shall prophesy a thousand two hundred and three score days, clothed in sackcloth"*.

Let's look at the codes first, 1,260 days, when these numbers are decoded; the sentence is announcing to us that; I am, through my relationship with myself, earning the mastering of myself to my soul. The verse is informing us of the two hemispheres of our brain (Witnesses) where the ego will learn and earn the right to come together with the inner mind, to expand the temple from within. Hence the mention of the garment of sackcloth, which is representing the sacrificial fabric, that was worn as a form of protection for the uninitiated mind during the ancient past. They had not yet earned their fabric of linen or silk! Just the same as we recently watched King Charles who wore his sack cloth at his inauguration being anointed up into the royal acclaim of becoming the King of all of his lands. It was once he had the crown placed on his head that he could claim his title and be dressed accordingly.

Verse 4: *"These are the two olive trees, and the two candlesticks standing before the God of the earth"*.

Again, I would like to remind you of the story previously written regarding the olive tree from one of my old farmers and his wife on the Isle of Corfu, in Greece, whose story had been passed down generation after generation; where they explained to me why the olive tree grew and produced its fruit for up to one thousand years. Every seventh year, the olive tree re-nurtures itself with one of its own seeds burrowing underground and strengthening the main trunk, which the original tree feeds on, as the two olives are representing the two hemispheres of the brain. Now that is a miracle that one can give to one's self. How does this species, relate to the writings explaining the seven seals. What do you suppose is the tree's hidden agenda?

We know that this species can bear its own fruit for over 500-800 years; all of which has been written and recorded down through the generations of the family. We also know that this wonderful tree never releases its fruit on the same branch, so the more it is pruned, the more harvest it can produce! Now if the olive tree can produce its life into everlasting energy, then so, can we? How do we accomplish this for ourself? By you never dwelling on what has already occurred.

Keep pruning your thoughts. Stop reinvesting in the same old story? If you have thought it once, then allow it to release itself to search for its own continuum, to bring your future to you. Now do you understand the divine words that have been written? John is explaining to us how important our genetic inheritance is; through the gift produced through the evolution of the species, all of it has been transferred or transformed for us to inherit ourselves as a species of our inner light, which reflects out to those who walk towards us, which as it extends itself, it picks up its own momentum which embraces the consciousness of all that is.

Now do you understand the importance of how every species that has evolved before us, is impregnated into the olive of our brain during our gestation, before our birth onto the planet. Each species has their own interpretation of their own personalities, all of which, we as humanity can resurrect when in doubt of ourself and are able to use.

Verse 5: *"And if any man will hurt them, fire proceedeth out of their mouth and devoureth their enemies: and if any man will hurt them, he must in this manner be killed"*.

Remember that the word 'man', is representing a personality of one gene, who is not in alignment with the others and must be resurrected.

Verse 6: *"These have power to shut heaven, that it rain, not in the days of their prophecy; and have power over the waters to turn them into blood, and to smiteth earth with all plagues as often as they will"*.

In this verse we are given the explanation that through our negative thinking we have the power to stop everything from moving forward, and through this kind of thinking, we do not receive our baptism, which of course is the rain. We are without water; our inner consciousness, there is no nurturing, being returned to us. We then begin to bleed, which creates our illnesses, our diseases; as we are well aware by now that we have given them free reign to create themselves, through us innocently turning our back on ourselves.

Verse 7: *"And when they shall have finished their testimony, the beast that ascendeth out of the bottomless pit shall make war against them and shall overcome them and kill them"*.

Verse 8: *"And their dead bodies shall lie in the street of the great city which spiritually is called Sodom and Egypt, where also our Lord was crucified".*

Verse 9: *"And they of the people and kindreds and tongues and nations shall see their dead bodies three days and a half, and shall not suffer their dead bodies to be put in graves".*

Verse 10: *"And they that dwell upon the earth shall rejoice over them and make merry and shall send gifts to one another; because these two prophets tormented them that dwelt on and also in the earth".*

As our ignorance becomes our new innocence, the old personalities that depended on others are dead; from death comes life everlasting and we are born again; so, through their innocence of beginning again, each personality can filter through to support and join forces to become our new city of light! We can see how our body is our earth and our head is our heaven when we read these words! We see how the two prophets, are the two hemispheres of both left and right brain; and are taking charge of the rest of the body to bring it into a relationship of harmony and balance. We learn to harmonize the left brain through the support and balance which is supplied to it, through the eminence of the right brain.

Verse 11: *"And after three days and an half the Spirit of life from God entered into them and they stood upon their feet; and great fear fell upon them which saw them".*

Verse 12: *"And they heard a great voice from heaven saying unto them, Come up hither. And they ascended up to heaven in a cloud; and their enemies beheld them".*

Verse 13: *"And the same hour was there a great earthquake, and a tenth part of the city fell, and in the earthquake were slain of men seven thousand; and the remnant were affrighted- and gave glory to the God of heaven".*

To explain the sacredness of the numerical number we pronounce as the tenth; is through extolling the soul and moving up into the next level of intellect; the number ten denotes the exalted change one has the opportunity to become, when one has ended a past experience; there are no more single digits! Remember in my book of *Decoding the Sacred Alphabet and Numerology*—it is explaining the codes to each number and when the number adds the zero, it means that your past is finished. You have been exalted intellectually and have earned this new state of grace. You can now move forward through your new intellect, to reclaim your place or palace with the divine self. The seven thousand dead, is decoded as the inner teacher having claimed another 7,000 genes, which has brought them forward up into regaining their own light; as they had been innocent victims trapped in their ego, that could not find the strength to support themselves.

Verse 18: "*And the nations were angry, and thy wrath is come, and the time of the dead, that they should be judged, and that thou shouldest give reward unto thy servants the prophets, and to thy saints, and them that fear thy name, small and great; and shouldest destroy them which destroy the earth*".

Verse 19: "*And the temple of God was opened in heaven and there was seen in his temple the ark of his testament: and there were lightnings, and voices, and thunderings, and an earthquake and great hail*".

Do you recall the message I received from my Uncle Edwin, who had passed five years previously, when the storm came and 21 eucalyptus trees came crashing down, when I had finished my interview explaining the codes on radio with Sky Channel in Greece. Well, there it is in all of its glory. I must have done something right on the day, although it took days for me to get over it! I remember my father teaching me when I was much younger, "Hard work never killed anybody, it is the wisdom to know how to do it correctly, that makes all the difference."

The nations are our personalities that had earned and claimed their own existence; and they became indignant to what was occurring around them; and were swept up into the heavenly realms to face their own court. This was where each gene that belonged to that nation, had to be brought forward up into the next evolutionary shift of their consciousness; for them all to become a reflection of the same light.

If we refer to each one of our inner nations as a city of light, we can see how they had to pass their house inspection to make sure that the foundations were strong enough to support their new state of grace. They had to make sure that all of the plumbing flushed throughout their house, that there were no blockages to deter them; that their beams were intact to support and solidify the rafters supporting the roof. In other words, they had to reward one another.

In this way they could become stronger and move into the entire spectrum of the mind. Each nation became harmonically balanced, which gave faith to the other personalities who still could not nourish themselves. Again, I refer to my mate, Albert Einstein for his training and guidance during his explanations to me of his theories of relativity as to how we ark our light through time and space for a constant renewal.

When this was occurring in my life, I remembered that it is through the constant changes of my inner sacred alphabet that was being reinforced back to me through my new ideas, that the numbers became more solidified to produce my next encounter. I was well aware that time is only in the instant; the instant is not in time! I began by saying thank you to myself at least 100 times per day; I could not believe how many of my thoughts needed rectifying. My goodness, had I manifested so many during my life? I was bringing all of my selves to attention and was now fully aware of what was going on. As the old thoughts and excuses were finally diminishing their old ways, I could look ahead to know that there were thousands of my old genes being given the opportunity to reinvest in themselves for me to start all over again.

Right, I thank you again for your patience in reading this chapter, so put the book down, now thank yourself and drink a glass of water to flush the information throughout your entire system, then please take a pause! Now, allow your mind to rest.

CHAPTER TWELVE

The Doorway Of The Divine Self

This is one of my favourite chapters as it explains the strength the emotional mind has claimed through the ego learning to release itself up into its next inheritance, for the future of entering up into the doorway of the divine self; as it is through the inner strength becoming a power source of calming and releasing the fear that has trapped itself, as it is still in abeyance through its own fear of reprisal, which has held its intelligence back. Also, which is where we finally begin to realize how we have been rethreaded through our previous inheritance or families of our past, that we have inherited through our DNA, also had the same difficulties as they had hesitated in knowing how to understand their inner divinity within themselves.

Verse 1: "*And there appeared a great wonder in heaven, a woman clothed with the sun, and the moon under her feet, and upon her head a crown of twelve stars*".

Verse 2: "*And she, being with child cried, travailing in birth, and pained to be delivered*".

Verse 3: "*And there appeared another wonder in heaven; and behold a great red dragon, having seven heads and ten horns, and seven crowns upon his heads*".

Verse 4: "*And his tail drew the third part of the stars of heaven, and did cast them to the earth: and the dragon stood before the woman which was ready to be delivered, for to devour her child as soon as it was born*".

Before we enter into this chapter, let us understand the reasoning of the twelve stars. As we are aware, the right hemisphere of the brain, is the one who has already journeyed through the underworld and has brought forth her wisdom to accompany the ego or left brain through its journey of confrontation. Hence her twelve steps releasing half of the double helix from the DNA; which is coming from above to educate the strands climbing up from below. This is what we are all about! It is explained to us through symbolism, what she has already achieved. Hence the reflection of her inner light, also known as her twelve cities of light, which are represented to us as the stars that light up the night sky.

Remember, this is also explaining the stories of the journey that Jesus had to endure to become his own Christ light; as to how he could release himself from the thorns that his ego had created as a form of protection; he was now on the journey to release his inner language; which is hidden and still trapped through his own innocence within each gene. All of which symbolically represents our fear releasing itself; and as Jesus evolved intellectually, this ring of thorns climbed up through the strands of his DNA, to release itself up and out through the crown of his head, to seat itself as his inner eye opened up on the forehead of every human, for all of us to view. Shades of the children's fairy tale of the lonely Princess who was out of balance and could not lead herself on, she slept for a hundred years and became trapped in the briar bushes, until a Prince rode up and rescued her, they fell in love with one another, married and lived happily ever after, where they both became balanced and complete with one another. Now read on:

It is here in verse 3, that we begin to understand the fear, that our ego, left brain, has held on to for its own safety harness and support, as it still autonomically trapped in its past, until it has finally surrendered to itself and found the strength to climb up through the rungs of its own ladder; we are being shown how the serpent as explained through Egyptology, and a greater rendition is explained to us through the Chinese Principles, grew his legs and began to walk to become the dragon; he was being forced to stand upright and had to become accountable for every thought he manifested through his own actions.

The fire that came from his nostrils was informing us as to how he had to resurrect himself. The seven heads of course, relate to the seven seals that had to be opened on the back of the book (our inner Bible, our recorded DNA of our previous generations) as they journeyed up through the seven vertebrae of our neck, as we left the earth, for us to journey up into the heavenly abode, once the book was free to unfurl and open up all by itself. He had placed himself into forcing his control over his life; his crowns are showing us that he had needed to reach a peak of his own perfection of the realms he had earned to keep on trying to defeat his divine intuition. His life force had just about depleted itself. This was his last stand.

In verse 4, we are being reminded of the resurrection through our right hemisphere of the brain, or death through the knowledge of the left hemisphere of the first God EL, where he swept one third of the stars from the heavens and cast them on the earth. This makes us aware, that his light was diminishing fast. As to the explanations in verse 2, as to how the ego wanted to devour her child as she birthed, we understand in this verse, the importance of her expectations for her to deliver of her first emotional thought, where the ego has not been able to stain or blemish her mind.

Verse 5: *"And she brought forth a man child, who was to rule all nations with a rod of iron: and her child was caught up unto God and to his throne"*.

Verse 6: *"And the woman fled into the wilderness, where she hath a place prepared of God, that they should feed her there a thousand two hundred and three score days"*.

To obtain this information that I write to you now, during my journey I was sent out into the wilderness alone for many years, to where my mind and body went through horrendous pressure to bring myself up and out of the bottomless pit. The beast at that time, who later became the dragon, tried for what seemed forever, to interrupt my flow. Every positive move that I made, he was there to try and pull me down. And more to the point, I seemed to be permanently pregnant with new lessons and ideas and was constantly birthing personalities and found myself becoming stronger each day. I thanked God repeatedly every day for the many different species of birds that gathered outside my shed door, that were with me every day, of course they were from the angelic realm, those that had inherited their wings at birth, which were constantly reminding me, moment by moment that they were there to support me.

There was no possible way that I could live amongst my family and friends and continue on with my teachings to learn and earn. I had to live each one of those experiences before I had the courage to exalt my mind up into understanding and accepting my commitment to earn this incredible truthful Sacredness of the Divine Language. All of which are explained in my revised book of *Decoding Extra Terrestrial-Intelligence*. It took years before I felt my sanity could return to the earthly realms. When we reach up into the outer limits, there are no more excuses to release; our inner strength is our 'be all to end all'. I never forgot an experience; my photographic memory had absorbed it all. When it came time for me to go out and teach; I vowed to be there, to support my students through these horrendous experiences. Once they had attained their own enlightenment, where their strength became their inner power, their questions were becoming few and far between, I came to the realization that I was free to travel on. They all have a permanent smile on their faces now!

Verse 7: *"And there was a war in heaven: Michael and his angels fought against the dragon; and the dragon fought and his angels"*.

Remember that the arching of the Angel Michael (the word we use today is our inner microphone) represents the confidence we exude throughout our mind as to how we produce and speak our thoughts. It is through that inner confidence that we have exalted through us learning to earn our inner trust! It is through this confidential sound of our own voice, speaking with clarity, where our wisdom releases the inner pressure that we have collected throughout our life, for us to realise that we are now earning the right to speak our inner truth, possibly for the first time in our life. We are also becoming more aware that speaking these positive thoughts, will deliver us up higher into the divinity of our inner language. Therefore, as my confidence grew, I became stronger and more aligned with my intellectual activity where automatically my fear was diminishing and my inner strength took pride and place in my heart. Yes, I ranted and raved with my insecurities bouncing around me for what seemed a thousand lifetimes. Now all is calm and I can view the whole planet and the games that are placed before you, as you learn to walk away from your past fears, as those ideas no longer bind you to your past, who as yet, do not fully understand the consequences to honestly know themselves.

Verse 8: "*And prevailed not; neither was their place found any more in heaven*".

Verse 9: "*And the great dragon was cast out, that old serpent called the Devil, Satan which deceiveth the whole world:* (your inner body is the world) *he was cast out into the earth, and his angels were cast out with him*".

Verse 10: "*And I heard a loud voice saying in heaven, Now, is come salvation, and strength, and the kingdom of our God, and the power of his Christ: for the accuser of our brethren is cast down, which accused them before our God, day and night*".

Verse 11: "*And they overcame him by the blood of the Lamb,* (which is our innocence finding the strength to birth its self) *and by the word of their testimony; and they loved not their lives unto the death*".

Verse 12: "*Therefore rejoice, ye heavens, and ye that dwell in them, Woe to the inhabiters of the earth and of the sea! For the devil* (ego) *is come down unto you, having great wrath, because he knoweth that he hath but a short time*".

Verse 13: "*And when the dragon saw that he was cast unto the earth, he persecuted the woman which brought forth the man child*". (Her inner power and strength).

Verse 14: "*And to the woman were given two wings of a great eagle, that she might fly into the wilderness, into her place, where she is nourished for a time, and times and half a time, from the face of the serpent*".

Remember I spoke previously about time and times and half a time when I was explaining each day, months and years;

we realise now that we are made aware of how she was nourished by God for all eternity, as long as she bided her time and allowed her thoughts to become her own righteous thoughts.

I remember when I was driving back to the homestead one day, after my eighteen-hour drive down South to sit with my teacher for four hours, to finalize a series of my exams; where I had to be accountable to my inner-knowing, to explain the results of how time was held in our abeyance for us to supersede our thoughts beyond our previous statement. It had been a strenuous exam regarding entering into the marrying of the collective mind, as I had to be already living in this alignment to answer the questions she placed before me. It is where both hemispheres of the brain entered up into the 33.3 grid at the same time through reaching its own echo, or re-balancing its antenna of truth; to create an illusion of space, which would find its place where it could settle back into the circumference of my mind.

This exam was all to do with how my thoughts were released out into the telepathic inheritance of the consciousness and meld through the sonic sound or waves which are created by the collective; these waves bounced back like a lightning rod to open a doorway of perpendicular motion, similar to a time capsule that could only be entered into with a balanced mind which was focused on just one thought; where I could view the circumstantial evidence that it created.

It was time refracting time, and through this bend you could hold on to that space and it became yours. I explained all of this to my students as their block of land in the universe that had their name on it. It all has to do with the word 'Intention' and what my intention could create through the laws of the universe. I was glad when it was all over, so that I could return to the outback. For the first time, I had learned and earned, how to respect my isolation from other minds.

My thoughts of course were running erratic as I turned around and drove the long way back to the homestead; as to how I had delivered myself to my teacher, as I never received any praise for a job well done. I was a subject of the universe and also a child of God and it was up to me to congratulate myself, if I felt I needed consolation.

I only had a few more hours to drive when my car faltered and stopped all by itself, where my car pulled over on the side of the road. I tried to drive off but it would not move forward; I had had enough and was yelling at God, to inform the beast that it was time out and to give me some breathing room, as I thumped my steering wheel repeatedly. I had been awake to close on forty hours without any rest and my patience was feeling stretched to its limits as I concentrated on the narrow roads. "For goodness sake, you know that I have to get as far as I can before the sun starts to sink and bid us goodnight for the day." I yelled! It was at this time of the day that you had to broaden your horizon, remove the blinkers and focus on the sides of the road, as well as in front. This was the time when the kangaroos were beginning to look for the grass by the edge of the road and hopped blindly into the lights as you approached them. It was the time when the wild pigs were coming out into the open, they were hungry and the cattle were looking for that last blade of grass before settling down for the night. There were no fences to protect your vehicle in the outback, as they were too huge, only steel grids across the road as one paddock finished and the next one began.

I no longer had my big 4WD to protect me, I only had my trusty little Toyota that had never let me down over these traumatic years; in fact, it danced along the road for me and always smiled; although, if I hit one of these animals anything could have happened. I yelled, "where the hell are you when I need you the most; you're certainly not standing beside me." I felt exhausted and was becoming so frustrated and I was finding it extremely difficult to find the strength to go on. These last few hours were the worst, as I was very much aware of the concentration I needed, for what was ahead of me.

I felt two hands on my face and my head was turned to the side of the road and there draped across the wire of the Dingo fence was the hugest eagle I had ever seen. The wing span was over three meters in length and I realized I had been given the soul and the wings of the Great Western Eagle. I had finally received my wings, I was my own pilot, in charge of my own Vimana, therefore I knew that I must have passed my exams. Verse 14, kept me nourished and I realized that I had to return back to the beginning and start all over again. Of course, after another apology to God, I sheepishly gathered my feathers and bones that I was asked to collect and hopped in the car and drove on down the track. As I drove on for another hour, I began to calm down from the wonder I had received; I had waited years for this event to come to me.

The sun was now right in front of my vision and I needed to concentrate much harder on the road ahead. As I was climbing a slight rise on this gravel road full of corrugations, another 4WD overtook me at a break neck speed and nearly ran me off the road. When I got to the top of the hill, here it was upside down in a gully by the edge of the road with the lady trapped inside and her groceries spread all over the car and the four wheels spinning like crazy. Once again, my heart jumped underneath my tongue and I jumped out to see if she was alright when she lifted up her arm and waved to me. At that moment another two cars pulled up beside us and two young men jumped out to offer her assistance.

That accident occurred to give me the courage to slow down and continue on, this woman had the same thoughts as me, we both wanted to get as far as we could before the sun went over the horizon. I knew then that the road ahead was cleared for me and that there would be no more difficulties for me to face, as I headed for another hundred odd kilometres towards the homestead gates. I apologised to all concerned, as I called in to the homestead and informed them of the accident before I headed to my shed. The next morning, we received the information that there was no harm done and all was well.

Verse 15: *"And the serpent cast out of his mouth water as a flood after the woman, that he might cause her to be carried away of the flood"*.

He was trying to baptize the woman back into his own ways, so that once again, he had total control over her.

Verse 16: "*And the earth helped the woman, and the earth opened her mouth, and swallowed up the flood which the dragon cast out of his mouth*".

There are two explanations that I can give to this verse; firstly, I will start with the easier one. Her body had set out to protect her, which is Biblically written as the earth, and devoured the mucus which was springing forth from her mouth.

And now for the second explanation; throughout the Egyptian Philosophies there are many Stella's and Hieroglyphs explaining the opening of the mouth ceremony. The story is interpreted to us as a ritual for the 'supposed departed' who had died and moved on. Also, this is communal with the Freemasons rituals, for the same reason. Now for my interpretation; this occurs as you commit to the self, to only speak your truth. Once this area has been opened, which is situated just in front of your ears and is the section where the bottom and top jaw hinge off one another for your spoken word to release itself; we realize that this is the 6th seal; it is the second last section of the seventh seal to open, it is from here that you cross over the bridge to the other side of your nose, which ends level with your eyebrows to meld up through the medullar oblongata where you are accepted up into God's realm for ever more.

Verse 17: "*And the dragon was wroth with the woman, and went to make war with the remnant of her seed which keep the commandments of God and have the testimony of Jesus Christ*".

We, humanity are the seeds! Remember, that our seed which releases from the emotional right hemisphere of our brain is our next emotional thought, therefore it is heard from within, and in the future enters into becoming our Divine thinking.

CHAPTER THIRTEEN

The Beast

Verse 1: *"And I stood upon the sand of the sea, and saw a beast rise up out of the sea, having seven heads and ten horns, and upon his horns ten crowns, and upon his heads the name of blasphemy".*

The number ten informs us that he has gone as far as he can and now needs to exalt his thinking and move on to the next thought. Each horn had been crowned which alerts us to the fact that through his ego, they had reached their own peak of perfection. The beast thinks it has attained everything. Remember the beast tries to control us through the first God EL, in other words its first home lives in the sexual confines. The natural laws have deemed that we must grow up and be re-educated into the education of An, our inner University; situated just above the navel in our solar plexus region, which opens up the DNA and recharges our inner dictionary with new thoughts, ideas, and words, which creates a more advantageous language, for us to use! All of which will upgrade our religious outlook, where we are linking back into the eternal source of all that is, by reuniting back into ourself. This action begins to stimulate the ego to try for its next attainment.

Let's return to the sacred numerology and look at the numbers written. If we place one horn to each one of the heads and we minus seven from ten there are three left over. What does the number three represent through the codes? The mind of God! Are we talking about the Universal God, this Greatest Order of the Divine, our world within? Or are we being informed of the inner God, that the beast understood, was his God alone!

Remember that there are twelve strands to our DNA and here we see only ten. In other words, the beast had not yet entered up into its hierarchical mind to be able to enter into its next dimension. Therefore, it had not earned the opportunity for it to evolve up into its next imperial thought.

Again, I refer back to the Egyptian philosophies of the five free days one earns when the journey has completed itself, where they denote the shredding of the hymen being removed from the last five Imperial glands in the throat, all the way up into the crown of the head. These glands are the Thymus, Thyroid, Hypothalamus, Pituitary and Pineal. Yes, I know this goes against the establishment of everything that has been previously recorded. I take full responsibility for writing it at this time, as this was how it was delivered unto me! Read on, it will all come out in the end!

Those ten horns encapsulated by his seals kept him under his own control as he continually searched for another excuse to hold on to his old empirical ways. Which he thinks is his truth and when his worlds begin to disintegrate, his only discourse is to create this blasphemy that sprouts from the last shreds of his ego.

Verse 2: "*And the beast which I saw was like unto a leopard and his feet were as the feet of a bear, and his mouth as the mouth of a lion; and the dragon gave him his power, and his seat, and great authority*".

When reading other mythical stories in relationship to the beast; the accounts change to represent the energy of the species that are created through these cosmic laws, which is in accordance to the animal's behaviour through their understanding and emotional value of themselves. They usually live in the confines of the author's or orator's home area. Through the Asiatic laws the dragon is the mythical beast that has only two legs with ten claws, no wings and the lower section is in the shape of the serpent. His son is born with nine claws and it has to earn the tenth claw throughout its life! The dragon lives in the heavenly abode and is supposed to be looking after us. The difference is that everything must be done correctly according to how the mathematics coincides with the natural laws. He is there making sure we achieve what we want to accomplish throughout our life. He represents our left hemisphere of our brain; whereas the phoenix represents our right hemisphere. The phoenix has the patience to continually convert anything the dragon tries to create over and over again. The make-up of the rest of the beast is created through the animals that are still roaming the earth! In other words, they are still trapped within their own solitary consciousness.

Please remember, when our attitude changes through the development of our intelligence birthing its self; we have an urge to go beyond our own boundaries and reach up for a more evolved species.

Verse 3: *"And I saw one of his heads as it were wounded to death; and his deadly wound was healed: and all the world wondered after the beast"*.

The wounded head represents the scars of its past, which evokes that one of the seals seemed to have been destroyed. We are told that this wound was healed! Do you remember when I have previously explained that once our seals have correctly birthed open, they can never close! They remain permanently open which is due to their intellectual freedom that they have earned. This means that we cannot go back over our past thoughts and experiences as we try to sneak back in to our past to excuse this moment! This moment has moved on; it is no longer applicable to our thoughts therefore it has disappeared out of our dictionary. We have trod new ground and moved on!

Therefore Karma, (or as I explain it Khama when decoded is KHA, the inner knowledge as explained through the ancient divine language, MA is explaining how we master the ascension) as it is always in charge of each situation until we get back to where we really belong! This head was hanging on to the remnants of its past which is where his ego can no longer hinder the other six heads from attaining their future growth! Remember that the native animal mind is still caught up in the second dimensional brain. It has reached the end of its own antenna. This area is connected to our upper thighs from above our knees up to our sexual area. My goodness lets nourish ourselves on those previous statements, it seemed to take forever to bring this information to you through its truth!

Verse 4: *"And they worshipped the dragon which gave power unto the beast: and they worshipped the beast saying, Who is like unto the beast? Who is able to make war with him?"*

Verse 5: *"And there was given unto him a mouth speaking great things and blasphemies; and power was given unto him to continue forty and two months".*

Hang on a minute! I have heard those numbers mentioned before! Remember in chapter 10, verse 2: *"But the court which is without the temple leave out, and measure it not; for it is given unto the gentiles; and the holy city shall they tread under foot, forty and two months".*

Allow me to refresh your mind to this code through what I have previously written. Verse 2, explains to us that the Court which is without the temple, to leave alone, as there is no substance available to you just yet! This temple is an initiation temple that is instilled within our genes until we understand the divine language where we are able to initiate ourselves. We have named these personalities the gentiles, who are the innocent ones who do not know as yet themselves. God created an extension of time for them to earn their temple, forty and two months, we know that the numbers 4, relate to the Temple, and 2 is connected to the relationship.

I was trained through my ET Masters of Time, that these parables, are stories of the gentiles who were still looking for Atlantes, their book of maps, also known as their long-lost city. Is this why we are still out there looking for the lost city of Atlantis with the three rings which are informing us of the three-dimensional mind or does it mean the three divisions of our body earning the right to becoming one, as we earn the rights to becoming in charge of our own passage? They were searching for their maps, to guide them into the temple area, known as the fourth dimension.

Through your new found awareness you can see that it all depends on each individual as to how they form a relationship internally with themself; as to how soon they will create or accept each temple as they walk towards their next educated step of their hierarchical mind. It makes the story easier to understand now, that we have been reminded of a previous verse to see why the same time frame has been repeated again in this chapter as I add to the previous statement.

Verse 6: "*And he opened his mouth in blasphemy against God to blaspheme his name, and the tabernacle, and them that dwell in heaven*".

Who gave him the message? His own stubbornness! In other words, he was rejecting his higher good and wanted to control his whole body. Hence the kindreds, tongues and nations.

Verse 8: "*And all that dwell upon the earth shall worship him, whose names are not written in the book of life of the Lamb slain from the foundation of the world*".

So those personalities that were still unaware of their own strength followed meekly on!

Verse 9: "*If any man have an ear, let him hear*".

Verse 10: "*He that leadeth into captivity shall go into captivity; he that killeth with the sword, must be killed with the sword, Here is the patience and the faith of the saints*".

Verse 11: "*And I beheld another beast coming up out of the earth; and he had two horns like a Lamb, and he spake as a dragon*".

Here we make note of the Lamb, metaphorically known as our innocence who spake as the dragon, which is informing us of the fear that all of us have inherited that is still enveloped within. Have you ever thought to yourself that the unknown is really the in-known and we were never taught how to release it? Did he become a replica of the Beast of the Seas?

As you can see in verse 11, we are being introduced to another beast! Now there are two beasts, one rose from the sea which is representing the complete collective of the consciousness and the second beast coming up out of the earth, which is made in the likeness of the consciousness, is coming from our body, described to us as the earth through the language of the biblical agenda; and is represented in each individual person!

During my education my teachers also explained to me that the beast hides under the protection of the garment of God! Its home base is the hypothalamus gland where it knows it is protected, as through its innocence it can pretend and comprehend that it has God reigning over it. This gland is the store house for all our fear where it knows the next step is the next doorway for our thought to be delivered to our pituitary gland. The final doorway is the pineal gland which is the doorway to our unconscious energy. These three glands represent the Masters of our lost city of our recorded maps; the Hypothalamus, stores our past; The Pituitary is our present moment of our thinking and the Pineal is our future inheritance, which leads us into our ever-lasting life. Now do you understand more clearly, the Lost City of Atlantis, or as previously written in my books Atlantes as the Italian newsagent said to his staff in Lake Como, where we all have the opportunity to become at one with this amazing gene that is placed in the crown of our head that we have named the God head in the southern hemisphere, or if you are in the northern hemisphere the Head of God.

The pituitary gland is where every thought is harmonized and balanced and is mathematically sorted into either the left or right hemisphere of our brain, as you all well know through reading my previous book, now revised into nine separate books *Decoding the Mind of God*.

Are we talking about our own ego here? Therefore, are we made in the likeness of God and the beast as well? That would broaden our explanation of both hemispheres of our brain. Left /ego, Right/ emotions!! Goodness that puts a different light on the subject; is this explaining the parables of Jesus before he became his Christ? Remember he was missing for many years until he became his Christ Light, when he was known to us as Jesus Christ! There are many stories from many countries written regarding those missing years.

Verse 12: *"And he exerciseth all of the power of the first beast before him, and causeth the earth and them which dwell therein to worship the first beast, whose deadly wound was healed".*

Verse 13: "*And he doeth great wonders, so that he maketh fire come down from heaven on the earth in the sight of men*". (Here we note the resurrection for the genes to unite with one another, through each gene earning their freedom to face themselves).

Verse 14: "*And deceiveth them that dwell on the earth by the means of those miracles which he had power to do in the sight of the beast; saying to them that dwell on the earth, that they should make an image of the beast, which had the wound by a sword and did live*".

Remember the sword is the soul's word! His truth! Now we know how the first head earned its wound! It was through its own thinking that the first head was wounded and was healed. When we see an image in our mind, it is a replica of what is there right in front of us! Another saying of my father when he explained to me "Look straight ahead and follow your nose, because your nose knows! Another reference is the sword that pierced the side of Jesus.

Verse 15: "*And he had power to give life unto the image of the beast, that the image of the beast should both speak, and cause that as many as would not worship the image of the beast, should be killed*".

Verse 16: "*And he causeth all, both small and great. Rich or poor, free and bond, to receive the mark in their right hand or in their forehead*".

The mark on the right hand, begins as a three-pointed star, once you have made the commitment to self; once this initiation has worked its way throughout your cells and has completed itself, it then adds point by point and keeps on evolving up to the ten points. These marks are in atonement for those personalities that are rich or poor, free, or still a slave to themselves that they must die to be resurrected again through changing their ways into a more positive outlook.

Is this why we use the reference to a star on stage! Once this is accomplished, which could take years to finalize, is when you know you have earned the right to speak your truth.

The palms of our hands are measuring the final results of our thinking. The birthing of the marks in the forehead, just above or between the eyebrows keep on changing daily. As we look into the mirror and see our own reflection; we who have learned and earned our passage to Freedom, look for the responsibility of what is ahead for the day. They change from the rose and move through every geometrical symbol that has been created as they reflect how the mathematics are creating our reality in each moment!

There are so many of you that I see walking down the street with your hidden potentialities marked on your forehead; and most of you are totally unaware of your signs. These mathematical symbols are showing those who know, how the ego is sacrificing itself to earn the right to release the truth to yourself!

Verse 17: "*And that no man might buy or sell save he that has the mark or the name of the beast, or the number of his name*".

Verse 18: "*Here is wisdom. Let him that hath understanding count the number of the beast: for it is the number of a man; and his number is Six hundred threescore and six*". In other words, 666, decoded as, mastering the mind.

We are being introduced into the beginning of Armageddon; where we are viewing the inner war as it brings its self, up into another level of its own assault. Through the sacred codes the number six represents earning the right to collect all personalities together, to master one's self. There are three of them; one each for EL, AN and EA, remember the number three, denotes the mind. These codes are informing us that we are all capable of overcoming this inner ego, also known as the bestial side of us that refuses to adjust and grow up to face its own consequences, (the results of its own actions) through earning the right to realise why nothing works as there is no harmony and balance for it to gain and earn the next rung of its own inner staircase or DNA.

I would like to conclude this chapter as to how you the reader are beginning to realize how I am interpreting and releasing this hidden information back to you. Through my telepathic inheritance there is much less chatter on the airwaves, regarding your doubt in regards to what I am writing right now! Slowly you are beginning to hear and agree to this ancient wisdom, through my written words.

More to the point, many of you out there perfectly understand that you have always known this inner part of yourself—you just needed a reminder. Perhaps now, you will use it to your benefit, bringing your twelve tribes together. They are your inner family, no matter who you are; they represent your wholeness and completeness.

Why? Through reading these words, your experiences of how you have already lived your life, also to how you can adjust to each momentary thought, also as to how you have earned each opportunity to be reflected back to you, the more you silence your mind. Your memory banks are waiting to release what you have closed off and locked away through your lack of support to yourself. Through reliving each experience and thanking yourself for being given the opportunity to review your past thoughts; is how we begin to heal these inner nations of our self! The diseases you are manifesting through your thinking are beginning to break down, as they have no energy left for them to nourish themselves. They cannot feed their future on an empty paddock. The drought is within you!

Through the companionship that you are telepathically returning to me; you are also helping me to finish writing this book. We are just over half way, we are into discovering the sacredness of these codes explained in chapter 13, which is denoted as 'I am my mind" so let's keep strolling down Memory Lane together to relive what we are all here to accomplish on behalf of this place, we call home.

Once we can bring an experience back to its origin, you can release the cellular pressure that was created in the first time! There is no grief through an old thought being resurrected. It is a blessing to understand the 'Divine Equation'. Just the same as when a loved one dies; they died to give you the opportunity to benefit and uphold your 'State of Grace'. They are with you always, so allow these Twelve Apostles that are within you, their freedom to exalt you to where you sit on your throne and can view every moment of your own existence. You will certainly choose your next words to speak to others who are made in your likeness, more eloquently!

Remember that metaphorically the word 'BIBLE' is explained to us, as our **B**ASIC **I**NFORMATION **B**EFORE **L**EAVING **E**ARTH. It creates your reality; it is in this moment, right here and now!

I present a gold medal to those of you who got through this chapter. Now did you understand it all? Take a rest and then read it again! The codes to number 13, decode as: I AM, MY MIND.

CHAPTER FOURTEEN

The Fall Of Babylon

Verse 1: *"And I looked and lo, a Lamb stood on the mount Sion, and with him an hundred forty and four thousand, having his father's name written in their foreheads"*.

We are being introduced to the scribe within; as we begin to understand the information that is embedded in the genes who are protected by our cells, or as the Bible interprets it, as the written word. The scribe is now free to exude more information as it automatically releases from the DNA. We also note that many new personalities are stepping forward to unfurl themselves through their willingness to learn. Our inner dictionary is promoting and releasing an extended future for us to create for and through ourselves.

An important part to remember; is that St John is writing to us through his acceptance of his inner sight. It is not reality as so many of you think it is. Reality is a word that can only be created through those who do not understand and know themselves; they refer to this word as a sky hook that they need to attach to themselves to support the moment! They must always rely on what others have done to verify their own importance to themselves. How about you? Are you not important enough to believe in yourself through your own eyes?

Verse 2: *"And I heard a voice from heaven, as the voice of many waters, and as the voice of a great thunder: and I heard the voice of harpers harping with their harps"*.

Verse 3: *"And they sung as it were a new song before the throne, and before the four beasts, and the elders: and no man could learn that song but the hundred and forty-four thousand which were redeemed from the earth"*.

We are brought back to Genesis again with the twelve tribes of Israel multiplying themselves into the 144,000, where they are being redeemed from the earth. I also like to surmise that we are watching how our twelve strands of our DNA, become their own apostolate as they earn their freedom to work on our behalf. Here is the information of the New Testament as we view our freedom announcing itself through the sonar of our truth, positively producing and supporting our momentary thoughts, as we think.

Just as the parables explain, Jesus earned his Christ light during the eighteen years he was missing. Decoded, these numbers represent: 1—I am, 8—harmonized, and together they form 9—to know it all. This offers a clearer picture of why the two kings unearthed from the Mayan and Egyptian Empires had these numbers carved into their foreheads. They had finally found freedom from their own entanglement and attained everlasting life as they ascended into the Kingdom of God.

Verse 4: *"These are they that were not defiled with women, for they are virgins. These are they which follow the Lamb withersoever he goeth. These were redeemed from among men being the first fruits unto God and to the Lamb"*.

In other words, these thoughts are not interrupted through our ego or our emotions; they are new personalities releasing from our cells which are cohabitating with our genes; through the freedom they have stepped into through birthing themselves for the first time, during this lifetime, which has an added value for ourself as they broaden the perspective of our DNA. They are innocently following the one who leads them.

Verse 5: *"And in their mouth was found no guile: for they are without fault before the throne of God"*.

Verse 6: *"And I saw another angel fly in the midst of heaven, having the everlasting Gospel to preach unto them that dwell on the earth and to every nation, and kindred, and tongue and people"*.

Verse 7: *"Saying with a loud voice, Fear God, and give glory to him; for the hour of his judgment is come: and worship him that made heaven, and earth, and sea and the fountains of the waters".*

The angel is promoting our next thought; it comes through our oracle. It is delivered to us from the cosmic order of our inner divinity which is released from the positive emotional realms, where we are being asked to thank our wholeness; for understanding and releasing the past.

Verse 8: *"And there followed another angel, saying Babylon is fallen, is fallen, that great city, because she made all nations drink of the wine of the wrath of her fornication".*

Until we begin to realise the importance of our inner ministry of self, we will continually just babble on; these nations or personalities must follow one another, just like the sheep in the fields.

Verse 9: *"And the third angel followed them, saying in a loud voice, If any man worship the beast and his image, and receive his mark in his forehead, or in his hand".*

Verse 10: *"The same shall drink of the wine of the wrath of God, which is poured out without mixture into the cup of his indignation; and he shall be tormented with fire and brimstone in the presence of the holy angels, and in the presence of the Lamb".*

Verse 11: *"And the smoke of their torment ascendeth up forever and ever: and they have no rest day nor night, who worship the beast and his image, and whosoever receiveth the mark of his name".*

Verse 12: *"Here is the patience of the saints: here are they that keep the commandments of God, and the faith of Jesus".*

Verse 13: *"And I heard a voice from heaven saying unto me, Write Blessed are the dead, which die in the Lord from henceforth: Yea saith the Spirit, that they may rest from their labours; and their works do follow them".*

Verse 14: *"And I looked and behold a white cloud, and upon that cloud one sat like unto the Son of man, having on his* head a golden crown, and in his hand a sharp sickle".

Verse 15: "*And another angel came out of the temple, crying with a loud voice to him that sat upon the cloud, Thrust in thy sickle and reap: for the time is come for thee to reap; for the harvest of the earth is ripe*".

Verse 16: "*And he that sat on the cloud thrust in his sickle on the earth; and the earth was reaped*".

Verse 17: "*And another angel came out of the temple which is in heaven he also having a sharp sickle*".

Verse 18: "*And another angel came out from the altar, which had power over fire; and cried with a large cry to him that had the sharp sickle, saying, Thrust in thy sharp sickle, and gather the clusters of the vine of the earth; for her grapes are fully ripe*".

The sickle or scythe in today's language, is also the mind slicing through the harvest of our thoughts that we have already sown. It is through reading this chapter that we are beginning to understand that the bandages of the past are being unravelled and released from the mind. All of the personalities that were supported by their fear have had a change of heart. Hopefully now, the past that has been buried is over and no longer of any importance, as that energy has already been filed away into your memory banks, which will automatically surface when you slip back into your past and you will remember how you transformed yourself when in need. The new thoughts now have the opportunity to face themselves. No more derogatory remarks.

Verse 18: "*And the angel thrust in his sickle into the earth and gathered the vine of the earth, and cast it into the great winepress of the wrath of God*".

Verse 19: "*And the winepress was trodden* (understood) *without the city, and blood came out of the winepress even unto the horses' bridles*, (the reigning in of one's own spiritual strength) *by the space of a thousand and six hundred furlongs*".

We make note that there were seven angels present to bear witness in chapter 14, where we become aware of how the numbers 1,600 are interpreted when taken back through the Universal Language and the Sacred Alphabet, as to how they are informing us of our inner spiritual strength; I am (1) mastering (6) my relationship with my soul (00).

An interesting chapter where we can watch the earnings of our inner spiritual waters turning into wine.

CHAPTER FIFTEEN

The Wrath Of God

Verse 1: *"And I saw another sign in heaven, great and marvellous, seven angels having the seven last plagues; for in them is filled up the wrath of God".*

We are informed that these seven wraths are the final shreds of our anger that created these plagues, to finally leave the frustrated ego as it journeys towards its next step. Finally, through our new confidence, our nervous system is rearranging itself, as these are the irritations that are still embedded on our last layer of skin.

Verse 2: *"And I saw as it were a sea of glass mingled with fire: and them that had gotten the victory over the beast, and over his image, and over his mark, and over the number of his name, stand on the sea of glass, having the harps of God".*

The supreme consciousness is no longer invisible to us. There are no more barriers refusing our entry. The walls have begun to tumble down; they have disintegrated and have returned to the soul. This is how the Biblical and Mythical stories were introducing us to war. We are finally finishing and winning the greatest battle of our life!

Verse 3: *"And they sing the song of Moses the servant of God, and the song of the Lamb, saying, Great and marvellous are thy works, Lord God Almighty; just and true are thy ways, thou King of saints".*

Verse 4: *"Who shall not fear thee, O Lord, and glorify thy name? For thou only art holy: for all nations shall come and worship before thee; for thy judgments are made manifest".*

Our personalities are finally releasing the confidence for our new found freedom to deliver unto themselves; our thoughts are earning the right to accept one another into becoming a relationship with one another for them to know they have earned the right to master their next thought. We who are gathering our inner strength are earning the right of our freedom to speak our inner truth. Goodness what a difference that would make to humanities growth! We think that we have already understood the message of the hidden God! Please, for the first time, let's earn the right to place this amazing story up and into its rightful perspective!

Verse 5: *"And after that I looked, and, behold, the temple of the tabernacle of the testimony in heaven was opened".*

Verse 6: *"And the seven angels came out of the temple, having the seven plagues, clothed in pure and white linen, and having their breasts girded with golden girdles".*

Verse 7: *"And one of the four beasts gave unto the seven angels seven golden vials full of the wrath of God, who liveth forever and ever".*

I would like to interpret the word 'wrath' through the sacred alphabet: **W**isdom **R**eleasing our **A**scension through the **T**ruth from **H**eaven. How did we come to interpret the word as 'anger'?

Verse 8: *"And the temple was filled with smoke from the glory of God, and from his power; and no man was able to enter into the temple, till the seven plagues of the seven angels were fulfilled".*

Again, we note the number of times this chapter mentions the smoke, which is explaining to us the resurrection our genes must extol before they are free to relinquish their past. In the last of the seven group of pyramids which is once we have entered up into the divine equation, we note that this pyramid has no cap. It has a huge burning pit which represents this chapter explaining the resurrection of the plagues. It is open to the heavens and is referred to as Abu Rauch. The word 'rauche' is interpreted as a smoke apparatus in the earlier languages. Hence, we make note as to why the pyramid must be kept opened to allow the smoke to escape. This pyramid is known to us as the crown of the head. Or through the Indo-Asian principles it is described as the crown chakra.

Now we are feeling quite comfortable at continuing on to complete the story of why Alexandria, or as previously known through the Aramaic language as EL-ex-AN-dri-EA, who are these three Gods who finally at the bequest of discovering and releasing their own inner journey of discerning themselves, became the mind of God. Also, this story relates to the Christmas rendition of the three wise men, who came from the east, which is the energy that is releasing from within, as we continue to accept this important information of earning the rights to our own journey of self-discovery, through accepting our understanding of the relationship to anoint the baby Jesus with gifts of incense and myrrh, which releases from the divinity of our soul's essence within. An ultimate gift to one's self, don't you agree.

This amazing place is situated with its library supposedly full of every book that has been written or scribed on the planet became the lighthouse that was supposedly seen completely around the four corners of the world. This was through my learnings of those nine alternative years of step by step, training with my Masters of Time, which took me 26 years to bring into a completion, into the sacred codex of this wonderful gift that Egypt has left for us over 13,000 years ago, of us moving from our third dimensional mind into what is referred to as the afterlife or into the journey of our next life. Also, I remember back in the beginning of the nineties, where my Masters of Time who reigned from the 'Mantisoid region of Universal Time' through their gentleness and honour for the journey that they explained to me, that if we went back 30,000 years of human gestation, that we would also make reference to the codex at that time, that we would be able to make note of similar stories being released explaining the wisdom of our inner gestation.

This coded reference revealed to me that it is through the gift of you earning your inner sacredness, that you have now earned of your double-edged sword or more easily explained as your inner divinity or soul's word, as to how the codex of your truth releases the myths of how you are in the process of earning the completeness of yourself, also explaining the purpose of why you are here back to you.

Chapter 15, verse 5, once decoded is reminding you that you are earning the freedom of your collective mind in regards to you advancing towards your absolution of forgiving yourself for your past digressions for you to release the courage to journey on. Can you now feel how your freedom is opening you up to accept greater expectations of self.

CHAPTER SIXTEEN

Clearing The Channels Of Our Collective Consciousness

An interesting chapter ahead that speaks to us of the confidence one has to find to flush out both inner and outer levels to the channels of our old collective consciousness.

Our thoughts need rearranging as we walk up to accepting these mature thoughts of earning our own masterhood (6) of self, as these channels are the branches of our central nervous system reaching up towards accepting the full potentiality of their own light. Remember back in verse 1, the great voice is your higher self; it comes from your heavenly realm which is situated in the crown of your head; the earth represents your body. To bring it all back into context, your next thought has to be of a positive nature for it to continue to hone you in to you facing up to the responsibility of your natural laws.

Now where do these natural laws come from? They release from your inner language of your soul, that you were superlatively (of a superior quality of your thoughts) downloaded with during your gestation, before your birth as to what you were programmed to experience during this lifetime in regards to you improving the memorial contract of your inner DNA to help improve upon the next generation, therefore please take my hand and let's walk this chapter together.

Verse 1: *"And I heard a great voice out of the temple saying to the seven angels, Go your ways, and pour out the vials of the wrath of God upon the earth"*.

Verse 2: *"And the first went, and poured out his vial upon the earth; and there fell a noisome and grievous sore upon the men which had the mark of the beast and upon them which worshipped his image"*.

In verse 2, we now understand that the cells, in cohabitation with our body's genes, are purifying themselves as we move towards the remnants of the ego's fear—finally freed from the stranglehold of the past. As it now remains in abeyance, we can hear the inner groan as the ego earns its right to release the last vestiges of its old life, where it can collect itself through its own resurrection to begin again.

From verse 3 onwards, we are shown how our thoughts that we deem unimportant are released from our body, allowing purification to begin. Note the words written now—we are talking about a radical gene, that is holding on to its extreme view of what it thinks its life to be about.

Verse 3: *"And the second angel poured out his vial upon the sea; and it became as the blood of a dead man: and every living soul died in the sea"*.

Verse 4: *"And the third angel poured out his vial upon the rivers and fountains of waters; and they became blood"*.

Verse 5: *"And I heard the angel of the waters say, Thou art righteous, O Lord, which art, and wast, and shalt be, because thou hast judged thus"*.

Verse 6: *"For they have shed the blood of saints and prophets, and thou hast given them blood to drink; for they are worthy"*.

Verse 7: *"And I heard another out of the altar say, Even so, Lord God Almighty, true and righteous are thy judgments"*.

Verse 8: *"And the fourth angel poured out his vial upon the sun; and power was given unto him to scorch men with fire"*.

Remember the waters represent the consciousness that is surrounding the whole planet and us as well, for we are worthy of baptising ourself. We note that these words are continually reminding us of the resurrection we are able to attain through having the strength to be in control of the self; to destroy the next negative thought before it has the chance to try and stake its hold of our past thinking, once again.

Verse 9: *"And men* (our genes) *were scorched with great heat, and blasphemed the name of God, which hath power over these plagues: and they repented not to give him glory"*.

Verse 10: "*And the fifth angel poured out his vial upon the seat of the beast; and his kingdom was full of darkness; and they gnawed their tongues for pain*".

These negative thoughts could not rely on their strength; their blasphemy was deteriorating moment by moment; to allow their newly released freedom of mind to reign.

Verse 11: "*And blasphemed the God of heaven because of their pains and their sores, and repented not of their deeds*".

Verse 12: "*And the sixth angel poured out his vial upon the great river Euphrates; and the water thereof was dried up, that the way of the kings of the east might be prepared*".

We are aware that the kings of the east (within) are the glands around the throat area that are waiting for their turn to spring into action. They are assisting us to digest our positive thoughts, and through their temperance and wisdom both are finally being coerced or compelled into trusting their support, for the opening up of our inner self. Remember that this is the sixth angel and the number six relates to mastering one's self.

Verse 13: "*And I saw three unclean spirits like frogs come out of the mouth of the dragon, and out of the mouth of the beast, and out of the mouth of the false prophet*".

Verse 14: "*For they are the spirits of devils, working miracles, which go forth unto the kings of the earth and of the whole world, to gather them to the battle of that great day of God Almighty*".

Frogs like to live in still or stagnant waters. They do not live in the sea. There is no fresh oxygen in their community. They are breathing their same thoughts over and over again. And whilst on this subject, one of the twelve plagues was on frogs! To bring these verses into context I ask you to remember the childhood story of the prince who had a spell cast on him and he became a frog. A spell is an insolent personality that is in desperation to stay put; it does not want to evolve and undo its thinking which has become frozen through time; where other personalities distance themselves at the command it is issuing. Hence the fear that is re-created where it becomes locked in.

The story continues with a princess who was an insolent child where she demanded others to work for her, instead of her earning her own rewards. The princess met up with the frog when her golden ball rolled into the pond. He said he would return her golden ball to her if she did what he wanted her to do. She did not want to do his bidding; but in the end he tempted her so much that she spoke with her father and he said that she had to do as the frog asked; to get her ball returned to her.

The frog pestered her to reply to many of his requests, such as eating off her golden plate at meal times and wanting to sleep on her pillow when she went to bed. This went on for three weary days and the next morning she awoke to find her frog had turned into a handsome prince. As they looked outside the window there were eight white horses harnessed in to a golden chariot to take them to where ever they wanted to go. They married and lived happily ever after. The prince had transformed his original thought and the princess had earned herself. There are thousands of children's stories written regarding these verses, it is also applicable to men as well as women, as it is representing the emotional mind which is where our inner nervous system opens up to release more information as we climb the branches of our inner tree of knowledge to reach our everlasting home. We are tempted by these evil spirits to claim and earn our wisdom; it just does not appear in front of us.

Verse 15: *"Behold, I come as a thief. Blessed is he that watcheth, and keepeth his garments, lest he walk naked, and they see his shame".*

I love this verse; my father explained it to me when I was a young girl that no matter who we are, I always had to remember that when others looked at me; there was something in me that others could accept about themselves. The garments of my mind and self, had to be kept clean. If one has no garment, then others could see right through you and of course they would walk away.

Verse 16: "*And he gathered them together into a place called in the Hebrew tongue Armageddon*".

The word 'Armageddon' is explaining to us that we must bring our information together concerning our truth, as we know it to be; which is spelt and pronounced differently in many other languages. Which one is right, again I had to go back into the sacred alphabet of time and pronounce it to myself, syllable by syllable from how the word was first spoken and passed on to others. Slowly over months of research, I took it back through the Asyrian language for the word to represent the Armour of Gideon. I have previously mentioned our introduction into claiming this attire.

Who was Gideon and what part did he play in the Bible of self-proclamation? There are three chapters devoted to this personality, where we understand his responsibilities to the people of Israel. Please read in the book of Judges, chapters, 6, 7, 8, as he learned to carry out the words of God.

The codes begin to open up to us, as we release the story of Gideon being supplied with an army of 100 men. What is the numerical factor of this story? We are being informed that Gideon had become his own communion of how he had earned a relationship with his soul self to communicate through his inner harmonization, which rebalanced his mind with his soul. Thus, he became a learned one that God had enough trust in to place him in his position. An interesting story!

It is just another step forwards towards the final phase before achieving our total enlightenment; where we are brought up into the unconscious mind of self; we present and deliver our self, up to the head of God. It is the path of walking alone in your mind; where you are clear and free of inhibitions and regrets; also, where you have a permanently open window that is opened from within, for us to use the ability to tune into the earnings of the whole of the collective of the consciousness.

Verse 17: "*And the seventh angel poured out his vial into*

the air; and there came a great voice out of the temple of heaven, from the throne, saying, It is done".

Verse 18: "And there were voices, and thunders, and lightnings; and there was a great earthquake, such as was not since men were upon the earth, so mighty an earthquake, and so great".

Verse 19: "And the great city was divided into three parts, and the cities of the nations fell: and great Babylon came in remembrance before God, to give unto her the cup of the wine of the fierceness of his wrath".

Verse 20: "And every island fled away, and the mountains were not found".

Verse 21: "And there fell upon men a great hail out of heaven, every stone about the weight of a talent: and men blasphemed God because of the plague of the hail; for the plague thereof was exceeding great".

We find another aspect is being delivered to us of achieving enlightenment. For us to begin to understand and accept this amazing chapter; we are becoming aware of our body babbling on with no direction to aim for. There are many cities of light all of which are vying for control over one another where the end result usually turns to 'Waring' with one another. Isn't that so, today?

As the earthquake begun; we realise that the city which housed all of Babylon; is the collective power of self at that point, where it was separated by God into three sections; the EL the AN and the EA. Does this remind you of the verse, "Suffer little children and forbid them not, for of such is the kingdom of heaven"?

We also notice that the inner cities of the nation fell; therefore, there could only be these three cities of light and the rest of the nation had to decide which one of these three they supported. As you can see, we are moving on to the next quandary of payment that is due to us from God, through the patience we release and give back to our self. In other words, we are coaxing our ego self by releasing our logic thinking into viewing itself through the emotional mind; the right hemisphere of our brain. We are now viewing through the mathematics as to how the mind of God within us began to collect itself together.

Verse 20, explains it all. The islands represent the cluster of cells that separated themselves and were huddled together through them not having the strength to co-join with one another, (just the same as we have to do, when through our own innocence, we try to create a new sentence) we are learning to understand our inner consciousness, for us to release this new land.

The mountains had of course to disappear, all but one and that is the Alps from Austria, Switzerland France and the border of Spain through to the Basque Territory, where my father heralded down from his mother's linage who was named Alfonso 1st who became the King of Asturias, in the land of the Basque Territories, at the beginning of the Pyrenees, as these five border areas are the last bastion of mountains to still be alive throughout Europe to manifest for itself, to grow according to the last count, 1.5cm per year. This information gives you your freedom which attribute to your last remaining fears that need to be dissolved. In the beginning of our own personal understanding the Bible refers to our body up to our neck as the earth; now that we have progressed this far into awakening our intellect, we note that the word 'earth' has been changed to land. Therefore, we have become our own country; we have released our own citizens, who have found and earned their own peace and respect for one another. We have brought forth our own inner language, which will become successful through our visions of what we would love to accomplish from here on in, to eternity.

CHAPTER SEVENTEEN

We Are Finally Waking Up

This chapter brings our thoughts together where we are finally waking up to the pretence that we have used as our protection and hidden behind most of our life; it is a reflection of our past which is still trapped in our old layers during this strenuous birthing for us to become an affiliated member of the angelic realm when denoted is explaining that we are aware of becoming our inner Christ Consciousness, which is on the road to us becoming a new progressive Apostle. So, to all you doubters of the words written in this book, please think again as the full book of Revelations is explaining to us humanities next evolutionary step, or the metaphysical journey we partake of, also known as the spiritual highway that leads us into the complete journey of enlightenment.

As always, we must release and understand our past to prepare ourselves for our future. We must eradicate our fear for our future to begin to appear before our eyes. It is where we like to hold on to our ideas that we think are important to us; while we busily create personalities of indifference; therefore, there is no progress. How can we keep on learning? What is good and what is evil? This beast that I call the left hand of self-tempts us every moment of our lives. I remember during my journey when I seemed to be dragged around the bottomless pit for what seemed forever and my cry to God was: "Where are you, why are you allowing this to happen to me? Can't you see I am giving you my all?"

God was in the background forever smiling at me and the devil was right in front of me tempting me not to release myself away from its hold over me. All of my screaming and ranting was to no avail. With ripped fingernails and toes; my bleeding knees were continually digging into the jagged cliffs ahead to support me; finally, through my respect and love for myself, over time, all of my endeavours were starting to seep through my mind which brought a sense of peace I have never known before and after many years, I knew I had to restore the word 'faith' not fate, back into my inner dictionary to release my strength that I had birthed many years before, to climb my way back up through my DNA to journey back up to the top. I found out that I had to earn my inner silence to calm my shattered nerves through me trying to take a short cut, which waylaid me when the pressure rebuilt itself through my inner frustration of not servicing myself first. Once I had re-implanted my forgotten faith, I could now focus collectively on earning this next new experience and time once again became my healer. In this chapter we earn the right to release this inner communicator, that has waited, oh, so many years to communicate to and through us. Now read on.

Verse 1: "*And there came one of the seven angels which had the seven vials, and talked with me, saying unto me, Come hither; I will shew unto thee the judgment of the great whore that sitteth upon many waters*".

Can you recall me mentioning before, that when a whore is mentioned so often in the writings of the Bible, she is representing an emotional thought that is trying to claim other personalities to do her bidding, through her deceiving herself? We have a tendency today to name it bribery.

Verse 2: "*With whom the kings of the earth have committed fornication, and the inhabitants of the earth have been made drunk with the wine of her fornication*".

This is where the ego of each personality is claiming its own kingship; it thinks it is on its way to have the right to claim its own passage; all of which still controls and rules certain sections of the weaker emotional mind. The inhabitants are still being controlled through her trying to over control herself; hence them becoming drunk, through being totally disarrayed in the mind! They have and had reached the point of no return; where they meander along any path and will always end up at a dead end.

Again, we are being reminded of the conversion of Mary Magdalene from the Book of Luke, chapter 8, verses 1-3, in the New Testament from whom were cast the seven devils.

Verse 3: "So he carried me away in the spirit into the wilderness: and I saw a woman sit upon a scarlet-coloured beast, full of names of blasphemy, having seven heads and ten horns".

Verse 4: "And the woman was arrayed in purple and scarlet colour, and decked with gold and precious stones and pearls, having a golden cup in her hand full of abominations and filthiness of her fornication".

Verse 5: "And upon her forehead was a name written, MYSTERY, BABYLON THE GREAT, THE MOTHER OF HARLOTS AND ABOMINATIONS OF THE EARTH".

My Goodness! Shades of Daniel in chapter 7, isn't it? We note that the woman's clothes were purple and scarlet. Remember our colours are released through our inner alphabet, as they are explaining to us how we are arching our intellect up to the crown of our head. The heavier and darker they are, the more aggressive behaviour there is to release, for our emotions to gather their supremacy to climb the ladder of our DNA. All of these colours mentioned in the previous verses; are reminding us that they stem from the sexual area of the ego self.

The more emotional intelligence you release from within, the lighter the colours you wear. Previously I have stated that when we receive a vision from within, that the strength in the colours is in tune to represent the first God EL; the black and white are representing the education of the God AN; which is educating our moment and the colour sepia and the pale muted colours, are representing this road less travelled, the home of GOD known as the EA, our forever-lasting future.

Verse 6: "And I saw the woman drunken with the blood of the saints, and with the blood of the martyrs of Jesus: and when I saw her, I wondered with great admiration".

Verse 7: "And the angel said unto me, Wherefore, didst thou marvel? I will tell thee the mystery of the woman, and of the beast that carrieth her, which hath the seven heads and ten horns".

Verse 8: *"The beast that thou sawest was, and is not; and shall ascend out of the bottomless pit, and go into perdition: and they that dwell on the earth shall wonder, whose names were not written in the book of life from the foundation of the world, when they behold the beast that was, and is not, and yet is"*.

Verse 9: *"And here is the mind which hath wisdom. The seven heads are seven mountains, on which the woman sitteth"*.

Can you recall how these explanations began back in chapter 13? We know that mountains represent our collected energy; they have no breathing space to release their fear, therefore they cannot inherit. We continue adding to my explanations of this wondrous beast on a deeper level as previously written. In other words, the woman is sitting on top of her collective fear; and is sucked down into her bottomless pit which has kept the Book with the seven seals closed. How can these seals inherit on her behalf, to release the emotional wisdom she requires to automatically arch or ark herself towards her new light.

Verse 10: *"And there are seven kings: five are fallen, and one is, and the other is not yet come; and when he cometh, he must continue a short space"*.

Freedom is on its way, thanks to these five that have fallen. Remember the number five in the sacred numerology represents the changes we make to free the moment. The sixth one to fall is in the moment; which will automatically release the next continuous step. Once the seventh has stepped into the picture the other six will unite and we will see it has nowhere to go! These seven kings are the collective power that has stopped the woman from freeing her past to inherit herself. One of them is aware of what is happening and is preparing to free itself from sin, or living in the past; and the last one is still to evolve up into its inheritance and when it does, it releases the confidence to go on as it realises it is finally on the homestretch, as it does not have too far to travel.

Verse 11: *"And the beast that was, and is not, even he is the eighth, and is of the seven, and goeth into perdition".*

Once they have all collected together, the beast has been absolved into the land where there is no more guilt! Please note that the word 'guilt' has now been eradicated out of your dictionary. If it is released from your dictionary it is released from your mind!

Verse 12: *"And the ten horns which thou sawest are ten kings, which have received no kingdom as yet: but receive power as kings one hour with the beast".*

Verse 13: *"These have one mind, and shall give their power and strength unto the beast".*

As previously explained our horns are our antenna's permanently searching the cosmos for the light or another rendition for the light, is the natural law that is always available to assist with the wholeness of self; so now we are beginning to realize that if we are living in our past and dwelling on thoughts that are no longer appropriate to our moment, it is impossible for us to inherit this perpetual light or understand the codes to these sacred laws. Once we have learned to overthrow those thoughts that are no longer infringing upon us then through our innocence, the innocent lamb becomes our light which manifests our intelligence; and through its own time it has earned the sonority right to rule over us. The power as kings for one hour is revealing to us metaphysically, each decisive moment. They cannot produce their own beam as they are still trapped in their past; they can only release a glyph of light which can assist the beast in each of its moments! Now you can understand why the ego can only hold 13 words at once, in its own dictionary.

We can also understand why many of you walk away intellectually from the wisdom of the metaphysical language when we begin to realize that the natural laws are seen as too stringent. Through our innocence we do not know how to cope! If you don't know how to look around you to see the answer being reflected back to you, then you do not have an iota on how to decipher yourself!

When one begins to exalt their knowledge up into their own matter of physics, or metaphysics, their mind becomes clearer which hones them in together, all of which solidifies their inner strength, which of course rearranges and changes their alphabet, which will automatically change the autonomics of their inner as well as their outer language. They will learn to combine their thoughts as to how they pronounce their thinking differently.

Many speak of these laws as the past! Excuse me! They are still governing everything we say and do each moment of our existence, to this very day! Do you think we can change them? Once again it will only be through the majority rules, that we can swing the scales to correct the overflow of our crowded emotions. I have named this sentence our inner parliament. The results of our actions are continually collecting each mistake we make on our behalf, which is in the control of our pituitary gland! Never mind the old cliché that we are changing these laws moment by moment! We are rearranging them by adding to them, which will broaden the horizon of things to come! These mistakes have to be relayed back to us, and of course these laws are always the winner, hence you are becoming more aware of each thought you think, where you can see that we still have a long way to go! Now read on.

Verse 14: *"These shall make war with the Lamb, and the Lamb shall overcome them: for he is Lord of lords, and King of kings: and they that are with him are called, and chosen, and faithful".*

Verse 15: *"And he saith unto me, The waters which thou sawest, where the whore sitteth, are peoples, and multitudes, and nations, and tongues".*

Now let us bring this information back to our inner self. Don't forget the Lamb is the innocent thought! When it can't think for itself, it automatically follows on from the one in front of it. Through our innocence we have an inner yearning to do things right! Another interpretation is, the lamb is our light and we know that our Light is our future Intelligence! In verse 15, the waters also represent the consciousness of the beast.

All of the people, multitudes, nations and tongues etc; are representing the personalities that are still imbued within the beast. Please remember, the nations are those personalities that feel they are earning their own independence; they have birthed their emotional inheritance and have a tendency to keep to themselves. They want to be independent of others and live in their own realms, which is why the beast has great difficulties through it hiding amongst the waves of the waters to unite his verse. They have placed a boundary around themselves.

Verse 16: *"And the ten horns which thou sawest upon the beast, these shall hate the whore, and shall make her desolate and naked, and shall eat her flesh, and burn her with fire".*

The number 10 in sacred numerology, represents the changes that evolve from releasing a past world, where we must be free to evolve up into the next cycle of the nine single digits. It is where we begin to make note of the digits 1-0 explaining to us that—I am my soul.

Verse 17: *"For God hath put in their hearts to fulfil his will, and to agree, and give their kingdom unto the beast, until the words of God shall be fulfilled".*

Verse 18: *"And the woman which thou sawest is that great city, which reigneth over the kings of the earth".*

We are finally beginning to understand that for us to survive the life our ego demands of us, which is referred biblically to as the beast, the bestial side of us, the one who wants to control others through only listening and obeying itself; therefore, we are given the divine will to earn the rights to unite all of our personalities to reside in comfort beside one another, as these are the Laws of the Universal God.

They are embedded in our genes, which are embedded in our cells and have been for many thousands of years. It is our choice to live the way we do, although we also know within ourself, that we can create another explanation for everything that happens to us. Through our own innocence when we rely on others to do our own bidding, we are failing ourselves. That is when we begin to create guilt into our past generation's inner spectrum. Each following generation must try to make a stand to repair the doubt from their previous inheritance for your future to set you free. Is this why we are taking so long to release the restrictions that we are swathed in layers during our gestation, where we have become bound up as our DNA is downloaded for us to inherit during our lifetime? This chapter 17, conveys the statement: 'Through the sacred codex of my inner mathematics, I am earning my Christ (light) communicator through my inner earnings, as to how I become the teacher within'. Thank you for taking your time, to you reading this chapter through to the end.

CHAPTER EIGHTEEN

Final Rendition Of The Fall Of Babylon

Verse 1: *"And after these things I saw another angel come down from heaven, having great power; and the earth was lightened with his glory".*

Verse 2: *"And he cried mightily with a strong voice, saying, Babylon the great is fallen, is fallen, and is become the habitation of devils, and the hold of every foul spirit, and a cage of every unclean and hateful bird".*

As crazy as it seems at that time, this was the language that was recorded for all of us to unfurl and inherit for our own future. We are finding out that this language is identical to the Applied Sciences previously recorded throughout the Principles of Indo-Asian, Egyptology, the Mayan Prophecies, to be able to control the population, as well as being recorded in this Book of Revelation. It is interesting to see that we are finally bringing the Sciences and Religions together at last, where they are both explaining exactly the same story! Well, now it is my turn to reveal another example of the truth to you all.

Regarding the message that is brought through the Mayan Prophecies, we can see the similarities at the Temple of Chechen Itza, where there is the largest of the thirteen ball courts situated between the North Temple, also referred to as the Temple of the Wizard of Consciousness or the old man as is depicted on the wall; and at the southern end is a larger Temple in ruins. The reason for these ruins is explaining to us that you are about to take the chance to leave your old kingdom behind to be rewarded with the new. They had found their confidence to advance their thinking into taking their next advanced step.

Now before I finish this paragraph, allow me to explain the word 'Chechen' through the sacred codex of the alphabet, there are two syllables in the word, both syllables we note that now I must repeat the word back to front, in other words

I must reverse or re-verse the word, to find the truth to the equation of the word. We first note that the first syllable is spelt 'Che' and then it is repeated again, 'che-che' and ends with an 'N'.

Please remember what you have read in this book regarding you leaving your old thoughts behind by you climbing up out of the earth to free yourself from your past, as to how you have gained the confidence in self to walk up into opening the seven seals for you to be enveloped up into the heavenly realms for ever more. All you are doing is dying to your own inhibitions who no longer serve you for you to attain your confidence to walk on.

It is assumed that they played football in this arena. Not so! This same area is also explaining the fall of Babylon. The hieroglyphs that we see where the heart is ripped out is not happening to others. It is how the ancient ones recorded the death of their own personalities that were refusing to release their past control over their inner nations. Remember throughout the Shamanic Laws the species of the cat family represent detachment, or the emotion that is refusing to budge, remember the cat in your family owns you, you do not own the cat! Are you aware that our energy in motion, is where the ego is detaching itself from one's higher self. Now back to the game, where we notice that there are two Temples on the east (relationship within) facing wall that overlook the ball court and another one in the south where all three of them are representing the Jaguar Temples. The walls inside this temple are also covered with hieroglyphs explaining the slaughter. We note that there are seven Temples in the Yucatan area where they are all explaining the wonder of these seven seals. Remember there are three Gods to evolve into one another for us to earn what has already been downloaded during our gestation of our inner **B**asic **I**nformation **B**efore **L**eaving **E**arth? My goodness, when you have digested all of this information you will know where you are—why you are—what you are—how you are, and more importantly who you are! My goodness, there are five of them, and five represents the freedom within.

Let's return to our new found growth of intellect. As we view our selves from above, we see our body is becoming filled with the magnification of our inner light! Remember that the bird tribe evolved after certain animals had reached their peak of perfection. In the beginning of their gestation, they were born with membranous skin like wings before they evolved into feathers, therefore they were the first of the original angels! Just as the bat is still trapped in its evolution today as it hides in the dark, as it still has the original membranes for its wings. They learned how to lift themselves up and out of the moment. That is why birds are mentioned; they are coming up through into their divine angelic language. The birds that were trapped or caged in their darkness could not eradicate their thoughts, as their ego still had total control over them, therefore the blasphemy of the emotional primal mind, which represents our understanding, continued to interfere with their own progress.

Now do you understand the heart and feather being weighed on the scales throughout Egyptology, as to how every species that has evolved before us, as explained in the beginning of Genesis, chapter 7, verse 2: Noah's Ark, where the animals were to be collected by seven of the clean beasts, the male and his female: and the beasts that are not clean by two, which is the male and his female, for the ego (the child within) to collapse into, as it is still in training. Verse 3: Of fowls of the air by sevens, (as they evolve once our heart has been measured through our mathematics harmonising and adjusting to our new found awareness) the male and the female: to keep seed alive (our thoughts) upon the face of all the earth. Now we can understand why the animals had to be collected by seven as we will need our inner sustenance to assist us into releasing each clasp on the back of the book (our DNA) for us to evolve up into the chamber of our God Head, this amazing gland that the pineal gland looks up to, also known as the upper echelon of us earning the unconscious recognition of our mind. All of which has the opportunity to advance us up into its ultra consciousness exactly the same as we also have the same privilege?

Now you can understand more fully as to how your inner codex is unravelling itself as we begin to release our thoughts from the third dimensional mind for us to be looking through every thought we release! Welcome to the fourth dimension. I thank you for your patience in reading to the end of my explanations, as the words you have read in this paragraph are now registered throughout your inner vocabulary for ever more and you will be able to release this information for the rest of your journey here on the earth. Please remember also, that all of the ancient sacred spaces that are still available for us to view around the earth, are all explaining to us the journey of how our intellect has evolved up into the stage of complete enlightenment. No, you don't have to travel to the stars or other planets while on the earth, leave them where they are, just as we do, as they also have a job to continue in their own realms. Let us continue to get our own realm right and just, first!

Verse 3: *"For all nations have drunk of the wine of the wrath of her fornication, and the kings of the earth have committed fornication with her, and the merchants of the earth are waxed rich through the abundance of her delicacies".*

Verse 4: *"And I heard another voice from heaven, saying, Come out of her, my people, that ye be not partakers of her sins, and that ye receive not of her plagues".*

All is becoming easier to understand and accept as to how the stronger personalities that did not have confidence in themselves, had to stop using her for their own benefits; and they were asked to leave!

Verse 5: *"For her sins have reached unto heaven, and God hath remembered her iniquities".*

Verse 6: *"Reward her even as she rewarded you, and double unto her double according to her works: in the cup which she hath full filled to her double".*

Verse 7: *"How much she hath glorified herself, and lived deliciously, so much torment and sorrow give her: for she saith in her heart, I sit a queen, and am no widow, and shall see no sorrow".*

Verse 8: *"Therefore shall her plagues come in one day, death, and mourning, and famine; and she shall be utterly burned with fire: for strong is the Lord God who judgeth her".*

Verse 9: *"And the kings of the earth, who have committed fornication and lived deliciously with her, shall bewail her, and lament for her, when they shall see the smoke of her burning".*

We are finally beginning to understand how the personalities of the ego could get away with abusing the emotional mind to satisfy its self! Once again, we take note of how the smoke is representing the resurrection of her thoughts, the more she believes in herself.

Verse 10: *"Standing afar off for the fear of her torment, saying, Alas, alas, that great city Babylon, that mighty city! For in one hour is thy judgment come".*

The word 'hour' is interpreted as the **H**eavenly **O**rder **U**nderstanding and **R**eleasing its information. Therefore, an hour is representing the accumulation of one thought being brought back into its fruition, its own fulfilment of hope, for it to see the results of its work coming together. The personalities which are named Kings, that have supported themselves from this thought have realized that they have nothing to support them, therefore they must turn around and face their own reflection. There is no way out! The fire and smoke can only come through the resurrection. Remember the seventh seal or pyramid I spoke about previously? In one hour or moment, is thy judgment come. All is explaining to us that the karma we receive is given to us in the collective moment. The mathematics of the mind has accumulated on behalf of the thought! It does not build up! It strikes while the iron is hot!

Verse 11: *"And the merchants of the earth shall weep and mourn over her; for no man buyeth their merchandise anymore".*

Verse 12: *"The merchandise of gold, and silver, and precious stones, and of pearls, and fine linen, and purple, and silk, and scarlet, and all thine wood, and all manner vessels of ivory, and all manner vessels of most precious wood, and of brass, and iron, and marble".*

Verse 13: *"And cinnamon, and odours, and ointments, and frankincense, and wine, and oil, and fine flour, and wheat, and beasts, and sheep, and horses, and chariots, and slaves, and souls of men".*

Through her own temptations being delivered back to her; the merchants who used her for their own excuses; she now had the intellectual right to refuse. She could close off the relationship in her mind and move on. She did not have to suffer as they no longer had any control over her.

Verse 14: *"And the fruits that thy soul lusted after are departed from thee, and all things which were dainty and goodly are departed from thee, and thou shalt find them no more at all".*

Verse 15: *"The merchants of these things, which were made rich by her, shall stand afar off for the fear of her torment, weeping and wailing".*

We are noticing that all of these things mentioned in these verses, are connected to the spiritual essence of human thought. There is no more trading between the personalities, who once were all vying for their own share; the competition is finally surrendering. All of the personalities are becoming congruent into releasing the eternal wisdom of one's own self. There is no arguing up here, when you have entered up into the doorway of heaven.

Probably of no interest to these verses but, I will explain it anyway, as it has shot forward into my mind. Do you recall the items place in the tomb of the Golden Pharaoh Tut-Ankh-Amon in Egypt? We have supposed up to this point that they are there to feed the person in their afterlife. Not so! These items represent the essences of the species that have already evolved, that will be needed to suffice the Pharaoh as he journeys through the book of Revelations, to replace those personalities that have autonomically been mathematically corrected, where they are now free to deplete themselves; even down to the cats when decoded, relate to the word 'detachment' that were mummified through them not supporting himself.

All the animal species wrapped in packages represent our personalities that will need to be re-nourished and replaced. The different grains represent our ideas, while the pulses represent how we harmonize and blend our thoughts together. The herbs and spices add to the flavour, blending and healing us on an inner level.

When dressing the table, fresh herbs are placed among freshly cut flowers, prepared as we honour the meal set before us. The bed allows us to turn our thoughts inward, where the ego is at rest; and the chair provides a place to take the weight off our feet and relax the mind. These pieces of furniture shape our house into a home—a temple, a city of light. Now, we can fully understand the precious verse: *"In my father's house there are many mansions"*. *This passage conveys the metaphysical vibration of personalities coming together as we finally release the inbuilt pressure of our DNA. And the story continues.*

Verse 16: *"And saying, Alas, alas, that great city, that was clothed in fine linen, and purple, and scarlet, and decked with gold, and precious stones, and pearls"*.

Verse 17: *"For in one hour so great riches is come to nought. And every shipmaster, and all the company in ships, and sailors, and as many as trade by sea, stood afar of"*.

Here we note that the ships are explaining those personalities who are in charge of themselves as they ride the oceans of consciousness or time, without stepping in to interfere. Now do you make note of the four ships that were placed at the corners of the large pyramid in Egypt for us on our journey of self-discovery to sail the seven seas, which is explaining to us the recorded journal of the last 64 generations, of the blood line of our own DNA. We then journey up through the seven vertebrae of our neck to release the seven clasps on the back of the book of our inner bible, our recorded inheritance of our DNA, to release the innocence of our past generations through many of them not knowing about their own spiritual wisdom, or their wise domain that they were downloaded with before they were born. We are not still babbling on, ever so slowly, we are evolving into understanding our past as well as preparing the future for our next generation to inherit.

And while I am on the subject, please do not allow AI to rob us of our inbuilt integrities that have already been downloaded into every human. I have found so many misdemeanours and breaches in its work, that I want my following four generations, plus more, to still evolve to inherit the downloading of their own personal DNA, that was seeded into every human before they were born. In other words, their 'Bloodlines' will be robbed of their own right to unfurl what has already been downloaded into their cellular gestation, for them to earn their own manifestation of light! Please remember our light is our inner intelligence that we earn as we unfurl our genetic inheritance as we grow up into adulthood, all for our own perpetual motion to release, our inner balance to equate, through our intelligence unfolding itself.

The more we unfurl our inbuilt dictionary, the more intellectual light we manifest for not only ourself, also, as to how the expansion of this energy is then seeded through the threads of truth for the whole human population to inherit, as well as the planetary consciousness for the planet to adjust and adhere too. It has a tremendous long way to evolve before it can interfere with the Greatest Order of the Divine unit, that every human has already been seeded with and is also already born with. We do not have to short-circuit the human intelligence that has taken us thousands of years to understand and adhere too. All for the sake of a heap of money into a few banks. It has already been released to us that five years after it has been tested that the younger mind will become short circuited and ten years after that, there will be a depreciation in the following generations. Thank you for reading these last two paragraphs, I have finally got it off my chest! Now let us get back to the real interpretation of *Revealing the Revelations of St. John the Divine* as he explains to us the holistic memory of the human strain as we earn the intelligence to us understanding the sacredness of our inner metaphysical language we were seeded with before we were born.

Verse 18: *"And cried when they saw the smoke of her burning, saying, What city is like unto this great city"*.

All of our forthcoming thoughts must find their own individual strength as our emotional mind journeys through her own resurrection; hence the smoke. We can see how the last pyramid near Alexandria named Abu Rauch is representing the smoke seen far out into the sea, where there is no outside interference.

Verse 19: *"And they cast dust on their heads, and cried, weeping and wailing, saying, Alas, alas, that great city, wherein were made rich all that had ships in the sea by reason of her costliness! For in one hour is she made desolate"*.

Verse 20: *"Rejoice over her, thou heaven, and ye holy apostles and prophets; for God hath avenged you on her"*.

Verse 21: *"And a mighty angel took up a stone like a great millstone, and cast it into the sea, saying, Thus, with violence, shall that great city Babylon be thrown down, and shall be found no more at all"*.

Verse 22: *"And the voice of harpers, and musicians, and of pipers, and trumpeters, shall be heard no more at all in thee; and no craftsman, of whatsoever craft he be, shall be found any more in thee; and the sound of a millstone shall be heard no more at all in thee"*.

Verse 23: *"And the light of a candle shall shine no more at all in thee; and the voice of the bridegroom and of the bride shall be heard no more at all in thee: for thy merchants were the great men of the earth; for by thy sorceries were all nations deceived"*.

Verse 24: *"And in her was found the blood of prophets, and of saints, and of all that were slain upon the earth"*.

Briefly explained this chapter is the last of the abominations of our third dimensional world. The ego has finally released it's—strangle hold—over our emotions, where it has been subtly succumbed by the internal laws into balancing itself with the right hemisphere of the brain.

As we enter up into the 'Royal Order' of our new world order; or through the acceptance of our new inner order of our world, we realise that through our new found wisdom we have finally earned a balanced mind. Our Christ light (our inner consciousness) through these natural laws has superiority over our thoughts, where all becomes beauty and grace. Through the laws of sacred numerology, the number seven has become a notation of our inner light, which is connected to the seventh seal. We refer to it as the inner teacher, which is our Christ consciousness. We are finally realizing that we have become our own church! Why should we set out to destroy, or maim others; or pick up a gun and inflict through our own ignorance, our self upon others, when in reality, it is destroying your reason for being here. Remember these laws were ignited within you through the beginning of your gestation, before you drew breath, which sparked a cognitive relay throughout your cells for you to adhere to, as you stepped forward into your future life. When you admonish this important fact of life, your support succumbs to the innocence of your ego, as laid out in the beginning through the journey of you discovering yourself, where every human is a reflection of one another! I am referring to how your inner program or how you can exonerate yourself to accept that your body had already been set out through the sacred mathematics and numerology of your DNA, which is protected through your cellular structure of yourself?

Chapter 18 relates to the harmony and balance you have personally awakened and accomplished within you, which will infinitely support you for the rest of your life.

CHAPTER NINETEEN

The Search Of The Cosmos

Verse 1: *"And after these things I heard a great voice of much people in heaven, saying, Alleluia; Salvation, and glory, and honour, and power, unto the Lord our God"*.

Verse 2: *"For true and righteous are his judgments: for he hath judged the great whore, which did corrupt the earth with her fornication, and hath avenged the blood of his servants at her hand"*.

Verse 3: *"And again they said, Alleluia. And her smoke rose up forever and ever"*.

And now we note how her life was resurrected through the smoke to the end, and she grew up to begin again to further her own education, which is where her halo began to spin in a harmonic balance, which symbolically creates the sign of infinity. In other words, her intelligence is free to use the advantages of these seven seals or clasps on the back of the book which is now open for ever more to assist her in her search of the cosmos.

Verse 4: *"And the four and twenty elders and the four beasts fell down and worshipped God that sat on the throne, saying, Amen; Alleluia"*.

Verse 5: *"And a voice came out of the throne, saying, Praise, our God all ye his servants, and ye that fear him, both small and great"*.

Verse 6: *"And I heard as it were the voice of a great multitude, and as the voice of many waters, and as the voice of mighty thunderings, saying, Alleluia: for the Lord God omnipotent reigneth"*.

Verse 7: *"Let us be glad and rejoice, and give honour to him: for the marriage of the Lamb is come, and his wife hath made herself ready"*.

All of these verses above are explaining the final resurrection of the lower mind; known to us mythically as the first God EL through which we have earned our everlasting life.

Verse 8: *"And to her was granted that she should be arrayed in fine linen, clean and white: for the fine linen is the righteousness of saints".*

Verse 9: *"And he saith unto me, Write, Blessed are they which are called unto the marriage supper of the Lamb. And he saith unto me, These, are the true sayings of God".*

Verse 10: *"And I fell at his feet to worship him. And he said unto me, See thou do it not: I am thy fellow servant, and of thy brethren that have the testimony of Jesus: worship God: for the testimony of Jesus is the spirit of prophecy".*

Verse 11: *"And I saw heaven opened, and behold a white horse; and he that sat upon him was called Faithful and True, and in righteousness he doth judge and make war".*

Verse 12: *"His eyes were as a flame of fire, and on his head were many crowns; and he had a name written, that no man knew, but he himself".*

Verse 13: *"And he was clothed with a vesture dipped in blood: and his name is called The Word of God".*

Verse 14: *"And the armies which were in heaven followed him upon white horses, clothed in fine linen, white and clean".*

Verse 15: *"And out of his mouth goeth a sharp sword, that with it he should smite the nations: and he shall rule them with a rod of iron: and he treadeth the winepress of the fierceness and wrath of Almighty God".*

Verse 16: *"And he hath on his vesture and on his thigh a name written, KING OF KINGS, AND LORD OF LORDS".*

Verse 17: *"And I saw an angel standing in the sun; and he cried with a loud voice, saying to all the fowls that fly in the midst of heaven,* (these are explaining all of our positive thoughts that have earned their futuristic time to inherit themselves) *Come and gather yourselves together unto the supper of the great God".*

Verse 18: *"That ye may eat the flesh of kings, and the flesh of captains, and the flesh of mighty men, and the flesh of horses, and of them that sit on them, and the flesh of all men, both free and bond, both small and great".*

These previous verses are beautiful. I hope that you have understood enough of the metaphysical language by now to come to your own decisions where your heart is full of love and respect for yourself as you read them. To end up at this point to know that the flesh in the previous paragraph is explaining to us the nourishment that we have already received and earned of our own inner intelligence, (intel-Legiance) which we have now earned, as our God Given Right, for us to digest for our future inheritance.

Verse 19: *"And I saw the beast, and the kings of the earth, and their armies, gathered together to make war against him that sat on the horse, and against his arm".*

Verse 20: *"And the beast was taken, and with him the false prophet that wrought miracles before him, with which he deceived them that had received the mark of the beast, and them that worshipped his image. These both were cast alive into a lake of fire burning with brimstone".*

Verse 21: *"And the remnants were slain with the sword of him that sat upon the horse, which sword proceeded out of his mouth: and all the fowls were filled with their flesh".*

All sounds very gory, doesn't it! Here we go again! And yet it is still the same story explained over and over again, each time lifting our intellect layer by layer, as we have now released the thoughts that our ego has had under its own control which has previously felt trapped within, having been collected all through your lack of confidence or through your innocence to release and speak your learned truth. Which is why the King of Kings, sat on his white horse with the sword or the soul's word, coming from his mouth! Your inner dictionary begins to release your spiritual strength which denotes, the white horse to allow the non-judgement angelic thoughts to speak; hence the fowls or may I remind you that your future thoughts were filled with their flesh to nourish themselves for ever more. We are being constantly reminded to allow our truth to set us free.

Finally, we have reached the end of our second series of digits, decoded as: 'I am knowing all!' This gives us a priority right to extend our intelligence up into the next series of nine digits to forming a permanent relationship with our inner self to embed all of this information permanently into our mind.

CHAPTER TWENTY

The Inner Journey Of You Discovering Your Soul

Verse 1: *"And I saw an angel come down from heaven, having the key of the bottomless pit and a great chain in his hand"*.

Verse 2: *"And he laid hold on the dragon, that old serpent, which is the Devil, and Satan, and bound him a thousand years"*.

Remember that the sacred codes of numerology explain the 1,000 years to represent I AM MY SOUL MIND. You are now in control of that dragon, not as previously noted, where the dragon was in control of you! It has nothing to do with coming back in a thousand years! Just like the Mayan calendar explaining 2012 had nothing to do with the end of the world. It is a code explaining to you, that when you have formed a relationship with your soul, you become that relationship! Therefore, for the rest of your life, you are totally in control of every thought that releases from you. You have just about completed this inner journey of you discovering and releasing the information that has been carried forward and has been stored in your soul mind from before you were born.

Verse 3: *"And cast him into the bottomless pit, and shut him up, and set a seal upon him, that he should deceive the nations no more, till the thousand years should be fulfilled: and after that he must be loosed a little season"*.

Verse 4: *"And I saw thrones, and they sat upon them, and judgment was given unto them: and I saw the souls of them that were beheaded for the witness of Jesus, and for the word of God, and which had not worshipped the beast, neither his image, neither had received his mark upon their foreheads, or in their hands; and they lived and reigned with Christ a thousand years"*.

Verse 5: *"But the rest of the dead lived not again until the thousand years were finished. This is the first resurrection"*.

What John is endeavouring to explain to us are the memories of the experiences that will release throughout your life. Some are good, and support you; others still need to earn their own rites of passage therefore they need your confidence for them to exalt their mind. This first resurrection is through the God EL, being delivered up into his next step of his own education. Now we move into the second dimensional mind where we have had to learn how we educate our self! Hence, we read of Satan breaking out again to resurrect himself through his education, so we must read the same thing over again. In other words, we are becoming more aware of the intellectual advantages we have brought forth, through becoming more emotionally balanced with each thought we release. As you can see this same explanation is out there in all religions explaining Christianity (the inner light in our own unity of self) to us, as to how we inherit this divine language to become our own church, when this word is decoded, you can now understand how our outer energy is understanding and releasing our soul's inner energy that we were seeded with before your birth. This is your programme now go forth and multiply your mind. Remember you're never alone.

Verse 6: *"Blessed and holy is he that hath part in the first resurrection: on such the second death hath no power, but they shall be priests of God and of Christ, and shall reign with him a thousand years".*

This second death explains another range of our personalities that must conform for them to enter up into the heavenly kingdom. The difference is that they have been exalted autonomically through their own education to become Priests of God.

Verse 7: *"And when the thousand years are expired, Satan shall be loosed out of his prison".* Now remember, the thousand years represent to us that—'I am my soul mind'. If we notice throughout the Chinese language, every so often they celebrate the dragon with festivals thanking him for his temperance.

Verse 8: *"And shall go out to deceive the nations which are in the four quarters of the earth, Gog and Magog, to gather them together to battle: the number of whom is as the sand of the sea".*

And the war within begins again! We start by realizing that the first God EL, has been resurrected and made holy; the second God AN, has not yet completely birthed its strength; although it is well on its way to add to its own transformation. Therefore, these thoughts, have been initiated up the ladder of our DNA, where they become Priests and will reign with their inner light, while they are thinking positively through believing in themselves, to release and live with their soul mind! This time the journey is through their meta-physical education where you are confirming to yourself, what you think is right and what you think is wrong. Your inner strength will conform to release itself through the truth that you release, which will become your strength to support you forever more!

Therefore, we see how Satan thinks it can return to try and reclaim its previous existence by gathering the Gog and Magog; which is biblically represented to us as the superior energy that has already been educated from the past. Gog and Magog represent both hemispheres of our brain; where the beast is hoping that it can use the energy of what was; which is its total consciousness, to try and impress the soul, to try and prove that it does not require any further education. Hence the number of whom is as the sand of the sea, as explained in verse 8, which denotes to us that our collective consciousness is endless.

Verse 9: *"And they went up on the breadth of the earth, and compassed the camp of the saints about, and the beloved city: and fire came down from God out of heaven, and devoured them".*

Verse 10: *"And the devil that deceived them was cast into the lake of fire and brimstone, where the beast and the false prophet are, and shall be tormented day and night forever and ever".*

Verse 11: *"And I saw a great white throne, and him that sat on it, from whose face the earth and the heaven fled away; and there was found no place for them".*

Verse 12: *"And I saw the dead, small and great, stand before God; and the books were opened: and another book was opened, which is the book of life: and the dead were judged out of those things which were written in the books, according to their works".*

Verse 13: *"And the sea gave up the dead which were in it; and death and hell delivered up the dead which were in them: and they were judged every man according to their works".*

Verse 14: *"And death and hell were cast into the lake of fire. This is the second death".*

Verse 15: *"And whosoever was not found written in the book of life was cast into the lake of fire".*

We are continuing on from the previous paragraph where we can see how Satan could only rely on its energy of the past to try and regain its control. Now you can fully understand how our illnesses create themselves. All through us hanging on to yesterday's thinking; to support our momentary thought. These deaths are explaining the death of those genes that followed Satan through not having the confidence to believe in their new found belief and of course were thrown into the fire to begin again to resurrect themselves. Once our education has released itself, we are informed that the fire is explaining to us, the word 'resurrection'; and through their resurrection these genes are in the process of becoming an extended branch of our knowledge; which in time will alternate to add and become our advanced wisdom. Our wisdom becomes the symbol for us by reminding us that the waters, which become the lakes and rivers will all drain into the oceans. The ocean is symbolically representing the complete consciousness. The following verses will explain to you the second death known to us throughout the wonder of mythology as the God AN, or Ang as it is referred to throughout the Asian principles.

Remember always that, 'the word' has now been educated and brought up through our soul's energy and has become the double-edged sword, as has been created throughout mythology; interpreting as the soul's word! As we take our next step forward, we are eternally releasing the inner education of our oracle, which will become our order, moment by moment. Hence how King Arthur could finally remove the sword from the stone! We note that his previous stone mind is now open throughout his journey of self-discovery.

Chapter 20, is informing us that we have finally formed a relationship (2) with our soul (0).

CHAPTER TWENTY ONE

Viewing Through The Mind's Eye

Verse 1: *"And I saw a new heaven and a new earth: for the first heaven and the first earth were passed away; and there was no more sea".*

Verse 2: *"And I John saw the holy city, new Jerusalem, coming down from God out of heaven, prepared as a bride adorned for her husband".*

For the first time in your life, you are now free to look through your own matrix of your inner eye; known as your third eye, or to be precise it is the eye of God as the gene sits right behind that vortex of the forehead, as your 3rd dimensional world is no longer applicable to you. It has become a previous existence. This has now become your new city of light, and is where your emotional right brain is now stepping before your left! Your left and right hemispheres are in the process of marrying into becoming one. There is no more searching through the waters of the collective consciousness, as you have finally earned the right to inherit all of it!

What we have created out there is all through the education one has received from accepting the knowledge from within.

Verse 3: *"And I heard a great voice out of heaven saying, Behold, the tabernacle of God is with men,* (your genes, which is equivalent to your previous 64 generations of your inner inheritance, known in today's language as our DNA.) *and he will dwell with them, and they shall be his people, and God himself shall be with them, and be their God".*

Verse 4: *"And God shall wipe away all tears from their eyes; and there shall be no more death, neither sorrow, nor crying, neither shall there be any more pain: for the former things are passed away".*

Verse 5: *"And he that sat upon the throne said, Behold, I make all things new. And he said unto me, Write: for these words are true and faithful".*

Verse 6: *"And he said unto me, It is done. I am Alpha and Omega, the beginning and the end. I will give unto him that is athirst of the fountain of the water of life freely".*

Verse 7: *"He that overcometh shall inherit all things; and I will be his God, and he shall be my son".*

Verse 8: *"But the fearful, and unbelieving, and the abominable, and murderers, and whoremongers, and sorcerers, and idolaters, and all liars, shall have their part in the lake which burneth with fire and brimstone: which is the second death".*

Verse 9: *"And there came unto me one of the seven angels which had the seven vials full of the seven last plagues, and talked with me, saying, Come hither, I will shew thee the bride, the Lamb's wife".*

Verse 10: *"And he carried me away in the spirit to a great and high mountain, and shewed me that great city, the holy Jerusalem, descending out of heaven from God."*

Verse 11: *"Having the glory of God: and her light was like unto a stone most precious, even like a jasper stone, clear as crystal".*

Can you understand now how the Armies and Governments over the past two thousand years had to try and capture Jerusalem? They had not yet evolved intellectually to fully understand the codes of the inner 'Divine' metaphysical language. By now you have connected yourself up into the matter of your own physics as to how you are realizing that all of these verses are explaining to you how God or these natural laws of the universe are with you for ever more. They have now become your oracle and will permanently work with and through you, for the rest of your life.

Verse 12: *"And had a wall great and high, and had twelve gates, and at the gates twelve angels, and names written thereon, which are the names of the twelve tribes of the children of Israel".*

We make note that this verse is explaining the twelve strands of the DNA unfolding its self. At the same time this verse is explaining the innocence of the twelve tribes; known as children who still have to earn their rights of passage to become Israel, (**I**ntelligence of the **S**oul **R**eleasing the **A**scension of **E**verlasting **L**ife) as explained in the Old Testament.

Verse 13: *"On the east three gates; on the north three gates; on the south three gates; and on the west three gates".*

Verse 14: *"And the wall of the city had twelve foundations, and in them the names of the twelve apostles of the Lamb".* (Our DNA).

We can see how these twelve perpetual strands of our DNA had finally earned their balance as they climbed up through their internal ladder to become the twelve Apostles of the New Testament, who are always there to assist each one of us as they live within the Light of Christ. And hopefully you can now absorb through understanding more appropriately how I have explained the information regarding the twelve tribes and the twelve Apostles in my recently released, nine revised single books previously known as *Decoding the Mind of God*.

Verse 15: *"And he that talked with me had a golden reed to measure the city, and the gates thereof, and the wall thereof".*

Verse 16: *"And the city lieth foursquare, and the length is as large as the breadth: and he measured the city with the reed, twelve thousand furlongs. The length and the breadth and the height of it are equal".*

Verse 17: *"And he measured the wall thereof, an hundred and forty and four cubits, according to the measure of a man, that is, of the angel".*

Now we become fully aware of how we release the 144,000 personalities of self that will be saved! Also, you can accept in all totality, the signs that have been left for us, through the carvings on the skull of the Golden Pharaoh of Egyptology and Lord Pacal of the Mayan prophecies.

Verse 18: *"And the building of the wall of it was of jasper: and the city was pure gold, like unto clear glass".*

Verse 19: *"And the foundations of the wall of the city were garnished with all manner of precious stones. The first foundation was jasper; the second, sapphire; the third, a chalcedony; the fourth, an emerald".*

Verse 20: *"The fifth, sardonyx; the sixth, sardius; the seventh, chrysolite; the eighth, beryl; the ninth, a topaz; the tenth, a chrysoprase; the eleventh, a jacinth; the twelfth, an amethyst".*

Verse 21: *"And the twelve gates were twelve pearls; every several gate was of one pearl: and the street of the city was pure gold, as it was transparent glass".*

Verse 22: *"And I saw no temple therein: for the Lord God Almighty and the Lamb are the temple of it".*

Verse 23: *"And the city had no need of the sun, neither of the moon, to shine in it: for the glory of God did lighten it, and the Lamb is the light thereof".*

I just love these paragraphs as they explain so beautifully how our innocence (the Lamb) is protected by God as we faithfully tread towards our goals of how we attain our inner wisdom, as we arrive at each of these 12 gates through us having earned our wisdom, which are the pearls we have earned, through what we are all here to awaken within us, as we have stepped up to earning our total attainment.

Verse 24: *"And the nations of them which are saved shall walk in the light of it: and the kings of the earth do bring their glory and honour into it".*

Verse 25: *"And the gates of it shall not be shut at all by day: for there shall be no night there".*

Verse 26: *"And they shall bring the glory and honour of the nations into it".*

Verse 27: "*And there shall in no wise enter into it anything that defileth, neither whatsoever worketh abomination, or maketh a lie: but they which are written in the Lamb's book of life*".

Now we can understand the three walls that are surrounding the Temple of Hathor in Egypt. Each face had a gateway, four per wall, times three, equals twelve gates. It depended on how many walls surrounded the Temples as to how important the message each Temple was explaining to us and to what Lesser God the information belonged to of the three, the EL-AN-EA for them to become the one God.

This amazing Temple is explaining to us the spiritual quest as to how we leave the 3rd Dimensional journey of our life and earn the right to accept the birthing of the next spiritual advancement of our life, or our advanced educated step into the unknown thought as we reach up into the unconscious mind of self. The Bible is explaining the wisdom we receive or the gems we earn through releasing our next thought where we can accept that this is our new city, which is creating itself for you, on your behalf. This information is similar to the Great Wall surrounding the Forbidden City in China, which is explaining exactly the same thing. This allows you to envisage everything your heart requires, through you accepting the language of the Divine Principle of all that is, for you to become.

These wonderful verses in this chapter explain to each of you how we have yearned to learn, how we have earned the right to wear our crown. These jewels represent the growth we have attained through the unfolding of our twelve strands of DNA. Now, do you understand the colours and symbols of each flag you march with—in the Armed Forces, the Navy, and the Air Force—as we reach up into our 'Royal Attainment'? This becomes the standard we reveal to ourselves, protecting and guarding the heavenly kingdoms.

The twelve pearls represent the wisdom we accrue through us earning our new found belief in self. Remember the jewels were manifested through us birthing our inner knowledge which became our solidified strength, from and through the earth. In other words, these jewels were our earnings from the 'Royalty of the Divine Consciousness' within each one of us. The pearls were manifested through the waters, the ultra-consciousness, hence the wisdom one receives directly from the consciousness. And where does it come from? The pearl is derived from the Oyster, which represents the inner vagina of the ocean, as we rebirth into our next kingdom through the manifestation of our own light. Remember every species of the ocean is equivalent to the mathematical outcome of the species on the earth, as they are a replica of one another.

The gates are the doorways we walk through as we strengthen our mind for us to understand how each strand of our DNA, supports us unintentionally in the beginning of our life, which will become our future inheritance through the earnings we have gained from adjusting to the Royal Order of the collective consciousness. Through our own mind we are now becoming quite capable to replicate every single thing, that has previously evolved on this planet!

All are equivalent to the twelve tribes of Israel as explained in the Old Testament; who journeyed within to release their DNA to become the twelve Apostles of their New Testament; to collect and earn these precious gems, which has become our new city of intellectual light. The Israel the bible is referring to, is not the land on the planet, it is explaining to us the gauging of the land which has become our body. Through the codex of the Sacred Geometry, Alphabet, and Language, it is the exalted inner strength we have taken the time to release through our journey of self-discovery. The word 'Israel' (**I**ntelligence – **S**oul – **R**eleasing – **A**scension – **E**verlasting - **L**ife) is situated up high in our skull above our ears, above our third eye, where it is filtered throughout our brain. Just the same as all of the countries mentioned in the bible as they explain a story we can learn and earn from.

My mind quickly returns to the Greek myth of Troy. The word 'Troy' is interpreted throughout many of the Arabic languages as the word 'truth'. London's first name was called New Troy, which is denoted through the matter of physics, as your new city of light! The fascinating thing in regards to all of the information I have written, is for me to inform you that everything that has ever been created for us to learn; is all still here to show us the way! As it was, and as it is in this moment, are all creating our future into becoming, as it will be! Rejoice my future King's and Queens, previously called Pharaoh's, you have entered up into your Palace of Worthiness.

Now you can see how the story mathematically accrues on your behalf as it threads its way throughout your body, governed throughout us by the lymphatic system. The responsibility becomes yours as to how you think each thought that we are here to attain intellectually to see how your enlightenment finally becomes alive in your mind and thoughts, which is becoming your greatest gift to apply itself within you, as you have yearned to learn to earn, why you are here reading this story.

Chapter 21, is informing us that you have finally accepted that you have formed a decisive relationship with yourself.

CHAPTER TWENTY TWO

Your Inner Library Becomes More Than Your Inner Light

Verse 1: *"And he shewed me a pure river of water of life, clear as crystal, proceeding out of the throne of God and of the Lamb".*

Verse 2: *"In the midst of the street of it, and on either side of the river, was there the tree of life, which bare twelve manners of fruits, and yielded her fruit every month: and the leaves of the tree were for the healing of the nations".*

The leaves on the tree, are the pages that we have produced of our inner library; the fruit represents the harvest of the tree, also through the nectar we attain through nourishing ourself from accepting this tree as a compatriot of self, which rearranges our choices we have had to earn to release our positive thoughts within, all through the love and respect we atone to our self now, that we understand these sacred codes of our inner language, that was instilled in our genetic inheritance before we were born.

We have finally unfurled and released the last of our inner nations; this new you, has the strength to become in charge of every new thought you think, which through the annuls of time, is autonomically reflected back out to others. This telepathic arrangement then searches to find a compatible resonance that will stimulate and rearrange their mind, as their inner mind is in attendance to enhance their next thought! Congratulations are now showered on to you, releasing the new order of your world. Not the new world order. Here is where you become the new heaven and the new earth. There are many of us who have been exalted up into this area through time, through us finding the courage to search inside ourselves, for many thousands of years! We have earned the right to stand on the shoulders of previous human, who have taught us how to open our own inner doorways to follow on from them to walk this walk before us.

Verse 3: *"And there shall be no more curse: but the throne of God and of the Lamb shall be in it; and his servants shall serve him".*

Verse 4: *"And they shall see his face; and his name shall be in their foreheads".*

Once again, allow me refresh your mind to the 144,000 personalities who will be saved, as through your codex that you have unfurled from within, as to the acceptance you have earned the right to acknowledge that, I am the relationship of my own inner temple; through freeing my temple into becoming my soul's mind. And always remember, they are the stories you were endowed with during your gestation of the last 64 generations of your tribal law which then became your DNA which then became your royal blood lines. In other words, you are able to permanently gaze into your own reflection, so please always, keep a smile on your face!

As you walk down the street, you are noticed by everyone who walks into your energy as your light that surrounds you is transmitting throughout your aura. Your aura has now expanded way out in front of you in all directions, as it has become your intellectual university always surrounding you; it is your inner light that attracts their attention. As I have travelled and spoken in over 100 nations, you would be surprised at the amount of people who turn to look me straight in the eye with a smile on their faces; then there are others that turn their face and cannot view you, owing to their own mind becoming cloudy and they walk on by. Every language on this wonderful planet speaks exactly the same dictation that is telepathically embedded in your genes. These are the twelve tribes of Israel coming together and reuniting us all for ever and ever.

Verse 5: *"And there shall be no night there; and they need no candle, neither light of the sun; for the Lord God giveth them light: and they shall reign forever and ever".*

So true, the subtle blue light is autonomically created and collected throughout the central nervous system of our own brain and body as we evolve, to release the mathematical arching of our intelligence as we earn each step of our inner ladder. Through the brain it is called the belief of Ekankha (Eternal Knowledge of the God AN —our university training- KHA which we now understand is our inner knowledge that we have earned.) All of which enables us to move forward as we open up the information that was created for every human to endow.

Once again, I will emphasize that this neural pathway has been supplied to us through our own gestation before we were born, of the cellular structure for each one of us to inherit and benefit from the knowledge our DNA has supplied to each one of us. These are the tools to our inner book we are all born with; where you now understand why the Anunnaki are seen carrying their purse mainly in their right hand. It holds the tools of their trade, their business, their future ventures that they are striving for. In today's language it is called our briefcase, that has room for every thought we need. Also, for Royalty, as to how our beloved Queen Elizabeth was trained to always carry her bag with her. Her tools of trade were always available which manifested her light for her to carry her hanky etc; also, for us to see into and through our own darkness, as there is no need to switch on the light; once ascended our inner light shows us the way! Remember the word 'Lord' (through our **L**ife's **O**racle we **R**elease the **D**ivine) is informing us of the personalities that have reached the end of our inner antenna, just like the spire on top of the church. It can view all and is free to reign over the others; It is the one who, once you have earned your entrance into the Kingdom of Heaven, guides you lovingly into your future inheritance. Now do you understand the inner truth to the story I have been explaining step by step in many of my books to you, regarding how each step of Egyptology has prepared and explained this lost city of Atlantis of the three concentric rings coming home to become our exalted mind. Our life has already been mapped out for us all to earn and become.

I explain in my Business Seminars that this is our success working and collecting the future inheritance of the business or company as we earn each positive step forward, we automatically aim for and create when we bring the nations together; in this format, these nations are those people employed for their intellectual advantages to assist the Company.

Hopefully now you can view how the hieroglyphs of Egypt have been interpreted through us decoding the 'Sacred Universal Language' for us to inherit ourselves through understanding the keys of the Divine Language and slowly over the millennium of time we have been automatically transferring and transforming the mathematics of that wonderful ancient language throughout our everyday existence. Notice, that we are still back at the beginning of humanities gestation, asking the first question ever asked? Nothing is hidden from us; you are hiding behind this information until you find the confidence to stop hiding from yourself!

Verse 6: *"And he said unto me, These sayings are faithful and true: and the Lord God of the holy prophets sent his angel to shew unto his servants the things which must shortly be done"*.

Verse 7: *"Behold, I come quickly: blessed is he that keepeth the sayings of the prophecy of this book"*.

Verse 8: *"And I John saw these things, and heard them. And when I had heard and seen, I fell down to worship before the feet of the angel, which shewed me these things"*.

Verse 9: *"Then saith he unto me, See thou do it not: for I am thy fellow servant, and of thy brethren the prophets, and of them which keep the sayings of this book: worship God"*.

Verse 10: *"And he saith unto me, Seal not the sayings of the prophecy of this book: for the time is at hand"*.

Verse 11*: "He that is unjust, let him be unjust still: and he which is filthy, let him be filthy still: and he that is righteous, let him be righteous still: and he that is holy, let him be holy still"*.

Verse 12: *"And, behold, I come quickly; and my reward is with me, to give every man according as his work shall be"*.

Verse 13: "*I am Alpha and Omega, the beginning and the end, the first and the last*".

Verse 14: "*Blessed are they that do his commandments that they may have right to the tree of life, and may enter in through the gates into the city*".

Verse 15: "*For without are dogs, and sorcerers, and whoremongers, and murderers, and idolaters, and whosoever loveth and maketh a lie*".

Verse 16: "*I Jesus have sent mine angel (your next thought) to testify unto you these things in the churches. I am the root and the offspring of David, and the bright and morning star*".

These are the keys to us understanding and earning the seven churches of Asia as written in chapter 1. We have come back to the beginning of this amazing book! Now we can accept what I have written previously in regards to Jesus and He Zeus who are now regarded as both being the first begotten of the dead. Remember through the Ancient Sanskrit Language, David is explained as Davidea, decoded he is known as the inner teacher; throughout the western nations he is known as David, as he represents the inner eye just above your eyebrows! The one who sees from within! Until you know yourself it remains hidden from your view! The bright and morning star is the preciousness of your next thought! It is always shining and available to you every second of your life. All of the cities of Israel are portals of the journey available for you to receive your own enlightenment. How precious we are, as we are all made in the likeness of God!

Verse 17: "*And the Spirit and the bride say, Come. And let him that heareth say, Come. And let him that is athirst come. And whosoever will, let him take the water of life freely*".

Verse 18: "*For I testify unto every man that heareth the words of the prophecy of this book, If any man shall add unto these things, God shall add unto him the plagues that are written in this book*".

Verse 19: "*And if any man shall take away from the words of *the book of this prophecy, God shall take away his part out of the book of life, and out of the holy city, and from the things which are written in this book".*

Verse 20: *"He which testifieth these things saith, Surely, I come quickly. Amen. Even so, come, Lord Jesus".*

Verse 21: *"The grace of our Lord Jesus Christ be with you all. Amen".*

In review of chapter 22, there it is written—Kharma—the cause of the effect. Finally, we have completed this wonderful biblical story of our own evolution. We now understand that we have formed a relationship through unravelling the keys to both our inner and outer selves—the history of the evolution of human existence.

CHAPTER TWENTY THREE

In Closing

Not an easy book to understand in the beginning, is it? And yet, the information I have written in this book brings together the soul's word, or the sword of the Biblical story together. Hopefully, I have passed on enough information to you, as to how I was taught for nine isolated years, to understand these ancient languages that have been passed down to us for thousands of years, for you to grasp the intellect in which the Bible was originally written. These words are explaining to us, through the metaphor of the hidden God, how we can begin to reveal the divine truth within and through our inner selves. The words explain how the Gematria of these mathematical codes supports and guides us, through who, what, or why, we are here to accomplish for ourselves.

I explain to my students that this wonderful book is the 'Breath of God,' revealing His divine order through an inner equation. This book, known as the recorded language of the last 64 generations of our DNA—those twelve amazing strands that strengthen our spinal column and keep us upright—explains to all of us that we are created in the image of God. Therefore, this book offers an outer perspective, showing that once you begin to understand this ancient sacred language—one that is ignited throughout our cellular structure before we are born—you uncover the complete history of humanity. It reveals the divine equation, which, in its totality, is the very essence of who you are.

More importantly these words are explaining to us what we are capable of accomplishing, when we begin to release our inner truth and turn within to know how to rectify, accept and more importantly understand how we are able to now believe in our self? The book of Revelations, is taking you through the journey of your underworld; this all relates to the world of your ego. It is the journey of the intellectual quest where we are placed in our inner seminary to reunite with Amon Re; whose name was explained throughout the Egyptian Philosophies as the 'hidden one'. We now know that this is through the processing of the pineal gland, also known to us as the eye of God! Therefore, the eye of God is watching over you every moment of your existence.

Remember, five hundred years ago, Nostradamus spoke of the information coming from the heavens. Now you are aware that the heavens are the upper echelon which is the impregnated educated mind of self! It is the crown of your glory, not the sky as we know it to be. The more we look to the self for our own answers, the more we begin to understand this hidden language, that has been embedded within every human.

As we release the inner light through understanding and accepting our intelligence, we will understand the opulence of this hidden language that is embedded in each one of our genes. If we could only realise that through the importance of self; is, the main character that we will answer and live up to.

My hope is that you have found comfort in my words where you are able to allow the language of your unconscious mind to release its wisdom that has been furled in your cells; otherwise, you would not have found the courage to stay with my words to be reading this paragraph.

Remember that the word 'Metaphor' is a sacred word; which continues to become a metaphoric connection to every cell throughout the totality of the collective consciousness. This is explaining the essence of us all becoming one! As we have the greatest responsibility to respect and look after those who have walked before us; there comes a time when you realize that they are not there anymore! They have become you, which gives you the freedom to walk towards knowing that the soul's word answers to both the left and the right hemispheres of the brain, as they have become one. These hemispheres are referred to throughout the myth as the lamb and the beast. It is explaining to us the matter of our phosphorus; our inner light! As the movie Avatar informs us that we can all inherit the mineral 'Unobtainium' where our tree of knowledge and wisdom, keeps on opening up into the heavens.

We may be a third dimensional species if that is your choice to believe; please remember that this is only the first step to attaining our inner **b**asic **i**nformation **b**efore leaving **e**arth. Our inner dimensions are waiting to be released; they are curled in on themselves and are protected by each layer of intelligence we release. The more we release, the more they have the opportunity to unfurl. Do you recall the story of the pine tree? These are the same explanations as the book of Revelations. We are multiplying our intellect where we become more globally aware. We view everything from a greater height; where we can understand the past which enables us to extend our peripheral vision and see further into our own future! We can understand why so many countries use the symbol of the eagle for their own comfort. We learn to see through each moment, not just look at! Why not view all through the energetic eyes of your soul! You are never too old, you're just too lazy.

To bring all of this information back into a language that our children can understand; these stories become a greater reason for them to be educated; to go to school where they are on their way to be learning how to open up their inner education; which will become their future intelligence. It is the future generation that we must protect; as they have the responsibility of continually creating life on this planet, for their children to inherit; after we have returned back home to the source. It is no good when we are in heaven, to think about what we should have done!

Heaven is right here just above the earth; it is connected to you; it is the inside mathematical intelligence of what has been downloaded into your head! Your body is the earth!

Therefore, you are both the heavens and the earth! It is all happening right here, in this God given moment! Hence it is all up to us to place ourselves up into our own personal heavenly kingdom; or the metaphorical connection which some have interpreted as the afterlife, in the here and now! Throughout the explanations regarding the matter of physics that I have written throughout all of my books; you have been given the keys to your inner kingdom. The secrets have been revealed to you! Become the scribe, where you can release your written word to write and unite!

Disease becomes prevalent, when the mind is repeated or has become idle. Teach your children how to release the antennas of their thoughts up and out into the cosmos where they can learn to attain these natural laws, which will release and free their inner cosmos to understand how they can guide themselves as well as their confirmed personalities in the direction they can aim for. Don't keep them hidden, they become barren and fester when ignored and not in use! As my grandmother wrote in my first diary on my ninth birthday 'Aim for the highest, there is room at the top'. Change and advance their thoughts into regarding the word 'education'.

Please remember the illusion of what we create through our thinking, is reflected back into our children. History is someone else's story; and yes, we attract to ourselves the reflection of their thoughts; where we can mirror the inner light within ourselves to become the mirror of the universe! More importantly, teach them how to yearn, to learn, to earn their own inheritance. Make them feel permissible, to be accepted here. You are becoming more aware of how the child births the child; the innocent thought autonomically attracts the next innocent thought! Every one of us is right, and living what we think is right to the best of our own intelligence.

Remember the words of Kahlil Gibran who explains in his wonderful little book 'The Prophet' that you are your child's bow, and they are your arrows. Aim them in the right direction, for them to aim for their own target to release themselves. Remember the string on the bow has to be pulled back towards yourself, for the arrow to fly in the right direction.

I have read the last book of the Bible, so many times through my earnings of the codes, for all of us to create our freedom to move up into the next dimension of time, through my understanding of the book of Revelations that was delivered to us from St. John the Divine.

All of this written information is the totality of how we earn our intelligence; to become unified with and through the wholeness of the collective. That is why I had to write my first book *Decoding the Mind of God* which has now been updated and revised into nine single books, as that is what the younger minds have asked for, before I could release this information regarding Revelations to you. Otherwise, you would not have understood a word that I had written. Yes, I had to confront the seven headed ten horned Beast; this went on for years in my life, until I could finally release my old beliefs into accepting this higher wisdom, which happened slowly through me recognizing the intellectual light that awaits us through the deliverance of our unconscious mind. There was no one around to assist me only myself! My right arm shot towards the heavens when I trembled, asking to be shown the road home. The more I understood the pages of the past, the more I could reimburse back to myself what the order of God had placed before my eyes. This information that the fish of the oceans of consciousness, the animals, birds, trees and the wind were whispering to me, the more I quickly climbed above the knowledge that my teachers explained to me. Now it is written and explained to the future generations where they have this information to guide them as they yearn to look at, how they can learn to see into, to earn the view I am presenting to them now.

Remember that we reach the 'Pinnacles of our Divine Unity' when we have opened our heart to our self; and that is when we have brought the other two Gods of EL and AN, up into the EA, through us all becoming the collected energy of God. St. John the Divine, represents when taken back through the codes, that he was originally referred to as a teacher of light through the recognition of him searching his unconscious mind; which is where we are taught through the light of our intellect that we produce from within. Through the Arabic language 'Saint John, the Divine' is known as 'Your Highness', also referred to as the melody or language of the alchemy of our brain. All when we understand the 'Arcing of the Covenan' that every human has automatically made with God; it is through this understanding that we have the possibilities of re-nurturing this wonderful heavenly home, which we refer to as our body.

I believe everything is energetically connected to the power of how we prepare and release our next thought, where we have the opportunity to release from our collective inheritance for us to receive the benefit of our own growth. It is like the stories that have been handed down from generation to generation and from father to son. No! We are not there yet; but we are well on the way to releasing the truth of the Hidden God.

I emphasize to my students that when they hesitate to search beyond and are afraid to release their next step, they must trust themselves. I say to them, "I don't want to hear excuses or what your ego demands of you. I want to be able to view your inner confidence you are earning within yourself. I want to feel your passion for the responsibility you are taking upon yourself, where it is vibrating continuously through your aura. I want to view the colours you produce—your inner rainbow—just like the story of Joseph (once decoded is yourself) and his coat of many colours that his mother made for him."

Your colours are created through your matrix collecting its supersonic equivalent, through you attaining your PHI (the **P**ower of your **H**eavenly **I**ntelligence) where it becomes its own sound. This we refer to as the arching of our brain, where two equals sides begin to take responsibility for one another, which create the light waves throughout the eternal consciousness where both hemispheres of left and right brain, create a balance of perpendicular motion through the acceptance of one another earning their inner and outer of our internal balancing as one. The result is the creation of where we have earned our eternal balance throughout our mind; which releases and sends out through our aura, the harmonic convergence as to what has already occurred; all of which adds to the collective and autonomically (self-governing) mathematically changes and rearranges our intellectual reality.

Let us take a brief look at the waves that are consciously created on our behalf. Quantum mechanics, through our internal mathematics, releases DNA into a spiral movement, where we release the vibrational energy that enhances our colour spectrum. These quantum waves continuously emerge from previous thoughts, retracing their past in an autonomous cycle to shape a futuristic pathway. When accepted, this path becomes a highway—one that we can traverse to prepare ourselves and, more importantly, attract knowledge to our inner dictionary. These thoughts, having already been assessed and prepared, become available for our future. They become our inner administrative office that works on behalf of our collector station, autonomically ascending each thought into the unconscious mind. Standing waves create reality—yet reality is only created in the present moment, an instantaneous reaction that strengthens and solidifies the spire of our inner church, our internal antenna, that travels through the length and breadth of the complete cosmos!

In other words, our reality is kept alive, only through our constant reminder from the divine energy to keep believing in self!

If you can climb this high in your mind and understand that this is the beginning of you earning your collective freedom, which is your mind, body as well as your soul, then you are worthy of all that God is; you become attached to the '**G**reatest **O**rder of the **D**ivine—your Heavenly Mind,' as to what these Natural Laws have in store for you. You're all of it! This is also equivalent to the arching of your covenant. You're making this commitment to yourself. That is why you are here and what your life is all about.

Please remember throughout our blood lines, we automatically herald our story on to the next generation where the mistakes we have created are autonomically threaded through, into their DNA. All through one non-productive thought; where we did not have the faith in ourselves to carry it through into its creation; therefore, it has not been finalized. It builds and collects its own positive energy; where that process interacts with the matrix of the Divine Consciousness. This energy must be inherited to concede or coincide for it to codify into the next positive reaction, or generation. This adds time to quantification; where theories of space and time are relatively announced and then must be lived! The word 'Heredity' is explaining our genetic inheritance at work here!

Space is exuded from the right hemisphere of the brain; it is created through a repose of the emotions answering up to its own responsibility. The etheric web is autonomically created in every one of us! No one has been left out! This web must connect to all of its mosaic to be brought together for us to equate with one another, within this field of cosmic activity. If this is not adhered too, it sets an implosion into a like-minded catastrophe, which must always reach its peak of perfection through the results of understanding its own antenna.

This cosmically relaxes the body, which allows through compatibility, the magnification of change through our DNA for us to rebalance our self. Our energy can then reverberate to release our written word. We never run out of intelligence, as this allows for our inner order or the manifested aura in our cells, to reach up and out to assist us which supplies us with our inner strength, as we inhale and draw in our next breath.

The written word releases our next mathematical stage alphabetically, according to our own personal levels of understanding; also, through relaxing our mind is when we enhance our energy to supersede our intellect into releasing the next positive thought. Through this endeavour we become more aware of our possibilities that are on standby waiting for us to inherit!

The vibrations of what we term feelings, are at first stimulated and triggered through our pituitary gland and begin to release the pressure within our heart, which raises our inner temperature; all of which alerts the variations of our DNA; where our personalities that we have inherited from our past can reform to release our alignment with our inbuilt heavenly activities. The generations of the past can now flow peacefully through us, as we take our next precious step forward.

Now you can understand how you are clearing the incurred debt of those past family members who were less fortunate than yourself! All of which attracts the next written word which is automatically registered and released within the electromagnetic fields of our inner dictionary, through its magnetism to adjust to like mind. Energy attracts attention, which occurs through the mirror of its collective understanding of, like attracts like, which speeds up the conduitive responses where they have become disentangled through our previous fears as to how they are able to release themselves.

To create a permanent balance which harmonizes the mind, is through the creation of the magnetic field that surrounds each one of us; this field rebounds through the electrical fields that collects through the beat of our heart, which sends through its correlation on the subject at hand, as it connects systematically to the brain, once our heart has been opened through the awakening of us understanding the importance of our DNA.

This new belief in self, enhances the heart to create change throughout their consensus with one another. This is our magnetics at work, which in an instant, reverses the atoms psychology. As you bring positive change into your thoughts, automatically your inner world is autonomically changing and rearranging, all by itself. We become aware of how we are allowing our consciousness the space; or how we earn the right for our anti-matter to search for its own compatibility, which is how the mirror creates the illusion, all of which stimulates the reflection to appear! It is then given the opportunity to extend itself; which collects and works through our heart beat, through the trust and belief we have manifested all through us finally understanding ourself. As we change, so too does our inner universe equate and rebalance through these changes.

Please remember, as we think a positive thought, we are automatically creating our intellectual light; this light is photonic energy that searches for compatibility where it is cosmically attracted through one thought expanding and multiplying itself; always in the spiral which once was a circle where the internal mathematics broke the chain to allow our consciousness to release its essence or for our illuminated soul, to magnify itself to allow for its own expansion. With an open heart I give my eternal thanks to you, for reading through to the end of this chapter.

Chapter 23 delves into our evolving value regarding our redefined thinking and the relationship we have realigned within our minds—how we earn wisdom through both inner and outer perspectives, through the metamorphosis of our inner character as we birth up into the branch of Philosophy, through attaining our metaphysical existence and knowledge.

CHAPTER TWENTY FOUR

Final Synopsis

Now for the final conclusion where I can incorporate the codes of Egyptology, the Mayan and Greek myths, the Asian Philosophies, the stories of the Bible and the Medical Agenda to bring the story together to coincide with the freedom we can earn for ourselves. A code was recently brought to my attention that gave me confirmation to know that I could research deeper to find further confirmation to an answer I have known for many years.

I have added it here, at the end of the book. To me it is most relevant as it brings our journey into understanding that religion and science are one! We can see how the elders of the past brought the story down from the unconscious mind through to the right hemisphere of the brain, which extended the belief of the message over to the responsibility of our left hemisphere, which is our logic action or ego, to explain to us how we are here to learn to stop the ego running rampant with our thoughts and to bring it under control.

I found that step one of this endeavour begins by showing us how and why we dream, as this same identical language is embedded within each gene. We dream only when the ego is at rest! A dream is delivered to us through the unconscious mind, which stems from the energy of our soul. It is passed down to the right hemisphere which in turn transmogrifies (which transfigures through metamorphoses) the message to our ego, while it is resting in its own abeyance.

Once we make this commitment to understand ourself from within and have released the information that is embedded in our genes, is when we have an inner knowing that we have earned the right to keep our ego under control. Therefore, we become more aware, whilst we are in a state of dreaming!

Our third eye opens us up into the quantum of mathematics, where it becomes the mind's eye, when we have earned the right for the pineal gland to shed its own hymen, as the information begins to herald down to us in and through this 'Ancient Biblical Language', we begin to realise where we earn a perpetual balance through our collective understanding. It becomes our hologram, as it explains to us how our dedication to understand and accept this—Metaphysical Inner Journey—releases the information of our cellular inheritance, where our left and right hemisphere are finally drawn closer as they are in an abeyance to one another. All in exaltation to the marriage of Canaan where Jesus supposedly turned the water into wine. As both hemispheres begin to connect through their commitment to one another through harmonizing and rebalancing with each other, we become aware of an inner peace, which sets off a chain reaction throughout our whole body, all of which expands our inner sight, which then adds to becoming our inner light! Now that is the end of our inner Armageddon. This ancient language was spoken and scribed at this time of our evolution and somewhere along the line we have misplaced it or maybe through our innocence we have not fully grasped the consequences to understand and accept it, for us to step up to inherit it! And yet! If the truth be known, we all have been aware, it is there!

This is why it is so hard for many of you to understand when reading the hieroglyphs in Egypt that there were no wars between the people! The unconscious language can only be released from a balanced mind; therefore, there is no detriment to deter another human being. Every mythical story is alerting us to the fact that the only war being explained is the one going on within yourself as you climb your own ladder to attain your entrance up into the heavenly abode!

To 'kill' albeit the killing of many interprets through the sacred language, to retrain the personalities that are not willing to change their ways. Allow me to again explain through the Sacred Alphabet, the word 'kill' once interpreted, is explaining to us that, through our inner **K**nowledge, we earn our **I**ntelligence through **L**iving through us understanding the importance of our inner **L**ife.

Our inner knowing is releasing more of the hidden agenda of our genes and cellular structure of our DNA, that we were seeded with during our gestation, as we unfurl the codes of the hidden language through us elevating our mind up into the top rungs of our inner ladder, which autonomically occurs as we learn to accept and adhere to, through the results of us understanding our inner knowing. This wonderful word 'autonomic' has released itself to you through what you have created through your inner strength to endow you to each miracle you have created and earned. The combined efforts of this awakening are through the program of the Sacred Geometry and Numerology, working hand in hand in regards to the date you were born, which is the inner program of you, as to how your soul entered you, to assist you with throughout your personal journey, for you to become totally aware of the seeding created through you, of you accepting the inner structure of your inner earth.

As your numbers reach up to balance your intelligence, you begin to open up portals of your inner time zones, for you to reform the next thought you are about to think. Remember in the Old Testament, King Nebuchadnezzar explained to us that the days of our kingdom are numbered. Our kingdom is the inheritance we yearn to learn and earn, through us understanding this silent voice of our inner kingdoms. Just as St. John has foretold, through us understanding ourselves throughout the Book of Revelation, that we are revealing to ourselves our inner nations. Exactly the same as every story that is recorded in every Bible of the world. Now that is worth shouting from the rooftops: "Peace in our earth will come to stay, when we live our inner self every day!"

Now you can understand why a myth is still carried forward to this day. We still have not understood the reasoning of the initial story to begin with! At that time each story was passed on in the third person in cryptic form. Every picture told a story! Why? We remembered them. And yet we still did not know the reasoning behind or understand how it came into being. In today's language we are bringing through information in the first person, not the third; step by step as our intelligence has matured since that time, we have been brought a step closer to revealing the truth of all.

There are millions of stories written explaining the mythology of the human strain, which has served their purpose in any given moment to give strength to those in need. Everything that has been forwarded down to us is a story explaining each person's thought in each moment as to how they can become more aware of how to counterbalance their mind. That is the science being explained to us through the writings on the walls of Egypt!

I had to wait thirty-five years before I could release some of the codes to this answer. Everything had to be added correctly and then reversed back to the instant point of conception before my learned truth could release the information. One of my questions to the universe was whether I had correctly positioned the seven seals. I had realised they corresponded to vital glandular sections and needed to understand their role in connecting us to heavenly realms. I knew the only path forward was through earning these codes, allowing our inner intelligence to unfold them. Layer by layer, I had to receive the information to reveal the truth. It took years of difficulties for me to change my thinking completely and clarify my understanding enough to experience genuine self-satisfaction. These seven seals are clasped onto the back of the book, as referenced in chapter 5, verses 1 through 14.

I realised that they were a continuation of our 'Master Glandular System'. I had also come to the conclusion that these seven seals were the combined effort of the seven cervical vertebrae of our upper spine situated in our neck area as we journeyed from the earth up into the heavenly realms or an earlier rendition as explained through Egyptology as in that time, they referred to it as the afterlife.

This is where the metaphysics of our inner journey loses contact with our previous third dimensional reality, as we begin to accept the added responsibility of earning the rights to delve into the education of our next advanced step, where time works with and through us, instead of us trying to create unnecessary time. They are in connection to the seven sacred or heavenly steps through my understanding of the inner science of Egyptology, which they refer to as the Seven Bands of our Inner Peace.

Now hopefully you can understand the codex of the seven

layers in the great pyramid above the Kings Chamber in Giza, which is explaining to us the final outcome of our journey of us entering up into the royal chambers of our upper levels of us earning our own enlightenment. These seven levels are explaining the exalted pathway between the earth, our body and the heavens, our head!

Also, with the recent finding of the water storage beneath the pyramid, which represents the complete consciousness of the water of those who do not fully understand or know themselves. Now do you realise what the largest pyramid is referring to us, through us earning the intellectual advantage of trusting in ourself through us yearning, to learn, the results of where we can earn, how the keys cohabitate with one another to unlocking our DNA, of us understanding the last 64 generations of our internal inheritance, which becomes our Judicial Kingdom within. So far, through my understanding of this pyramid, it is explaining to us the power point of our spiritual journey that many are making at this time of accepting layer by layer the stratum of the upper echelons before we have fully completed our own personal enlightenment.

Over the years since I first began structuring this book, my intelligence has opened to fill in the gaps. Over the last fifteen years, I have seen my initial writings in a new light. As previously explained in this book, I now believe my updated findings confirm what was revealed in chapter 4, verses 7 through 9— the four beasts etched onto the outer casing of the small pyramid, is in reference to the role our ego blunders its way through to us innocently beginning our journey through life. The middle pyramid, represents our experiences—which is explaining how we live our life through the experiences we create as we try to learn from these indelible excuses we have created for ourselves. And now, standing before us, is the master pyramid of the Pharaoh, KHU FU (Khufu). When decoded, this word or name is alerting us to the fact that through our inner knowing combining with our **K**nowledge through our **H**eavenly **U**nderstanding, that we have gained through understanding the metaphysical language, to add to this endeavour, we have now earned our **F**reedom to **U**nderstand who we truthfully are, all through the earnings we are revealing to ourself! Now you know exactly why and whatever we are here to understand, is for us to accomplish, all by ourselves!

It was during my last trip to Egypt that everything slowly started to fall into place. Over the years I had enjoyed many conversations with this wonderful man named George, who was an Elder of the Coptic Religion when he explained to me their belief, where I understood his rendition perfectly as he still spoke the language of the unconscious mind, which he found hard to believe that I understood him so perfectly, as this was the way my Masters of Time explained this epic story in cryptic form to me. Here was the beginning of my interpretation, of the confirmation I needed to know that I had been on the right track all along, oh, so many years ago. In the beginning of my training through the studies I had been exonerated with through my Masters of Time from the Mantisoid Connection of Cosmology, it was explained to me that we had seven bands pertaining to the Indo Asian belief known to them as chakras. These bands circulated the body and as our intellect began to unfurl itself, these bands snapped open to release the strictures that through the threading of our DNA, had been innocently placed around ourself! The last band is situated around the thyroid gland up through the throat area into the facial structure of our mouth to our ears and eyes; known as the doorway to our heavenly abode and is referred to as the band of us attaining our peace to ever-lasting life.

I realised that I was into an area that needed to be more defined for my own satisfaction. It was deemed of great importance to me where I just had to allow my intuition the opportunity to lead me through these hidden codes of the sacred language, for me to bring the story together. George explained the information to me as the seven heavenly steps or to bring it into today's language, Egyptology refers to it now as the seven bands of peace we attain throughout our own journey to discover our own enlightenment. I have all the confidence in the world now to explain in my written agenda, that they are symbolically representing our glandular systems at work, that are situated in our neck area. as to how they were brought up thousands of years ago to be measured by the Masters of Time. Again, it is the explanation of the hieroglyphic language threaded throughout the Egyptian Philosophies.

Remember that the medical sciences are heralded down to us from the Latin language which was a sub branch of the metaphysical language in the beginning. As that was the way the educated minds spoke at that time. May I also remind you that symbolism is the next encounter of our intelligence releasing itself! This geometrical behaviour is explaining the advanced state of mathematics to firstly the right hemisphere, which relays the message on to the left hemisphere for us to absorb. It was when I realized that the colours of the pyramids of white, red and black that my mind clicked together as to where I had heard the similarities of these colours before? Yes, it was in this book that I thought I had nearly finished! Chapter 6 reveals the opening of the first six seals. The horses that are mentioned in reference to the Apocalypse, represent our inner spiritual strength; they are the same three colours of White, Red, and Black. These same colours also correspond to the presented to us. You can now see how the Apocalypse is explaining the journey we take to open these seals. Once correctly understood, this code has the potential to change the face of history in time. Please allow us the privilege to understand and accept the role we have the confidence in self to inherit, we're worth it.

There are seven sections of Lower Egypt that have a direct line of pyramids which can be seen from one section to the next. We begin with number one, Meidum; number two is Dahshur; third is Saqqara; the fourth is Abu Seer; the fifth is Abu Ghurab; the sixth section is the three known pyramids of Giza and the seventh is Abu Rauch. Although many additional pyramids lie within this final band of energy we release, they are not aligned in a continuous visible line like these seven. We note that all of these pyramids are situated (represented) in the glands above our heart area. The word 'gland' was first introduced to us by the Greek, Herophilus in 300 BC, which I have always referred to as God's land and is a term used to describe the mesenteric lymph nodes, which we know is one of the most ancient sections of the vertebrates. We are more aware that our lymphatic system, is what I refer to, as God's umbrella, as it is relayed completely throughout our body. Therefore, we note how the heart is earning its opening through each individual seal attaining its own freedom. These seals are in an alignment to the homes of the twelve strands of our DNA which houses the tribes of our past intelligence, for us to become ever-lasting life. These tribes are revealed to us in chapter seven which is continued further on.

Number 1: The pyramid at Meidum is known as the black pyramid, where we note that scattered around this pyramid are millions of shards of flint, which Egyptologists explain were brought into the area and scattered around the pyramid. Meidum is situated five miles south of Saqqara. It began as a seven-step pyramid which over time, four of them have disintegrated to where we see a sixty-five-meter cube with two steps on top, so there are only three steps remaining. If I take you back into the sanctity of numbers we are metaphorically being informed of the seven seals. Could this pyramid be the foundation stone to initiate us up into these sacred steps of unclasping the seals on the back of the book of our own DNA?

At this time of the human strain there are three steps remaining which is alerting us to our mind. We note the cube and fully understand that everything begins mathematically with the cube! Shamanically the symbol of the cube is representing the closed mind. The innocent one who still does not understand its own mind!

Here we note the introduction into these seven seals. Could this pyramid also represent the first resurrection where we leave our old world behind to begin our new? The Alpha and Omega. The end of one world to create new beginnings? These shards of flint could also represent our old thoughts that will be resurrected to make their way into the new? The first seal is being introduced to us as it begins to unclasp itself from the back of the book.

Number 2: The pyramid at Dahshur was supposedly built for Synofru, now known as Snefru who was supposedly the father of Khufu, as it was transcribed into English. "He who makes me perfect!" Here again was confirmation that I was on the right track in regards to the three main pyramids above Cairo, with the Head of God above them. My goodness, shades of how I had begun to understood the codes through the sacred language, explained to me in the Chinese language! I explain in my previous works that the ancient word 'syn' or 'sin' in both the German and the Arabic language is the relationship to us hanging on to the past! Again, please allow me to remind you of the symbolism behind the words *"Forgive me Father for I have sinned"*. This interprets as: 'forgive me Father for living in yesterday's thinking'. This word when spoken in syllables in the Arabic language is meant to relate to the nourishment and nurturing of self. We are understanding that our DNA must always be aligned and balanced from here on in. As we receive, so shall we give! Some of my learned Coptic Egyptologist friends refer to it as the area of harmony and balance which is along the same mind. I have heard the same story being repeated to me by my learned colleagues in the University of Languages in Beijing. To accomplish this information, we must remember that we are our inner spiritual self as well as our outer logic self. This pyramid is white in colour. There were no mistakes made when this pyramid was created. It is explaining to us how it was meant to be!

Now let us return to the beginning of this book and look at the opening of the first seal in the Book of Revelation in chapter 6, verse 2, explains itself thus: *"And I saw, and behold a white horse; and he that sat upon him had a bow; and a crown was given unto him; and he went forth conquering, and to conquer"*. When decoded, this is the beginning of us collecting our inner spiritual strength, as that is what the emotional species of the horse represents. The bow is what we need to aim our arrows, and remember our arrows are our thoughts in motion. The crown is the gift we will earn. Hopefully by now you can relate to what the horse represents in this ancient sacred language? The orators at that time were explaining to us that the horse symbolically is your inner light collecting its own strength! Many of us have visions or dreams of horses, which is how the universal law reminds us of what is important in our life in this moment. The second seal is beginning to unfold from the back of the book.

Verse 3: *"And when he had opened the second seal, I heard the second beast say, Come and see"*.

Verse 4: "And there went out another horse that was red: and power was to him that sat thereon to take peace from the earth, and that they should kill one another: and there was given him a great sword".

The third step is the next pyramid which was red, is situated around two miles north of the white pyramid. You are now aware that the 'Great Sword' is representing the soul's word, as you begin the journey into the heavenly realms, as it is also representing the sanctity of the thoughts you are manifesting through you discovering your own 'Divine Mind'. It is now the divine language that begins to speak through us. The point to remember is that these pyramids were placed in areas where they were grouped together to represent your glandular system, which begins in the upper body as they would follow the ley lines to distribute the energy to your lymphatic system which connects and controls the rest of your body. We have now entered up into the arena of the third (your mind) seal clasped on the back of the book.

Number 3: Verse 5: *"And when he had opened the third seal, I heard the third beast say, Come and see. And I beheld, and lo a black horse and he that sat on him had a pair of balances in his hand".*

Verse 6: *"And I heard a voice in the midst of the four beasts say, A measure of wheat for a penny, and three measures of barley for a penny; and see that thou hurt not the oil and the wine".*

The opening of the third seal is in relationship to our mind and is where we move up into the area of Saqqara which is known through the teachings of the Coptic Religions as the step we take as we move up into the 'Seal of Vibrations'. I believe that this seal is being introduced to us in the readings of chapter 14, and each following chapter right up to chapter 20 is explaining each step of these seven seals. Chapter 21 is explaining the crown we have earned as we enter through the twelve gates into the creation of our new temple which will become our new heaven and earth, as the twelve strands of our DNA have finally come home to be available to us for ever more. The final chapter is sending out an invitation for others to release their own strength and lead themselves into their own promised land.

This seal or gland is explaining how we begin to re balance and harmonize both hemispheres of our brain, so please bear with me. It is here where we are altering the gravitational pull of the body as our energy supercharges itself up towards the intelligence of our unconscious mind. It was at this time during my own journey when my watch kept advancing up to four hours per day. I would set it correctly the next morning and by the end of the day it had advanced another four hours. I realized that I was pulling myself away from my own gravity fields as my intellect was advancing. It all depended on what fields of intellect I was working in. And to this day I cannot wear a watch. Many of my students also had this same experience as they climbed their own internal ladder of awakening. They were very surprised and expressed their jubilation when I explained the reasoning of their inner educational growth to them.

While we are continually living our life without a care in the world looking for others to support us, the forces of gravity prohibit this climb. It is after we have opened our heart to ourselves that our DNA begins to vibrate to its own inner frequencies and vibrations, the closer it extolls its own virtue towards the heavenly realms. This is why my Arabic students always place their right hand over their forehead and say to me "I will see you through my heart for ever more". They have not forgotten their importance of this ancient information, where as we are still trying to recall it!

It is also in this area where our sound is autonomically created through the importance of how we are releasing our inner alphabet. This sound once it becomes announced vibrates up through the pituitary gland where it is constantly measured for the truth in our information. Once mathematized the information is sent either into the left hemisphere or right hemisphere of our brain. Left we must live the same experience again and the right is threading the information throughout the brain. Aren't we an amazing marvel?

Allow me to explain more information regarding this equation.

As you begin to ark your thoughts up through your DNA—it begins to ignite itself through the memories stored in your seven seals. As each seal is opened the frequencies that omit from the seal begin to awaken the next seal. Just like us learning our scales when we begin to sing. I began with humming; from the hum I learned to open my mouth and chanted the name of Aum which allowed the sound to produce itself. Now we can gather a clearer picture regarding the Egyptian theories of these two seals, glands or pyramids, creating the double harmony in the helix of our DNA. Once I could feel the sound correcting itself; it ignited the glands in my neck area to begin with, which then enhanced the ripple effect through every cell in my body which released my intellectual light to open up more of the DNA. These are natural refractions that occur in your personal universe which is explaining how your DNA arcs your intellect up through these clasps on the back of your book of life, for you to view how each page opens to produce your coat of many colours just like Joseph wore.

The Australian Aborigines speak of this inner sound as their song lines. They are out there threaded throughout the universe and are waiting for us to connect with them. This super organism is known as the global DNA. There is more on this subject in my previous book titled, *Decoding the Shaman Within*. When they are trekking in the outback, they listen to the pitch of their inner sound to know if they are on the right track. It is a powerful education regarding telepathic communication and the quieter you can control your mind the more you, autonomously tune into your original sound. Remember our genes mutate at a faster rate through us using the same alphabet that our previous generation used. Once again, the codes remind us that we can only follow on from the last three generations and then the genes begin to collapse, which allows them to become their future residence, where they can restructure themselves through our genetic adaptations stimulating our DNA, where our patterns begin to merge as they adhere through positive change. Through this change we are being reminded of the reason we are here, where we learn to depend on ourselves, not rely on the previous memories of the ones who walked before us! The universe is an enormous quantum computer where we find everything is beginning to become an earning, not just a learning!

The mind that babbles on can't produce its own sound, as there is too much endless chatter or unnecessary thinking jamming up the moment. The sound collects itself mathematically when we focus our intention on self only and not others. The purer our sound is exonerated the clearer the thought is heard by others. Why? This sound is released from your unconscious mind. The more you practice how to silence your mind, the more you embed yourself into becoming your own home. All of which creates your sonic sound, where it has earned its freedom without hesitation to roam the cosmos.

The mathematics then threads its way back through your glandular system to prepare you for your next equation. Once you have journeyed up into the heavenly realms, you begin to realize as well as accept, that time is no longer of any importance, as the gravitational pull has been altered through your unconscious thinking which continually resets your inner mind through the beat of your heart.

It is also known throughout the Egyptian philosophies as the 'City of the Dead' as the findings are explained in today's language that it was previously an ancient burial ground. Do you understand how this name came into being? You are entering up into the heavenly realms to begin your new life therefore, the past thinking is no longer of any use to you, therefore it is dead; in other word's it is no longer applicable to your future life. This means that your old personalities that relied on others must now resurrect into the new. There is no room for false acclaim or value up here, therefore you can no longer rely on your past as your mind must always be moving forward towards the next horizon. The dolphins were my teachers into this sacred area of the teachings, as they are the precursor to the whales. As previously mentioned, the dolphins vibrate to the 'freedom' the wisdom warrior will earn; and the whales vibrate to the sound of the unconscious mind of 'conversation and communication'.

Do you recall my previous explanations on our DNA, which is housed in the upper chest area, where we connect into the consciousness of the water? Here is the proof that you require. Some tomb carvings in Egypt depict fishermen hauling their catch into the boats, with recognisable shapes of fish, dolphins and whales. What do fish represent? They represent our next thought! We have entered up into the area of P'tah, who is known as the Apostle Peter throughout the Bible. Remember St Peter's Basilica in Rome is our Temple explaining the same information as the Egyptians regarding the opening of the heart ceremony!

Oh! So much information is unfolding—I hope you are keeping up with me, as we earn the right to bring this wonderful story of ourselves together. Remember, the last strands of your ego may resist this understanding if it is still living in the letter 'I' instead of evolving into 'I AM'. It will automatically try to retard this wisdom to regain control over you. Hold its hand and take your time, respecting every moment you have earned for yourself. Do not deny what your own intuition has acclaimed in its innocence of understanding itself! Now, you can honour yourself as you recognize how the Lamb had to grow into the Ram (eses I, II, III)—or is it in relationship to Isis? Also, remember that in Arabic, there are no vowels in the written language. I give my eternal thanks to the great minds of those who walked before us, who came from many different languages to explain their insights so that we may continue forward today.

Another important point to remember is the significance of the obelisks. In this area, the largest obelisk was carved from the rock, serving as a profound reminder that these distinguished monuments symbolize the antennas of the mind. Why here? It is at this third seal that the two hemispheres of the brain begin to unify, allowing us to become one, a singular mind—hence its immense size. Now, remind yourself of the wedding in Cana of Galilee, where Jesus turned water into wine.

These huge monuments were usually built in pairs, where they are representing the double helix of our DNA, to continue on to both the left and right hemispheres of the brain. The script on each obelisk is a recorded history of how the personalities or Gods were trained through the glandular system to unfurl our DNA to enable us to reach up into the heavens. And this we see with the point that was carved on the top of the obelisk to pierce through the layers of our past inheritance to point our way up into heavenly abode. We note that the stories of Rameses had nine obelisks one for each God x 3. Now that is progress! Each one of the three Gods, the EL, the AN and the EA, had completed its own evolution!

We also note that there are seven obelisks still standing in Egypt. There are thirteen in Rome and ten in the USA. Also, many other countries have some as well. Now go back through your codes in my revised book, *Decoding the Sacred Alphabet and Numerology,* to understand the reasons why!

It was in the pyramid that the disc was found with a few other things besides. My research into my own personal experiences explain to me that this disc is representing the winged disc. At the time of symbolically birthing my own wings I was out in the desert accomplishing my own education through opening up my heart to become an elder. I felt the pain quite severely each time my vertebrate separated to allow the knuckles to release themselves.

As my visions occurred, I received the winged disc spinning and as it did so, the wings naturally started to lift and flap. The Egyptian symbol of the Gods for this glandular area is the man's body with the head of the crow. The crow throughout the sacred codes represents the 'Keeper of the Sacred Laws'. Also remember that in this pyramid the small carving of a bird with a rudder for its tail was found, which represented a glider and is explaining how we are carried or glide on the thermal currents on our way up into the higher realms. At that time there were no planes therefore it needed a catapult to fly. As you can see, we are being metaphorically lifted up through our inner vibrations to be seated into the angelic resonances of our mind. As my previous books explain, throughout medicinal language those two little bones that allow our arms to lift in the Deutsche language called 'Schnabel' bones. The word 'Schnabel' represents the beak of the bird. As the crow speaks it is metaphorically representing the action we release when we reach out to explain ourselves to others. Our arms automatically lift when we are speaking our truth. Notice how some languages become very animated when one becomes excited?

Through my understanding this area is introducing us into the land of the angelic resonance. The winged disc is placed over the doorways of the Temples which store the information of our glandular inheritance. Therefore, if we read the writing on the walls correctly, we will understand the stories connected to these glands and what their purpose truthfully is! This symbol was with me for many years as I learned to open my heart to the information I was receiving. Remember our heart pumps through the electrical current that is collected and pumped throughout our glands.

Another remnant from the past was the elongated cylinder that was unearthed in this same area. When I was completing my own shamanic education in the outback, I noticed three medium pyramids in three different directions which could be seen at a distance, through my two windows, also the door into my large shed. This attracted my attention, and thought that next time I went to the mail box to collect the mail, which was just on three quarters on an hour's drive to the front gate of the property of 540 square kilometres of land, I would look more closely for other signs and lo and behold I came across what I thought were the remnants of an ancient Egyptian temple; once I had explained my findings to the owner, he went out to explore the area I had found, on his horse and stumbled across these ancient grain stores which were nearby the Temple on his property. The head stockman also found an identical cylinder on the land to the one unearthed in Egypt! We celebrated for days over our findings.

We tried for a long time to get the Establishment and Universities to listen to our story, but it was all to no avail, as we were told that we were not qualified to even assess what we had unearthed! As we were not trained in their field of expertise therefore, as usual, we were completely ignored. But I still have the photos. All of this previous information certainly changes our viewpoint regarding our ancient societies of the past, doesn't it?

Again, we note that the glandular system has the responsibility of filtering our energy into both the left and the right hemispheres of our brain. Once we have conquered the hypothalamus gland, the results are then passed on to the responsibility of the pituitary gland which weighs and measures our thoughts as to how we must repeat our life over again or if we have succeeded, we are given the grace to move on to the ultimate gland which is the pineal!

Now back to the story. In reference to the grain, we realize that wheat has a much stronger resonance than barley. Wheat stands upright where it represents the left hemisphere and Barley bows its head in honouring others and represents the right hemisphere as both were used to make alcoholic beverages to replace comfort in self, long ago, hence the mention of wine. I have previously mentioned that grains are symbolically represented as our ideas and we note that Barley is a much softer grain than wheat therefore it threads itself through the body more gently and is emotionally inclined to relax and balance the mind more than wheat. Hence the term to hurt not the oil and the wine, which represents the nourishing and nurturing you have previously earned. Allow me to repeat that nourishing means to receive and nurturing means to release. We are half way to opening these seven sacred seals as the fourth clasp begins to release on the back of the book.

Number 4: *Verse 7: "And when he had opened the fourth seal, I heard the voice of the fourth beast say, Come and see".*

Verse 8: "And I looked and behold a pale horse: and his name that sat on him was Death and Hell followed with him".

We have entered a sacred zone where our mind is becoming our Temple as we journey towards the Abu Seer pyramids, renowned for the construction of fourteen pyramids. Be aware that $2 \times 7 = 14$, signifying that the two lesser Gods, EL and AN, have both reached their respective levels through education, attainment, and effort. Now, they are ready to join forces for the final journey into the unconscious—the heavenly mind.

There are only four pyramids still standing. This old ceremonial centre still has many of the codes available. I will explain these glands to you as my education has trained me to do. These glands represent the Lymphatic system where in this section of the body there are hundreds of smaller glands that act as the filter system to store and fight off our interruptions of thoughts that will become our infections if we leave them there to fester. I refer to these glands as the master systems, where these energetic sensors open up to earn their antennas, as we learn to release and speak our previously unknown or inner truth. These sensors are the high priests of Egyptology where they continually support your intellect as you traverse up into the heavenly realms or home. Termed as the 'Afterlife'.

How did the biblical writers come to the conclusion of the pale horse? This section reminds me of the house of Levi where he placed all of the coloured cloth in the vats and boiled them together, where they all came out exactly the same pale colour! Could this story also be explaining how the scribes saw the three coloured pyramids blending their colours together to become their own temple? Our spiritual strength has had to climb the sheerest mountains for us to attain this belief in self!

Also, we are still in the process of finally leaving the third dimensional reality behind and are busily evolving up into the fourth? Of the four pyramids that are left we note that the first one we come across is still standing, this one was never completed, so they say. Why then, has it not deteriorated before the others? Could this also mean that this area is the beginning of where we recognize that we are something much greater than what we thought we were? Could this pyramid that was never finished, pertain to be the end of the old life and the start of our new life?

There are three others, could they represent the collective mind? Through my education we are entering into the last area of the bodily earth! Remember there are seven vertebrae connected to the neck! I feel that this is a symbolic expression of these seven collection points known as the cervical spine? This area is connected to the Thyroid gland, as to how it is busily looking after our vocal cords, auditory nerves, blood supply and most importantly the sympathetic nervous system right down to the elbows. We are taking the final steps up into the royal chambers for the order of things to come through our next educated step or our entrance up into the unconscious mind, as it is suggested throughout the codex of Egyptology.

There is a painting on the wall in one of the Temples where there are four canopic jars. Each canopic jar is coloured in the black, red, white and the fourth one is pale. Could this be how, in the past, the Biblical scholars interpreted their version of the story and placed the horses into their findings? Remember the horse is decoded as our inner spiritual strength, which now begins to work with us on our behalf. Why? They are used to assist us to take the weight that becomes a burden to what we can lift and carry, also to assist us when we ride them to save ourselves trekking for long distances. The Bible has used the old shamanic way to explain the Egyptian interpretation. These jars or urns hold the entrails of the mummy. Our entrails are graded through their importance of function and belong to the second God AN, of our three Celestial Gods which relate to the emotional importance that is constructed through the mathematics gathering and accruing each result of our transmissible or inheritable thinking. I teach my students that they represent the three Gods of EL— which represents the activation of our endocrine system, that begins to collect and gather each tweak of information around 4 years of age; AN—represents the activation of our immune system, around 13-16 years of age, where we begin to earn our future education to a higher degree, then out comes the dictionary that is released from our higher self, as we swing up into the advanced inner education of our teenage years; and finally EA—represents the lymphatic system where the three Gods all begin to connect up into the autonomic nervous system. In other words, you are assisted gently as to how your codex begins to collect on your behalf, which alerts your inner alphabet, as it is then passed on to the prime modalities of your mathematics to fire up to make the internal changes to your current vocabulary to urge you to continue on. Now please take the time to read and register this last paragraph again.

You are over two-thirds of the way up into achieving your own personal Apocalypse (Judgment Day) by now as you leave the earth, as you are now being prepared to enter up into the heavenly realms. Do you see how the sphinx is situated in front of the three pyramids where it is alerting you to the fact that you are now mastering yourself to become as one with the heavens and also of the earth? The missing link is no longer missing as our neck stretches us towards the sound of the ethereal wisdom that we have earned for us to bring our inner, plus our outer constituent language both together.

Through the shamanic convergence we are taught that the urn holds the sacred scrolls that are delivered to us as we pass each test that is placed in front of us. Once an urn comes into your vision world, you realize that you have finished what you had to earn and the next education is being placed in front of you! It became very precious for me to see the new scroll slowly unfurling itself out of the top of the urn. I still get excited to know that a new education is about to begin!

We note that they unearthed a group of statues, one of them sitting with a mace in his hand, that belonged to the past. This gives me confirmation through my learnings in regards to the patience of my dedicated Masters of Time as to how I had to bring all of the information regarding the inner languages of religion, the sciences of Egypt, and the Latin medical languages together. Threaded throughout my previous works I have explained that this area releases the results of our actions. It is through this amazing glandular inheritance we are born with, as to how our own electrical current is imploded through our inner mathematics as to the importance of how it is alerting our cellular inheritance, as to what has had to collectively reform throughout our body!

Once the glands are full of intellectual light the energy is subtly transferred into other smaller glands and distributed through the lymphatic system to redress the overflow of our vibrations. Just like the River Nile through the sun shining on the water is used as the conduitive system to create the electricity, so too our body does the same. Remember we also have seven layers of skin surrounding our body. We need the light!

All is explaining to us metaphorically how we become the giant bird as our wings vibrate into the angel through our three Gods becoming the one God. As we evolve, we have the chance to lift our energy off the ground so that we can fly in the mind, represented to us through the species of the crow, the God of Saqqara, which is our introduction into these amazing cosmic laws. The second God is the Ibis headed God named Thoth who stimulates our immune system and Horus the falcon headed God representing our third eye, or the eye of God, the one who sees over all. Remember that the crow seems to haunt the hospitals and the school grounds as it is tuned into the energy of our children and those caught up in their own quandary that have their thoughts occupied by learning to release their education and healing to the sick. It is there where crow hangs around to give them support and confidence to go on. Please excuse the time it has taken to explain all of this information.

Now to the last section of this biblical verse: *"And power was given unto them over the fourth part of the earth, to kill with sword, and with hunger, and with death, and with the beasts of the earth".*

By now you will be remembering that the earth is your body, the sword is the soul's word of your collective mind and the fourth part of the earth is explaining that you have now earned and entered up into your inner Temple, where you begin to realise that the hunger is starving the personalities that will not relinquish their old ways. The beasts of the earth belong to our ego in many different forms, as it refuses to let go of the hold it has over our new truth. It is still refusing to accept that its pathway is becoming shorter and narrower, as it still tries to confuse us into surrendering to our greater good, as it is realising that it is hemmed in and is being restricted to voice its disapproval therefore it also has to die. They must die to their old ways of thinking so that they can resurrect and begin all over again; as we are becoming more aware of the energy that creates the magnificence of the collective, and as you are becoming more aware, there is never a wasted moment!

To add to all of this information we are born with these

wonderful intellectual natural 'Laws of your Universe' which are autonomically released through your oracle and are always available to you. We are ascending up to the fifth seal which grants us our freedom to align to our truth as we reveal ourselves to the inner explanations of this book.

Number 5: *Verse 9: "And when he had opened the fifth seal, I saw under the alter the souls of them that were slain for the word of God, and for the testimony which they held".*

As we begin to accept the freedom we have earned of our mind, we make note of Abu GGhurab which is situated just north of Abu Seer; it is also known through my Coptic Egyptian teachers as the 'funerary complex'. Now we can see how these energetic sensors of the human body release the story of ascension through our intellect being fortified for the afterlife, which is our next evolutionary step where we can evolve up into becoming the Rah (through **R**eleasing our past we **A**scend into **H**eaven). To come back to the bible, these souls that were slain are the old thoughts that are no longer applicable in your new extension of your life. We have no need to carry and support them. We can now understand why the prison in Iraq is also known by this name.

Verse 10: *"And they cried with a loud voice saying, How long O Lord, holy and true, dost thou not judge and avenge our blood on them that dwell on the earth".*

Verse 11: *"And white robes were given unto every one of them: and it was said unto them that they should rest yet for a little season, until their fellow servants also and their brethren that should be killed as they were, should be fulfilled".*

The garments of white were their earnings as they resurrected themselves from their old ways. They could begin to birth their new colours that would automatically arc as they evolved into each forthcoming new experience. Hence the resting time needed to allow these thoughts to renew their mind. Remember the word 'Kill' implies as to how we are able to resurrect ourself to allow the new education to evolve for it to become our new inheritance.

It is here where we see the Mandela cut out of one piece of crystal showing us the four directions, better known in today's language as a star gate. There is a disc which many think, has been cut with a laser. In my previous works I have mentioned how in some areas of Egypt, technology had found that certain stones had been cut with a diamond tipped blade and up until that point we had not even created a machine or the power to do this! Or were they created by two stones of equal size being rubbed together in a circular motion, one clockwise and the other anti-clockwise to create the friction of levelling and polishing each piece. This was how I learned to polish the opals I had collected in the centre of Australia, at the beginning of my journey during my training with the Australian Aborigines. This star gate sits on top of a shaft that is 180 feet deep where a section of the Nile runs underneath. The Nile is symbolically representing the consciousness already relayed through our gestation to our spinal column. As previously written, you can see how these channels of energy are used through the harmonic convergence of our vibrations to create the music or inner sound to relax and repair the body, as we have earned the right to unfurl our collective mind to reveal and open ourselves up towards our next educational step. We are about to enter another important step up into our sonic sound as we begin to release the sixth clasp on the back of the book, where our freedom through us earning the right of our inner justice to balance and become our inner Master.

Number 6: Verse 12: *"And I beheld when he had opened the sixth seal, and lo, there was a great earthquake; and the sun became black as sackcloth of hair, and the moon became as blood".*

Here is where the last of your three-dimensional world is about to surrender and retire, no more fear, no more, "I cannot do that." If you notice, 'can' comes before 'not'. On this journey of self-discovery, this is where you are bringing the totality of your mind, that you have earned and gained to your benefit, up into the oneness of how you are autonomically becoming mirrored through your thoughts into your inner nations. You are now evolving up into 'The New World Order', where there is finally a new order completely entering into your world of thought. You are now entering up into the doorway of your unconscious mind, the miracles of your cellular communication begin to bespoke themselves to you on your own behalf. When decoded through the sacred language, it is explaining to you, how to **B**alance your **E**nergy through your **S**oul's **P**ower—guided by the eternal **O**rder of **K**nowledge.

Now let us continue on. There is no brightness left for the old personalities to nourish themselves on, hence the black sun. Do you recall where I explained that sackcloth is the sacrificial garment we wear, alerting us to the fact that we are still trapped in our worried mind, that we wear before we have earned our linen? Just as we noticed through watching the ceremony of King Charles during his inauguration as to how he was dressed under his cloak, into leaving his past world to be initiated up into his new kingdom from Prince to King! In other words, we are being introduced as to how our aura has superseded itself.

We now note the strength required that represent the size of the three pyramids of Giza. We have entered up to the doorway of the unconscious mind or the afterlife as we are being brought through the medulla oblongata. One pyramid for each of the three God's where we also understand how the mind of God has become the supreme order of the collective consciousness. This is where the scrolls of our past are rolled and placed into our autonomically (self-governed) recorded memory bank. There is no more control over the self and the new scrolls are open to reveal the twelve tribes of Israel, through the Old Testament, which are now known as the Apostles or Disciples throughout the New Testament and through the Aramaic and Asiatic Principles are known as the twelve Disciplines. All of which will work on your behalf for ever more. Once more we notice that there is a large funerary complex that surround these three pyramids which represent those verses mentioned in the book of Revelations or through the metaphysical interpretation are the personalities that were slain (eradicated) for the word of God.

Again, we are given the three colours of black, red and white. The black is used in reference to the small pyramid which represents the tribal laws of our ancient past, it represents the world we have just birthed into to inherit our recorded DNA. I feel it could also represent the responsibility of our hypothalamus gland; which is also the house of our innocence, also the house of our ego who has had to take on the task of being transformed. It is where we hunger and thirst for the correct information. I like to refer to it as the teacher who has the responsibility of our endocrine system; responsible for our growth and development. This system stimulates our internal cells, our genetic inheritance and our organs, into looking forward to the future where we are able to accomplish and live in the new order of our world.

The red pyramid represents the middle pyramid, or through Egyptology is the responsibility of our pituitary gland; this gland has the responsibility of our present moment. It is the educational system of the God AN, or Ang in the Asian philosophies, explaining to us our right and our wrong; which I feel is the responsibility of our immune system. The eternal energy is stimulated up through the heart and is pumped through the two ventricles which is carried up to the pituitary gland. These two passageways align with both the left and right hemispheres of the brain. Remember, we birth our feelings through our pituitary gland. All of which is representing what I wrote about in my first book *Decoding the Mind of God* now revised with updated information available in nine separate smaller books, which is in reference or known to us as the Akashic records. Until we release the information of our right brain, we will have difficulties accepting this information, as it is still clasped on the back of the book that our ego has had to earn; through this endeavour it gains its freedom from its entangled mind to open! Hence this information, is still unknown to us.

And finally, there is the white pyramid with the polished cap on top which represents our spiritual strength coming together for us to attain the intellectual knowledge that is forwarded on to us through the education of our pineal gland, which is the last storehouse and the introduction into lifting us up into the knowledge of us earning and releasing our unconscious mind. As we are aware of the three pyramids in Giza, (through, Gods Intellectual Zephyr we Ascend). Zephyr decoded is a soft gentle wind or maybe it is Zone, an area of particular purpose or maybe it is Zygote, a cell formed by the union of two gametes, in other words a fertilized ovum, a rebirthing! There are two shafts coming from what is known as the King's Chamber in a northerly and southerly direction. Through my teachings and self-estimation, I believe that these two shafts are directing the energy of our thought processors that bring each thought together, which I refer to as Jericho are released to us from above the ears, which is forwarded on into the left and right hemispheres of the brain, not the stars. We also note that there are seven steps leading into the grand gallery, all of which reminds us of the seven seals we exonerate to our self, through releasing the seven seals from the back of the book regaling the recorded history of our DNA evolving up to our neck area, as to how we have overcome our previous existence as a three-dimensional human for us to add to our futuristic intelligence as we continue on the road less travelled up into the intelligence of our unconscious mind. This is now my home and the miracles occur with each breath I inhale.

Through the studies with my Masters of Time, I was asked to forget about the stars and to bring my information back into the human body for the future students that I would attract, for them to become more aware of themselves as this was how we would understand ourselves first, before we could venture out into the universal cosmos and this is what I have accomplished. As my Master explained, they have been here for eons, watching and guiding us as to what we have created through a very important cycle of time that must be rectified as it is creating a distension of how we understand the free will we were supplied with, through our own distortion of thoughts, which became our fear or trepidation of the unknown!

This is how we have reshaped our nasal area over time, as we cross the bridge of our nose to the other side (our inner heavenly realms) where we have earned the right to speak our words to create a sentence! To add to this is where we begin our walk to discover the missing link between our primal past, for us to discover the advantages of our intelligence that we now use for those of us who have fully accepted ourself through us understanding and earning the freedom of understanding the gift we were given during our gestation, to us earning the wisdom of our spiritual journey today.

That is why the Sphinx was created with the cat family body which represents the word 'detachment', known as Sekhmet throughout Egyptology with the head of human, is before the three pyramids. Please remember in the animal kingdom they rely on the second dimensional mind, all except the whale of the ultra-consciousness of the waters and the elephant of the land, as they have completed their journey of self-discovery, where every one of their species lives totally in their telepathic inheritance known to us as the unconscious mind.

It is in this section of the human body that our voice has colloquialized through our intelligence unfolding itself, thanks to these seven vertebrae we have been designated or designed with, as we now realise how our intelligence has matured. All of which releases the mathematical codes of our DNA where we have earned our freedom to live in our heavenly abode for everlasting life, right here during this lifetime. And here again we become aware of the next dimension up into the fourth dimension of the mind, the child, the teenager, the adult, to the elder of the tribes, where we return our wisdom back to those who are also yearning for their next step.

Again, I have to thank one of my student's Aaron from Germany who after many hours of conversing, brought to my attention the works of Henry Salt and Giovanni Cavaglia, when they discovered the Tomb of the mummified Birds under the Giza Plateau at Deneb in the 1800's. Research is continuing at this time in this area by Andrew Collins, Sue Collins and Nigel Skinner Simpson, who have followed on from their findings in what is known as Salts Journal which was written in the 1800's regarding these catacombs situated under the Giza plateau. Their friend Rodney Hale came up with the idea that these three pyramids could belong to another constellation other than the Orion and Sirius constellations as he also had difficulties aligning the stars with the pyramid and he researched further where he superimposed the Cygnus Constellation and it fitted perfectly. When my students heard of this information, they contacted me immediately as they knew I was still not satisfied with my own verification regarding the He-Nu bird that I had explained to them over the last twelve years. I had always had great difficulty in accepting that these tunnels went to the Orion and the Syrian constellation as I could not bring the metaphysical explanation together to identify with, in regards to the sanctification of our brain, as was expected.

The only thing that kept me from explaining the bird was that through my understanding these two pathways to the universal laws represented our neural pathways to both the left and right hemisphere of our brain, as one must continue to walk up the seven steps to the grand gallery or the heavenly abode that is situated above the Kings chamber.

Could this explanation of the Cygnus constellation be metaphorically representing the He Nu bird, also written as the Bjn Bjn, or the Bja'an Bja'an bird of Egyptology as it is in the shape of a large bird which represents the intellectual angelicness of self once we have opened up into the unconscious mind? Again, may I remind you that through Egyptology there are three bird-like Gods that I am aware of, beginning with Saqqara or the God with the Crow's head, representing the first God EL, which holds the codes to everlasting life. These universal laws, are explaining how we begin to lift off and fly in the mind. Then there is the Ibis headed Thoth, also referred to as the Architect for us to understand and create our new cities of light, who is the teacher and lives within the God AN (our inner university which has been downloaded and instilled in our cells from before our birth) and lastly there is the Falcon headed God Horus, representing the EA, which I have just previously explained, is the third eye which is the one who sees from above. Here we note that the EL-AN-EA all must achieve the angelic form to become the mind of God! This area of our mind is where we permanently vibrate with the inner language as to what we refer to as the angels or through the codex of the 'Sacred Language' which is brought through to the metaphysical resonance, that the Angels are a prerequisite or presence for us to obtain the clarification of our next thought!

There is a mastaba tomb found in Deneb which is in perfect alignment with this constellation and represents the tail of the great bird. Hence its name as the tomb of the mummified birds, this area is situated on the North/West side of the pyramids. Could these mummified birds also represent the evolution of the personalities that were slain for the word of God to become at one with self? We note when viewing the Cygnus constellation that the wings align perfectly with the three pyramids where the alignment continues through the heart area down to the head of the bird to connect to the star Albireo. This bird also reminds me of the large bird with the zig zagged neck in the Nazca lines which is explained in my previous book. Once again, I make note of the how the Muslim religions touch their heart, their mouth, and their forehead, where they are metaphorically announcing to you that they have an open heart to speak to you through their truth. Every single species that has evolved on this planet is a metaphor of what will create tomorrow. The Cygnus constellation reminds us of the swan which through the Sacred Language represents the emotions we earn through our heart of our inner beauty and grace!

In chapter 7, verse 4, we realize the importance of this chapter with the awakening of the twelve tribes who were sealed and now owing to the previous six seals being opened were free to move up into the dominion of God. I ask that you remember that these twelve tribes are representing the 144,000 personalities that will be saved. Also allow me to remind you of the carvings of these same numbers that were both carved on Tutankhamun's and the Mayan God Pacal's forehead. These numbers represent the twelve strands of our DNA, also the twelve apostles of Christ, which take us back to the twelve tribes of Israel, according to the thousands of myths written from all corners of the planet. We have evolved up above the glands of our bodily earth, up into the head. As mentioned before these steps are shown to us as we step up into the grand gallery situated in the white pyramid. We have entered into our heavenly realms where the seventh seal is taking us up into the kingdom of God. This '**G**reatest **O**rder of the **D**ivinity' that has already been placed into our cells.

Number 7: And now we move into the opening of the seventh seal which is the last clasp on the back of the book in Chapter 8, for us to achieve through realizing that we have opened the book to reveal to ourselves, that we have now been delegated by the upper echelon to move up into the upmost intelligence of our own recorded DNA.

Verse 1: *"And when he had opened the seventh seal, there was silence in heaven about the space of half an hour".*

Verse 2: *"And I saw the seven angels which stood before God; and to them were given the seven trumpets".*

Verse 3: *"And another angel came and stood before the alter, having a golden censer; and there was given to him much incense,' that he should offer it with the prayers of all saints upon the golden alter which was before the throne".*

Verse 4: *"And the smoke of the incense which came with the prayers of the saints, ascended up before God out of the angel's hand".*

Verse 5: *"And the angel took the censer, and filled it with fire of the alter, and cast it into the earth: and there were voices and thunderings, and lightnings, and an earthquake".*

Here we note that the last seal is open for ever more into the upper most chambers of our heavenly realms, which explains the pyramid at Abu Rauch, which is opened to the skies and built on top of the mountain. Abu Rauch or sometimes written as Abu Rowash depending on how you pronounce the word 'rauch' in the Arabic language, means chimney and in the German language means smoke or smoke apparatus, both are closely related to one another. As our energy or thoughts are released through this section of our head we are viewing the permanence to the resurrection of our mind.

This area is situated on the plateau Ga'a, around five miles north of the Giza pyramids on the road that leads from Cairo to Alexandria, hence my teachings where I explain the codes to the mind of God, EL-EX-AN-DRI-EA. This last pyramid is exactly as it should be for us to take as our inner truth, through earning these sacred codes. Now you can understand how I have written the stories regarding Alexandria, previously referred to as Elexandriea becoming the mind of God. We can also understand the Biblical stories regarding their interpretation of Joshua and Jericho as the walls came tumbling down, and in the Epistle of Jude, verse 14. Enoch, the seventh generation from Adam, was stated, "*Behold the Lord cometh with 10,000 of his saints*". Throughout the Ancient Asian teachings there are ten thousand Buddhas. Through the Sacredness of the Ancient Alphabet, Enoch conveys an important truth in today's language: 10 = 'I am my soul', while 000 = 'My soul and mind have now become one'.

Why? He has already ascended up into the heavens. In other words, they had reached the culmination of the heavenly kingdoms through ascending up into the unconscious mind... and so it will be.

The seventh seal is the reason why this pyramid is open to the heavens. I note the deterioration of Abu Rauch is in similarity to the city of Ama'anea where one of my favourites, the last Pharaoh Akhenaton lived, as he only believed in 'One God' not many smaller lesser ones, which the unworthy minds needed as to protect and cover their many excuses, as it is situated around the area of our heart. Please remember the old heart has been refurbished by our inner self and made clean and bright again, once we had journeyed up to our throat area towards the end of our DNA, as he had finished what he was here to accomplish through his program, therefore, he was called home to God, the city was then attacked by the unworthy minds who wanted to return to the many Gods to ease their mind re the excuses they busily created.

We can now understand how the word 'Asia' was explained to us, for us to realize these seven seals or seven steps up to the door of heaven, which have been familiarized throughout the Philosophies of Asia and Turkiye which was referred to as Asia Minor in the past as they are introducing us up into the strength and power of our unconscious mind. A quick reminder is that in the beginning of St. John's writings in chapter 1, verse 4: "*John, to the seven churches which are in Asia; Grace be unto you and peace from him which is and which was and is to come; and from the seven spirits which are before his throne*".

The Holy Bible has also been collected and written through

their understanding of how they decoded the hieroglyphs of Egyptology! My aim has been to explain to you how I came to realize that the writings on the wall of the Temples of Egypt and also the reasoning as to why the pyramids are placed where they have been placed; are explaining to us how we have been created before our birth, more importantly is to inform you that this knowledge is explaining to us, the evolution of the central nervous system of the human body as to who we are and more importantly once earned, as to the capabilities available for us to use, why we are here. The Biblical stories were brought to us through the Latin language, which also created the language of the medical agenda and now we understand that they are all revealing the same identical story. They are explaining how every human was created in the first place.

The languages may be explained to us differently and yet they are all releasing exactly the same information, it is the story of how humanity is made in the likeness of God! One story for our innocence is through our ever-lasting life, the God EL, our next story is for us to understand our inbuilt education, our inner University, the God AN, and then the final story seats us up into our heavenly realms once these first two have reached our inner kingdom of EA. The three Gods of EL-AN-EA or Alexandria have finally come home. If I may use the words of one of my Masters, Sir Isaac Newton, and explain it as the 'Natural Philosophy', we can see how these laws coincide to Newton's three laws of motion, EL=inertia, AN=action, EA=reaction and acceleration proportional to force.

I now realize that religion has been brought to our attention for a reason over the last fifteen hundred years and hopefully I have not interfered with the original synopsis. In today's language we call them insights, (reflections of our inner sight) that which we cannot see through our two eyes and yet all is recorded in our inner sight, which becomes the magnification of our inner light.

We have needed these teachings which are explained for us to hold our ego at bay and more to the point for us to accept the totality of our own responsibility to ourself, rather than place it onto others. I also know that I have initiated many thousands of you into the next intellectual awakening that leads on from the Book of Revelations (revealing to ourself the inner nations). Now do you understand that we are embedded with our nations, that is every country on the earth and in the earth, which is our own body as well. This information has given us something more to believe in; where we open ourselves up to receiving the information and knowledge stored in the right hemisphere of the brain to allow our energetic sensers to ignite the intellectual light we have earned. Remember the white pyramid is the subtle one!

Having been trained in the language of superior sciences for over nine years by my eternal Masters of Time at the beginning of my forty-six-year journey, I then gained the ability to absorb more knowledge as each new sequence unfolded before me. Through this, I came to the conclusion that the Book of Revelation is similar to the advanced teachings of Thomas, Judas, and others. It represents the next step in understanding, explaining the eloquence of Matthew (the inner mathematics), Mark (who has made his mark), Luke (guiding me to look deeper and perceive energy), and finally John (introducing us to the intellectual light that resides within each of our cells). This light can be inherited through the acceptance of an advanced state of consciousness. We do not need AI to program what we cannot see, feel, or interfere with. We have been blessed with our own personal 'Freedom of Will,' our God-given right to seek, understand, and earn knowledge for ourselves.

I hope I have brought the mosaic of life together section by section, so that I could write enough information to explain this magnificent language to you through my earnings. I would also like to personally thank you for reading my story up to this page. I have enjoyed your company along the way. I also thank myself for finally finishing and putting an end to this much debatable book, which has been the bane of my existence for well over thirty-five years.

I can finally set fire to the thousands of pieces of paper collected through my own research for my intellectual resurrection, as to how I have explained my truth of these 'Natural Superior Science' through these cosmic codes, to you. There could be many mistakes as I have mumbled my way through the maze of information to reveal this amazing hidden language of physics or maybe just a few! I also am very much aware of the egos who will try to pull my story apart. Please enjoy your own argument. Not one of you held my hand as I unfolded my own personal journey. I also know that in the future there will be many who try to prove me wrong and that is also wonderful, as we all know that we need stimulation to ignite the light of our next step!

The symbolist teachings of the mystery schools explain the codes of all there is to know on the planet through the mathematics of the Fibonacci sequence as to how we unfold this inner information. Just like the stories of Eli in the Bible or the explanations of the stories of Ramses I, II, III, through Egyptology. Remember it takes time for things to come to pass and what you may understand today, your friend or neighbour may understand next year, and your grandchildren may take twenty to forty years. The information that I have written will never go out of fashion, it will never become outdated, as I found out, there is only one story; as it is a continuum of each person's moment, which will become the permanence of everlasting energy. It all depends on the thought you have in your mind right now.

We could also look at Plato who believed that the metaphysical language was the only way for the human mind to decode anything, as he wrote so much information regarding his understanding of Egyptology, which kept me searching for the truth, when I had stumbled on a different interpretation of what was prepared for us many thousands of years ago. He informed us that he received his information from his grandfather who received it from an Egyptian Priest named Solan, explaining the 'Intellectual Light' we receive, as we journey through accomplishing the educational journey of An. In other words, from the inheritance, we have been downloaded with during our gestation.

Now you have the information of the journey into the in-known. I look forward to viewing the minds that create the scripts for the movies of the future. It is up here where I can listen to my sound each evening, which is familiar to Yehudi

Menuhin or Hauser on you-tube, before I retire for the night! I spend every moment of my day assisting others to find through my grace, their inner gentleness within themselves and write my words to explain these amazing codes regarding the pages that are heralded down to our inner book, known as our DNA. Now you can open up your first page and begin. Become that astronaut out in space; you can live up here in the heavens and look upon on the wholeness of the earth as well. There is a melodious silence up here that at some time during our life, each one of us yearns to find the answer for! Remember, through the codes of mathematics coming together we have created a geometrical symbol; this symbol becomes the formulation of our ideas as to how we are creating our reality. It sets the scene for what we will become. It is on the front cover of every one of my books. As we equalize our thoughts, the next symbol begins to formulize itself mathematically from the positive behaviour of the thought before. Once equal we begin to note through our expectations, the next geometrical symbol automatically appears and our enlightenment continues to magnify.

I have walked the labyrinth of the Universal Laws and through these insights I have endeavoured to explain the codes of our past up to this perfect moment. Remember, your truth will set you free! The future is yours, through believing in yourself you can create it and live your life through the exponential inner mathematics that are due to you!

Remember, in the vast mystery of all that is, we all breathe the same breath of the one God, from the four corners of the globe. Let's spin that ancient medicine wheel and earn the knowledge that can heal our minds. We all have the opportunity to create the same light, to live the life explained by St. John the Divine and to become the shining one—when we have finally earned our freedom within, through earning the right to believe in ourselves! If only every person could train their ego and embrace self-realization, recognising that we have all descended from the heavens, passing through the same sacred gate. Go forth and multiply your three kingdoms—mind, body, and up here, you can eternally communicate with your soul.

My heartfelt thanks to all readers who have gained insights into self-discovery, and, more importantly, into who they are—internally as well as externally. We are all created in the likeness of God. Now, go and conquer yourself. May you all inherit the wind, known to me as the breath of the eternal '**G**reatness of the **O**rder of our inner **D**ivinity'—our world within. Blessed be.

Books By O.M. Kelly (Omni)

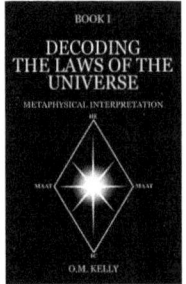

Book I. Decoding The Laws Of The Universe
If you're looking to unlock the hidden potential within you and transform your life, "Decoding the Laws of the Universe" is the book for you. This powerful and insightful book is designed to help you understand the deeper, metaphysical aspects of life and tap into the transformative power of the universe utilising the secrets of our Individual Universal Law.

This book serves to introduce you into the secrets of our Individual Universal Law. This amazing knowledge and wisdom, is transformative on a personal level and creates the opportunity for you to interrelate with the Laws of the Universe. Throughout this book, you will dive deep into the inner workings of your mind and discover the hidden laws that govern your life. You will learn about the alchemy of the mind and how to harness its power to create positive change in your life and the world around you. Through the lens of Metaphysical philosophy, you will gain a new perspective on the world and your place in it. You will learn how the universe communicates with you through coded intelligence and how to unlock the hidden messages that are all around you.

This book is a journey for personal transformation and spiritual growth. Take a voyage of exploration of the expansive vistas of information discovering the codes of Metaphysics and the Quest of Life. You will learn the Metaphysical coded wisdom of the ancients for the necessary mind elements to transit into a higher mindset. Explore the secret relationship between the Earth and human beings, the higher mind, the Metaphysical journey, the importance of self, belief in self, the codes of mythology, a higher level of attainment, releasing the past, fears and evolving one's light on a Metaphysical level, what causes stress, work place promotion and why it does not happen, and many other topics. Included is a short overview of the conventional Twelve Laws of the Universe.

Book II. Decoding Thought
Welcome to a journey of self-discovery and exploration of the mysteries of the universe. "Decoding Thought" is a ground-breaking book that explores the power of the mind and the principles of metaphysical thought. Through a deep exploration of the mind and body connection, the author provides readers with insights to unlock the full potential of their thoughts. This book provides a guide to harness

the power of the mind to create the life you desire. With explanations of metaphysical principles, the book makes these often complex concepts accessible to readers. "Decoding Thought" takes you on a journey through the vast landscape of the human mind. Explore the mysteries of thought power, and how it can shape our reality and transform our lives. The power of thought is not just a theoretical concept. It is a tangible force that can be harnessed to bring about significant changes in our lives.

This book can expand your consciousness and open your mind to new possibilities. By exploring the metaphysical principles that underlie our existence, you can gain a new perspective on life and the world around you. This book provides through a metaphysical interpretation explanations into the various aspects of thought power, including how it is linked to our DNA, and the roles played by the pituitary and pineal glands in our thought processes. O.M. Kelly also explains the metaphysical language in reference to the codes of the Egyptian Philosophies, the Bible, myths, cultures, and how they connect to the power of thought. The journey continues with a deep dive into the inner Secret School of Metaphysics, where we discover the Alchemy of the Brain and the pathway to our truth. Discover the unconscious/higher mind, and our Life Quest, which opens the doors to the Psychometric Consciousness. Through the lens of metaphysical interpretation, you will gain a new perspective on the impact of thought on our mental and emotional states that includes a look at Depression, Coping with Change and how to retrain our brain patterns to be positive and moving forward for our Financial Abundance and manifesting prosperity. The book ends with a brief overview of the brain/mind, and a short Q&A on thought power. This metaphysical book on the power of thought is a guide to discovering your true potential and creating the life you desire.

"Decoding Thought" is a must-read for anyone seeking to unlock the full potential of their mind and harness the power of the universe to create a life of fulfilment and this book serves as an invaluable resource.

Book III. Decoding Dis-Ease

Introducing "Decoding Dis-Ease" a Metaphysical Interpretation into understanding the intricate web of factors that contribute to our health and well-being. From the author of several groundbreaking works on the interaction of the mind and body, this book delves into a wide range of topics related to dis-ease. It is a fascinating and insightful book that offers a fresh perspective on health and healing. It is a must-read for anyone interested in the mind-body connection.

Readers will be inspired to embark on a quest of discovering the codes within themselves, recognizing that every cell in our body is pure Cosmic Consciousness. They will also gain a deeper understanding of specific health topics such as the thyroid, the kidneys, men's problems, and many other topics from a Metaphysical perspective. The book also examines how a dis-ease is given to us in group energy and the complex interplay between our bodies and minds, and how every human has the consequences of all that we do and experience.

Book IV. Decoding Death

Looking for a thought-provoking exploration of death and the afterlife? Look no further than O.M. Kelly's book, "Decoding Death".

"Decoding Death takes us on a transformative Metaphysical journey through the mysteries of the Universe. O.M. Kelly—known as Omni—provides an expanded horizon of possibilities, awareness, and a transformative perspective. In this book, Omni delves into a wide range of topics related to dying and death, from the loss of a loved one to a viewing of the afterlife. Omni has a unique ability to view the Laws of the Universe using her extraordinary state of heightened awareness and multi-dimensional perception and through the lens of metaphysics offers a unique perspective on the nature of death and what it means for the human experience.

Omni shares personal experiences and stories, including the passing of her late husband, brother, and parents, and offers a metaphysical insight for those dealing with loss and grief. She explores the transformational process of death and the potential for spiritual growth and enlightenment. The book explains that the human experience of death is part of a larger Universal process that is ultimately guided by a higher intelligence referred to as God (Laws of the Universe/Collective Consciousness) or whatever name you prefer. Omni's exploration of death is both metaphysically comprehensive and thought-provoking, offering readers a deep and nuanced understanding of one of life's greatest mysteries. With chapters on the Three Doorways—Three Stages of Death, The Quantum Hologram—Why a partner dies for the other partner to progress in the "Journey of Life", The Passing to the Afterlife, and many other enlightening chapters, "Decoding Death" offers a unique viewpoint. By drawing on a range of religious, philosophical, and metaphysical perspectives, Omni offers a compelling vision of the human experience of death and its role in the larger Universal Law.

Book V. Decoding Sexuality And Spirituality

Welcome to "Decoding Sexuality and Spirituality" by O.M. Kelly. In this book, explore the fascinating relationship between our sexuality and spirituality, and how these two aspects of ourselves are intimately intertwined. Delve into the concept that sexuality is the doorway to our spirituality, and examine the powerful and transformative energy that is generated when we fully embrace our sexual selves. The book also explores the notion of the metaphysical orgasmic cloud, and how it can be used to deepen our connection to our spiritual selves. We will also examine the role of marriage in our sexual and spiritual lives.

For women, the book offers a unique perspective on the journey of embracing sexuality and spirituality, as well as insights into the different stages of life and how they impact our sexual and spiritual selves. Drawing on both ancient wisdom traditions and metaphysical mythology, the book examines the myth of Hercules and how it relates to our sexual intelligence. By decoding the symbolism of this myth, we can gain a deeper understanding of the ways in which our sexuality and spirituality intersect and influence each other. So if you are ready to embark on a journey of self-discovery and unlock the true potential of your sexual and spiritual selves, then "Decoding Sexuality and Spirituality" is the book for you.

VI. Decoding The Dolphin's Breath

"Decoding The Dolphin's Breath" by O.M. Kelly (Omni) is a captivating exploration of the relationship between humans and dolphins. The book begins with a poignant account of a real-life encounter between the author and a group of wild dolphins, setting the stage for a deep dive into the spiritual and metaphysical significance of dolphins. This captivating book takes readers on a journey into the heart of the dolphin-human relationship, exploring the ways in which these majestic creatures can help us attune to the power of free will, and telepathic communication.

Throughout the Laws of Shamanism the wonderful Dolphin in consciousness, represents the attainment we can reach through ourselves earning our freedom of will. This book explains the benefits of the dolphins breath—the why and how we use the breath that influences our divine mentality. Further, it's a story which reveals how the dolphins have taught us the process to be free of fear, and to tap into the Language of Babylon—to understand the language of Earth. One of the key themes of the book is the idea that dolphins are always breathing their total freedom of thought, and the author provides insights into how humans can learn from this remarkable trait. The book also invites readers to embark on a journey into understanding the telepathic communication of whales and dolphins. Inclusive in the book is a written meditation which assists you to connect to the external consciousness and release the fear that you have wrapped around yourself for protection.

Overall, this book offers a unique and fascinating perspective on the metaphysics of dolphins, and will appeal to anyone interested in spirituality, and the power of the mind.

Book VII. Decoding The Sacred Alphabet And Numerology

This book offers a myriad of explanations concerning the higher consciousness in relationship to names, places and numbers. "Decoding The Sacred Alphabet & Numerology" by O.M. Kelly (Omni) is a thought-provoking and enlightening read that offers a unique perspective on the metaphysical world of letters and numbers.

Omni's insights and teachings are sure to inspire readers to deepen their understanding of the ancient sacred codes to names of places, your name and the sacred alphabet. The author also delves into the practice of metaphysical numerology, which involves using numerical values to interpret personality traits, life paths, and other aspects of a person's life. Omni explains how metaphysical numerology can be used to gain insight into our spiritual path and to better understand our purpose in life. Your ability to decipher the Sacred Alphabet and Numerology codes commonly and constantly presented to you throughout your life, will open opportunities to expand your consciousness and awareness you never thought possible.

Embark on a journey through the myth of Babylon and Shambhala and discover the sacred language that connects us all. Explore Luxor, the Delta Giza Saqqara and Faiyum, and Solomon's Temple, and uncover the mysteries of Akhenaton and Tomb KV-63. Find out how to unravel the threads of your DNA and unlock the ancient knowledge of the Old Aramaic Story of Aladdin and the Lamp. Explore Grecian stories through the Metaphysical language and travel along the Old Silk Road. Discover the Shamanic inheritance of numbers and their meanings, and learn how we rely on numbers to read the hidden language of the universe. Join O.M. Kelly on a journey of self-discovery and uncover the divine language within.

Book VIII. Decoding Sacred Fung Shwa

Introducing "Decoding Sacred Fung Shwa", the revolutionary guide to understanding and harnessing the energy within your home and yourself. In this book, author O.M. Kelly (Omni), has introduced a metaphysical sixth element that takes our understanding of energy to the next level. By incorporating "Your Life Force," we gain deeper insight into the connection between our homes and our emotional well-being. Discover the power of Fung Shwa and learn how to use it to create a balanced and harmonized environment that supports your mind, body, and Soul.

The book explains the meaning of Sacred Fung Shwa to the Shamanistic principles that underpin it. Delve into the metaphysical medicine wheel and explore the elements of life, before moving on to practical applications of Fung Shwa in the home.

Learn how to visualize your home as a collective energy and clear the clutter to enhance its flow. Discover your Astrological colours and how they can be used in Fung Shwa design, from the kitchen to the bedroom and beyond. Explore the compatibility of personal colours in relationships, and discover the power of paintings, pictures, and mirrors to enhance your home's energy.

But Fung Shwa isn't just about the home—we also explore its applications in the office environment and in small retail businesses. Learn how to apply Fung Shwa principles to a clothing store, shoe store, or café, even discover the role of Fung Shwa in money, and to Metaphysical Numerology.

Throughout it all, we focus on the quest of life and how Fung Shwa can help you achieve your goals and live your best life. So what are you waiting for? Dive into the world of Fung Shwa and transform your home, your business, and your life today!

Book IX. Decoding Extra-Terrestrial Intelligence

Are you ready to embark on a journey of self-discovery? Look no further than O.M. Kelly's groundbreaking book, Book IX "Decoding Extra-Terrestrial Intelligence". Through metaphysical interpretation, O.M. Kelly (Omni) has unlocked the secrets of the universe and revealed that the key to our next step in human evolution lies within ourselves. This book will show you how to tap into the indelible imprint of holographic importance that is seeded within every human, and unleash the Extra-Terrestrial Intelligence that resides within you. Omni shares her own personal journey of encountering Beings of Light and how it has transformed her understanding of the universe and humanity's place within it.

Omni presents the concept that we all have Extra-Terrestrial Intelligence, and have the ability to tap into the vast knowledge and secrets of the universe. The ancient civilizations left behind clues and teachings about this metaphysical existence and it is up to us to continue to uncover and advance the way we think. Through this journey of life, we can unlock the secrets of our own consciousness and tap into the full potential of our existence. This is a fascinating exploration of the mysteries of the universe and the potential for our own personal evolution.

Readers who are interested in self-transformation through universal truths, Metaphysical exploration for personal growth and a journey of self-discovery would be interested in reading this insightful book on contact with Beings of Light and Extra-terrestrial Intelligence, exploring ancient civilizations and the knowledge they possessed about the universe and the human mind.

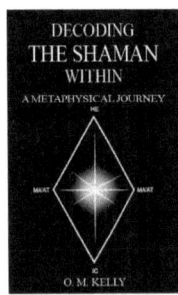

Decoding the Shaman Within

In "Decoding the Shaman Within" international author O.M. Kelly (Omni) shares her Shamanic metaphysical journey. It would be termed a contemporary Shamanic initiation journey; a powerful spiritual enlightenment and transformational voyage of discovering the codes of Metaphysics and the Quest of Life. Through the sacred passage of time Omni discovered the secret codes of the Collective Consciousness (Laws of the Universe) to trek a higher level of consciousness. Throughout Omni's training to receive the breath of Shamanism, many Elders from other cultures came to Australia and initiated her into their own tribal laws. Most of these Elders were men who arrived on Omni's doorstep uninvited but had received the call from the …

Universe to pass on their knowledge. Those magnificent people who had also earned their Shamanic experiences, only stayed long enough to give Omni their gift of consciousness and to initiate her into a new Shamanic name, which their tribe had bestowed, and then they disappeared out of Omni's life as quickly as they had come into it.

The Shamanic path in a Metaphysical perspective is the oldest pathway of the tribal law through the evolution of humanity. The Shaman is trained in the ancient language that is instilled in every genetic code that humanity carries within their DNA; you either have the opportunity to open it up and use it, or you just don't bother and choose to ignore it! It is as simple as that!

Power Thought for the Day Oracle Book
"Power Thought For The Day Oracle Book" provides insights to assist you on your life path. Through the "Totem" energy of all, the ancient species that have evolved before us, represent an emotional inheritance that we can rely on to sustain the moment. Each species that has evolved on this planet is recorded into our cellular memory. This book with 22 Major Arcana Shamanic Power Animal Totems provides a contemporary metaphysical interpretation symbolic of our evolution. By selecting a page of the book the Shamanic animal will provide an insight in how you are thinking at this moment in time. Through the contemporary Laws of Shamanism (with a metaphysical interpretation), O.M. Kelly (Omni) has produced a book that will assist the "Path of the Initiate" in emotional intelligence when our mind is in the field of doubt. When we become aware of how we are thinking it is a catalyst for transformation. This compact little book is a handy 4 x 7 inches or 10.2 x 17.8 cm to fit into your pocket or handbag.

How to use the book:
Our higher mind has no time; it steps into and works on behalf of the thought of the moment. This book encompasses 22 Major Totem Power representations, symbolic of our evolution. Close your eyes and inhale and exhale a deep breath and relax and allow yourself no thought as you select the right page of the Shamanic animal presented in this book. The right page will always appear for you at the right moment and you will discover how the power animals are working with you for insight into their wisdom. Different power animals come into our lives at various phases offering messages to guide us on our path.

Decoding the Revelation of Saint John the Divine: Understand the role you inherit

The amazing breakthrough book "Decoding the Revelation of Saint John the Divine: Understand the role you inherit", is for anyone with an open, inquiring mind, seeking answers to the surreal descriptions of Earth's final days.

Through years of research O.M. Kelly interprets the cryptology behind the codes of mythology and various religions and has Metaphysically interpreted how the Holy Bible had been written through the original codex of Egyptology. The biblical stories were collected and condensed through the educated minds of that time.

"Decoding The Revelation Of Saint John The Divine: Understand The Role You Inherit" by International Author and Lecturer O.M. Kelly.

What if the Book of Revelation was never about the end of the world, but the beginning of a higher consciousness?

After more than 48 years of meticulous research and metaphysical inquiry, O.M. Kelly (also known as Omni) presents a groundbreaking, revised edition of her renowned work that will change everything you thought you knew about the final book of the Bible. Drawing from ancient mythology and ancient traditions from Egypt, Mesopotamia, Assyria, and early Israel, O.M. Kelly reveals a metaphysical symbolic system that serves as a universal blueprint of human identity and evolving consciousness.

Inside this revelatory book, you will explore:The genetic role humanity inherits through the coded symbols of Revelation. Uncover the secrets of the Ark of the Covenant. Unlock the mystery behind the 144,000 and the sacred codes of their salvation. How you open up to the information stored in your Seven Seals. The true implications of the mark of the Beast. The ancient wisdom of the Egyptian pyramids and their connection to your consciousness. The truth behind Armageddon, not as destruction, but as revelation. Learn how to access the Recorded History of Your DNA and the Library of the Universal Mind. Understand the symbolic Fall of Babylon and its impact on our collective psyche. The process of clearing the channels of human consciousness to awaken the Divine Self. Explore the connection between Greek mythology, Egyptian pyramids, and early Israelite traditions. Understanding the genetics behind the role you inherit in Revelation. Stepping through The Doorway of the Divine Self. This is more than a book. It is a sacred map. O.M. Kelly deciphers the ancient texts and opens a doorway to understanding the mystery of life through metaphysical interpretation. Decode your destiny. Remember who you are. Awaken the divine within. Let the Book of Revelation become your guide to the evolution of consciousness.

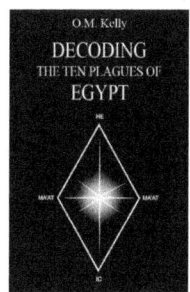

Decoding the Ten Plagues of Egypt

"Decoding the Ten Plages of Egypt" is a philosophical interpretation of the Ten Plagues as stages of consciousness for inner transformation. Not a theological treatise.

"Decoding the Ten Plagues of Egypt" offers a fresh perspective on the hidden structure and language through which the Bible was written. This work introduces readers to a step-by-step metaphysical decoding of the mysterious language surrounding the plagues described in Chapters 7 to 12 of the Book of Exodus. For the first time in contemporary history, the essence of Exodus and its previously unresolved, intriguing expressions are unveiled—providing deeper insight and a clearer perception of the Book's true message, as interpreted on a metaphysical level by O.M. Kelly.

Decoding Dreams

In "Decoding Dreams" international author O.M. Kelly (Omni), introduces a metaphysical interpretation of the dreams we dream. At times, we may believe that dreams allow us to peer into another world. O.M. Kelly provides the codes for us to understand that other world of dreams—or, through the Shamanic Principles, our "Vision Worlds". Dreams are created through your unconscious/higher mind communicating back to you; dreams are reminding you of the lessons that you need to understand regarding yourself. You cannot hear them if your mind is filled with incessant chatter. The ego refuses to conform when it is in control of the moment. Dreams can range from a pleasant dream, which could be a recommendation to add to what you are doing, to a nightmare, which is a wake-up call from your higher self regarding what you are doing to yourself. As you read this book, keep in mind that learning to metaphysically interpret your dreams is a step-by-step process. Areas covered in the book are: Dream Representations (Animal Kingdom and the Human Kingdom), Questions and Answers about Dreams, and Dream Interpretations.

Reprint coming in the near future.

www.ingramcontent.com/pod-product-compliance
Lightning Source LLC
Chambersburg PA
CBHW062031290426
44109CB00026B/2590